Praise for Christopher Keane
How to Write...

"Keane's *How to Write a Selling* ... dard book for aspiring young authors. It covers every asp... the writing process from initial conception to the completion of the script, finding an agent, and placing the project with a production company. A masterful contribution form a leading authority."

—James Nagel, *Hemingway in Love and War*,
Eidson Distinguished Professor, University of Georgia

"Chris Keane's book, *How to Write a Selling Screenplay*, is the new bible on the art of writing screenplays. It is a must for any new or experienced writer." —Michael Pressman, executive producer, *Picket Fences*

"Keane's book is a method, a set of observations, from which an aspiring writer can discover his own approach: an approach to discipline, to work habits, most important—a discovery of process—so that if there is any talent there and a personal vision, it has a chance to survive and find a practical means of expression. Comprehensive, instructive, and filled with illuminating and helpful personal anecdotes."

—Marshall Brickman, screenwriter, *Manhattan Murder Mystery*
and *Annie Hall*; cowriter, *Manhattan* and *Sleeper*

"Keane effectively combines theoretical considerations with hands-on applications that are easy to understand. His experience as an educator is abundantly evident on every page."

—Richard Walter, professor and screenwriting chairman, UCLA

"Keane has written a great guide to screenwriting. If all young screenwriters and studio execs would read it, American movies would be better."

—Ralph Rosenblum, professor of film at
Columbia University Graduate Film School
and editor of *Goodbye, Columbus*; *Annie Hall*; and *Sleeper*

"To call this a book about screenwriting is to underestimate it enormously. It is about good writing and each superb rule and suggestion can be used for plays, novels, TV, and movies. The greatest accolade I can give it is to say, 'I wish I had written it.'"

—Stanley Ralph Ross, writer, *The Cosby Show* and *Columbo*

Also by Christopher Keane

HOW TO WRITE A SELLING SCREENPLAY
KEANE ON SCREEN
THE HUNTRESS
THE HUNTER
LYNDA
THE TOUR
HANDBOOK FOR THE MARTIAL ARTS AND SELF-DEFENSE
DANGEROUS COMPANY
MR. & MRS. BLISS
THE MAXIMUS ZONE
THE HEIR
THE CROSSING
CHRISTMAS BABIES (with William Black, M.D.)

HOT PROPERTY

screenwriting in the NEW Hollywood

Christopher Keane

BERKLEY BOOKS, NEW YORK

B

A Berkley Book
Published by The Berkley Publishing Group
A division of Penguin Group (USA) Inc.
375 Hudson Street
New York, New York 10014

This book is an original publication of The Berkley Publishing Group.

Copyright © 2003 by Christopher Keane.
Cover design by Rita Frangie.
Text design by Kristin del Rosario.

PRINTING HISTORY
Berkley trade paperback edition / August 2003

To contact the author, please visit *www.keanewords.com*
or e-mail him at Keanewords@aol.com.

Library of Congress Cataloging-in-Publication Data

Keane, Christopher.
Hot property / Christopher Keane.—Berkley trade pbk. ed.
p. cm.
ISBN 0-425-19040-4
1. Motion picture authorship. I. Title.

PN1996 .K33 2003
808.2'3—dc21
2002038523

PRINTED IN THE UNITED STATES OF AMERICA

10 9 8 7 6 5 4 3 2 1

For my students

For the person who feels, life is a tragedy.
For the person who thinks, life is a comedy.

—Federico Garcia Lorca

Contents

Contents

PREFACE
The Twenty-Minute Method

Believe it: The best way to break into the movie business is to write a well-crafted, low-budget screenplay from your heart and mind, and from passion and craft. The script will get around and, if it's good, it will attract agents, producers, bankable actors, and money, and you might get it made.

You can't compete against the big studios that want blockbusters and give their writing assignments to seasoned pros. Write small with big implications. Read *Monster's Ball, Good Will Hunting, American Beauty, A Beautiful Mind, The Opposite of Sex, Igby Goes Down,* and the scripts plucked by distributors from Sundance and Slamdance. There's your market.

Believe this, too: Impatience kills. A writer goes through a slow process to reach that point where the screenplay is ripe, when it's ready to pick, then is shipped off to market. The process takes time. You build yourself as a writer as you build your work, and nothing should go into the market until the time is right.

This book is about how to write a screenplay that will have a chance in this rag-tag, highly competitive world of movies; it's about how to build an idea into a "hot property" that people who make movies will want to make or that will get you jobs.

Hollywood's changing. When *Memento,* about a guy who has

misplaced his memory and spends the movie trying to find it, wins with both Los Angeles and New York critics for best 2001 screenplay, you know there's something afoot.

When *In the Bedroom* and *Mulholland Drive,* both low-budget, quirky pictures, win top awards at the Oscars, you know that if you want to write for the Industry you can shift your focus. When studio pictures are left on the sidelines, replaced by quirky, independent pictures, you know that the way the Industry looks at moviemaking has been altered forever. The Industry is changing.

The studios will always be here. Let's forget about them for the moment. The independent market (the indies) ebbs and flows, always looking for funding and distribution, but the independent market is the place for new writers to find their niche. Showtime and HBO films have opened doors for new writers and new audiences. So how does a new writer walk through these doors? The key is to write a great screenplay that will not cost a bundle but will act as a showcase for the writer's talent.

My Big Fat Greek Wedding and *Memento* were both passed on by the studios' specialty labels (Fine Line, Focus, Fox Searchlight, Miramax, Lion's Gate) and were quickly gobbled up by smaller distributors, where they went on to make big money and gather major kudos. The studios are beginning to catch on somewhat; Focus did get *Monsoon Wedding,* Fox picked up *Kissing Jessica Stein,* but everyone but one passed on *How to Kill Your Neighbor's Dog,* which did only $60,000 in theaters but $12 million on video sales and rentals.

Write out of your passion, and if it's original, it will find a market. The big-budget jobs are studio-generated. Chances are slim for breaking in. *Good Will Hunting* started out as a high-tech thriller until Rob Reiner told Matt Damon and Ben Affleck to dial it down to make it the smaller, more personal story.

I'll give you the same advice. Write small and personal, lower budget, and brilliantly. If you want to work in the Industry as a screenwriter, forget about retread thinking, that mistaken notion that you need to write derivative garbage. What's hot is your vision, not what the marketplace says is currently in fashion. If you write for the marketplace, by the time you finish, that train will be gone and you will be left with a piece of material no one will want.

As a writer, you can't afford to follow old directions or read screenwriting books that *exclusively* use examples of movies made ten or twenty years ago; or that focus on big studio pictures. *My Big Fat Greek Wedding* never would have been made back then and certainly wouldn't have succeeded at the box office as it has—beating the extraordinary numbers of another indie, *The Blair Witch Project.*

Audiences will not put up with tired premises, no matter how strong the actor might be. Witness *The Mexican,* a $17 million piece of Warner Brothers junk that, after Julia Roberts and Brad Pitt came onboard, became a $77 million piece of junk. Or *Insomnia,* directed by Christopher Nolan (who also directed *Memento*). Nolan went from writing and directing a sharp and quirky award-winner to a quirky but tired old dog.

This book is aimed toward original thinkers with something fresh to say, to the new breed of screenwriters who will usher the New Hollywood into the future. Yes, there are rules to follow and rules you must know in order to break. But you cannot succeed or even get into Hollywood with old thinking, no matter how many books or teachers insist that the old rules are the ones to follow.

Storytelling, on the other hand, is as old as mankind. Subject matter is not. Craft, story, language, and perception change over time. To survive, you have to make the adjustment.

My students convinced me to write this book because, as they said, there is no substitute for getting the scoop from somebody who writes screenplays for a living—for the Industry, in the Industry, every day—someone who is deep into the process of the New Hollywood.

I teach two graduate courses a semester at Boston's Emerson College. And every summer at the International Film Workshops, in Rockport, Maine, I teach a one-month, first-draft screenplay class. It turns out that Emerson, along with UCLA and USC, pumps more students into the Hollywood screenwriting system than any other school.

So what does it take to write a successful screenplay? You can read every screenwriting book out there and all the guidelines, but there's no substitute for the daily grind and reading produced screenplays. I work on a screenplay every day, either a spec or one under contract. I put in my time every day; otherwise I don't feel right. I work under the dual umbrellas of love and guilt.

Call it fear-driven. I fear what my life will become if I work only for other people with their own agendas. I fear giving my entire creative life to other people. I don't want to work on their time rather than on my own. I know I have to make a living, so when I decided to write I knew I had to go after it and learn the rules.

I also read a lot—tons of screenplays. I read what others write. I love movies, and I try to see them all. I yearn to see movies that are coming out next week, next month, next year. I can't wait to read reviews. Every day I log on to Variety.com and HollywoodReporter.com to see what the industry is buying and making. I speak whenever I can—at Harvard, at the 2002, 2003 screenwriters Expo in Los Angeles, where the attendees designated me a "Star Speaker" (whoa!), and at the Maui Writers Conference (why not?).

I teach to get out of the house and to have some sort of steady income in an unsteady business of big paychecks or no paychecks for long periods of time.

I've written in hotel lobbies, in coffee shops, on park benches, in cars, on trains, on planes, and on buses. I crave maple walnut scones at Starbucks.

There is no way I'll ever own another desktop computer. I live on the road. Give me my laptop with battery juice and software from Final Draft and I'm golden.

I have been turned down at least five times by every Hollywood studio. But I keep plugging because steady work gets the job done, good work gets better, better work gets attention, attention gets jobs, and jobs get produced.

It all starts with consistent work habits and a knowledge of the game and how its played. Screenwriting is a process leading to a conclusion. In almost all cases for the new writer, the process is generally missing a key element, which begins long before the writer starts to write page one.

This pre-writing stage is the gut work that sets the foundation for the screenplay. If you don't do the gut work you have no shot. Period. It's not surprising that every working writer in Hollywood gets work because he or she discovered the gut work stage before beginning to write. It's called building the story. In fact, the gut work stage *is* writing—a crucial part of the process.

When my students suggested I write this book, they suggested that I use them in it. They've been through my screenwriting classes, some of them a half-dozen times, and many now work in Hollywood. I have included some of their stories here: what they had to go through to climb the Hollywood ladder, what they learned to avoid, and what they knew to chase after. There's no substitute for firsthand experience.

They also suggested that I organize the book in the way I run a classroom, as a kind of workbook—from the tiny sliver of an idea to the finished product, the screenplay itself—and then later show what happens to the screenplay when it leaves your hands and finds its way into the Hollywood machine and beyond.

So here goes. The journey. The process. Even the most seasoned pros struggle in this capricious business. These are the chances we must be willing to take for a writing life worth living.

The biggest lesson of all is in the work itself—the time alone with your thoughts, plugging them into the computer, spreading them out on a page, structuring the story, and laying out the story beats.

For those with regular jobs, I recommend writing twenty minutes a day, minimum. It's like having kids. If you don't feed them every day, malnutrition sets in. If you don't want your screenplay to suffer that fate, feed your story and your characters on a daily basis. As you get more interested, you will find more time. After the twenty minutes, shut down, get up, and go. The work isn't going anywhere; it will be waiting for you tomorrow. Meanwhile, all day long, the thoughts will be rolling around in your subconscious.

My students don't worry about tomorrow. They concentrate on the work today. Tomorrow will take care of itself. Then one day they have the first draft done. Like magic.

Except there's no magic about it. It's twenty minutes a day, and the script will take care of itself.

For starters, I recommend these movies to see and read.

Igby Goes Down
Kissing Jessica Stein
Memento
Story Telling
Tadpole
Y Tu Mama Tambien
Amores Perros
The Fast Runner

So have fun. I did, writing this book. It's part of my writing life. I hope some of it spills over to yours.

Chris Keane
Cambridge, Massachusetts

Acknowledgments

Thanks to: Denise Silvestro, editor extraordinaire; Brian DeFiore, agent exemplar; and Michael Schiffer and William Martin, good friends and fellow writers. To all the good people on both coasts, students and friends, who contributed enormously to this effort. And to Susan Crawford, with love.

INTRODUCTION

Why screenwriting?

GO TO A DARK CORNER AND
WAIT FOR THE FEELING TO PASS

They're called the Emerson Mafia. Hundreds of grad students and interns from Emerson College's Boston campus streaming to, living in, and working in Hollywood.

For one semester, Emerson Mafia interns take nonpaying jobs at studios, production companies, and talent agencies as part of their program requirement in the Emerson College writing program. Most all of them end up staying, sucked into the phantasmagoria known as the movie business.

They move into small apartments, with palm trees sprouting out of grassy backyards and roommates piled on top of roommates. They have been hooked on industry juice, they are talented, and they have ambition.

It doesn't hurt that the Emerson Mafia is a well-respected and trained cadre of young, smart, high-energy drivers with sharp focus.

I've taught screenwriting to most of them. They tell me the American Poetry Society has a hit out on me. Many of these students enter the Emerson Boston program to write poems, and after taking my classes end up working at Paramount or Creative Artist Agency (CAA) a year later, writing and analyzing movie scripts. If *I* were the American Poetry Society, I'd put a hit out on me, too.

I didn't mean to do it. It's not my fault. It's this form of writing—the evil screenplay—that caused all these poets to turn their backs on John Donne, Walt Whitman, Elizabeth Barrett Browning, and Ezra Pound.

This new manna from heaven, screenwriting, is a bastard art. After months, sometimes years, of toil, drilling images to the page, in a empty room, all alone, living on Tender Vittles with mayonnaise, the Hollywood powers yank your art away and pass it on to fifty strangers—producers, directors, other writers, grips—who mess with it, rip the originality out of it, and slap it up on a screen. It's an industry with no room for egos. If you go into the business, expect to be stepped on, pushed around, screwed over, and knocked down.

As somebody once said to me when I told them I wanted to write screenplays: "Go to a dark corner and wait for the feeling to pass."

I didn't wait for it to pass, nor did my students. We were already addicted. Making movies is the most highly collaborative art in the world. The screenwriter is the architect. The building is built by others off our original dream and conception. That's the way it is, the way it happens.

If you're afraid of losing control over your work, stop reading. You *will* lose control over your work. But if your vision is strong to begin with, if that 107-page screenplay you've busted your butt writing has the guts and the gumption and the heart and soul of a great story, with wildly compelling characters and dead-on structure, your chances of seeing that work make it up on the screen, in its original conception, is pretty damn good. That keeps me going.

Hot Property is about that process of getting your work to the screen. It is also about what the Emerson Mafia has gone through to get their bodies and their work out there in this highly competitive business, and how they take what they learned in the classroom and carry it out there in the best shape possible. The book is also an up-to-date account of the expanding world of making movies, in and outside of the studio system.

The process and the people are intertwined. I have interviewed dozens of former students who work in the business at all levels. They have stories to tell, stories filled with hopes, realized and dashed. Some have left Los Angeles, their cautionary tales filled with frustration and grief. Many have gotten jobs with studios or production companies or they teach or have become script doctors. They all share one thing in common: They know story. They know what a good script is and what it takes to write one, which is a lot more than many people working in the business know. They also know what a bad script is. This information gives them a giant leg up. They all know how not to write a screenplay. They've all done it. They have been in the trenches of despair, and they have learned from the experience.

They know character. They know concept. They can take you from the beginning of a story to the end by showing you character arcs and motivation. They can make the reader sit up and take notice.

They know what's been done and what hasn't, and they know how to take a single character at the most critical moment of her life and make her so appealing in her turmoil that a bankable actor will be attracted to the part.

When William Goldman said that in Hollywood nobody knows anything, he meant that nobody has any idea if a project will be a success, artistically or financially. It's the big gamble in the big game. It's why people go to Hollywood, to see if they can make it in the most volatile, unpredictable industry in the world.

The Emerson Mafia knows what it takes to make studio execs respond and say yes to screenplays. They know how the story must play out on the page. They know when to get into a scene and when to get out, when to get into a story and when to draw the curtain on it. The Emerson Mafia knows what genre is, and they know that crossing genres lines, no matter how well a script is written, is like signing your own death warrant. They learned a lot of these things in my classes, then they carried the information and applied it to life in Hollywood as screenwriters.

Today, many of the old principles of screenwriting hold fast. But the face of Hollywood has changed. What used to be accepted is no longer accepted. What used to be taboo is no longer taboo.

I am astounded by the misinformation I hear from people about what is and what is not acceptable in story, character, pitch, and genre. Misinformation, and disinformation, are big sports in this town.

I have heard seasoned producers get their terms mixed up. They say one thing and mean another. As a writer pitching a project, you have to listen carefully to sort it out.

I have put tape recorders in front of my former students who have been through the life, are *in* the life, and know the ropes. They have things to say.

They learned in a hurry how to write and rewrite on the job and, as in the Bob Seeger song, they learned what to leave in and what to leave out. They cut corners and cut to the chase. They waded through agents and managers and producers, sharks, wannabe scribes, naysayers, and nurturers, and always went back to the fundamentals they learned in class.

The New Hollywood seems to reinvent itself seasonally. The fundamentals of storytelling have not changed nearly as much as story sense. Topics once unsavory are now sought out. The independent market craves odd-ball stories—well-written stories with strong characters, stories that will lure A-list talent, or at least bankable talent, in order to get the movie financed.

Consider low-budget features such as *The Man from Elysian Fields* (with Andy Garcia, Mick Jagger, James Coburn, Juliana Marguiles), *One Hour Photo* (Robin Williams), *The Dancer Upstairs* (directed by John Malkovich, starring Oscar winner Javier Bardem), *Jerry* (Matt Damon, Casey Affleck), *In the Bedroom* (Cissy Spacek, Marisa Tomei, Tom Wilkinson).

Talent wants to work. Actors need to exercise their skills. Today, many solid mid-level actors who used to demand big dollars are paid scale, or they don't work. They look for work out of the mainstream.

And why not? Why should they take a tiny part (or any part at all) for low pay in a studio picture, when they could get the lead or second lead in an independent feature that might break out and put their names back where they belong?

A-list talent has done that. We all know Travolta's story. *Pulp Fiction*. How grateful he was when Quentin Tarantino asked him to play a hit man. Billy Bob Thorton, a wide-ranging, theater-trained actor of immense talent, plays parts big and small. If a script grabs him, he takes the shot. That could be your script.

The old studio days are over. The big movies are in-house creations that live for the most part in development hell. Hollywood admits that the best stories, stories so original and dramatically shocking they take your breath away, come from the Provinces (anywhere other than Hollywood) and are written for the most part by new talent who have learned the fundamentals of screenwriting—story, structure, and character. These are often used as writing samples that get writers jobs on other projects.

Two distinct types of writers live in Hollywood: the writers of original screenplays and the work-for-hire scribes. Once the original writer gets one or two scripts under the belt, he or she becomes a studio writer. They can't afford to write spec scripts anymore because they're too financially chancy. They have families and homes, a big monthly nut. Their agents put them up for studio jobs. The work chooses them; their choices are limited. There are some writers who do both, but those are rare exceptions. On occasion, if time allows, a writer will fiddle with a spec script of his own.

When *The Huntress,* a book I wrote about a mother-daughter bounty hunting team, metamorphosed into the USA series, I got a dose of reality. I was under the impression that I was hot and Hollywood would want anything I wrote. My next script—an $80 million thriller—hit a wall. You're not as good as your last picture. You're as good as your current screenplay. Your last project will get you seen, but you had better top that last project.

Rejection? Getting turned down is the nature of the beast. It's a staple of the industry. Actors get about one of every thirty jobs they audition for. At those odds, you need a powerful antirejection shield. Call it tough self-love.

But you soldier on. That old saw—if it doesn't kill you, it will make you stronger—has always been in the Top Ten of Hollywood's survival kit.

Who cares if they all don't love you? After rejection, give yourself permission to sit on the pity pot for twenty-four hours and then get on to the next thing. It hasn't killed you, and you will get stronger.

Or—you've heard the tales—you can wither away like some sad flower and blow out of town. You might get angry at those bastards who didn't snap to your brilliance. Or you can become disillusioned. Look at what happened to the poor girl in David Lynch's *Mulholland Drive.*

Or you can put the "fun" back in fundamentals.

This book is as much about writing in the New Hollywood as it is a workshop about the process. I will take you through a series of classes, and together we'll build a screenplay, from a simple notion to the complete manuscript.

My students have finished first drafts in a month, in six months, in a year. There is no time limit as long as the work is steady. Devote those twenty minutes each day to keeping the characters fed and clothed, and their story will live. Otherwise, they will wither away, relegated to that drawer or cabinet where all partially finished screenplays go to die.

One of my students who has a full-time job as a graphics artist in Cambridge, Massachusetts, a wife, and two children, devotes an hour every evening after work, five days a week, to his scripts.

After the hour, no matter where he is in the script, he leaves his computer and goes on with the rest of his life.

For the rest of each day the story spins through his subconscious. His characters confront one another. The plot moves forward. The story unfolds.

He's been doing this for five years. He has taken on a good agent who likes his work. He's had two scripts optioned and one sold. He's been hired to write two scripts by production companies. One hour a day. Every day. Steady work.

Philadelphian Michael Schiffer (*Crimson Tide, Colors, The Four Feathers*) graduated from Harvard, went to Europe, fell in love, and moved to Hollywood. He wrote two published books and fourteen multi-drafted screenplays before he was hired to write the script that was to launch his career. He busted his ass and didn't give up. He knew what he wanted and how to get it—by hard, back-breaking work, day after day, until he got good. It took him six years to hit. Now he's a top Hollywood screenwriter. He hasn't slowed down. He takes vacations with his family. He goes to the office every day. He takes meetings with studio execs. He's a working man who practices the art of his choice: writing movies.

I can't teach you the art of writing, but I can show you the craft. The art is yours. It's what makes you tick, makes you see the world as you do, and satisfies your need to express your feelings through story and character.

I can show you tricks, ways to do things, and methods to build story and character. How to lay the story out on the screenwriting page. How to stay connected to your story and not go rambling off somewhere and, with your characters, get hopelessly lost, usually in the desert of Act II.

I can also show you, once you're done, how to get your script read, how to sidestep the pitfalls, and how to confront the inevitables of the business, directly, without flinching.

I can offer you these things, just as you can offer your characters the things you know from the well of your experience. I can't write it for you, I wouldn't presume to, just as you should never try to do it all for your characters. Instead, let *them* run the show, as they should. They are the masters of the story. You are their servant, just as I am your servant. You give the characters guidance; I give you guidance.

One of the big problems with most writing programs is that there is too much hand-holding and not enough of the reality checks that writing on a daily basis throws in front of you.

How many times has one of my students come up to me and said, "Why can't I get this? My teachers have always liked my writing, all my teachers, all through high school."

"I like your writing," I tell him. "But your story needs work. Your structure needs tightening. Your writing will mean nothing if you don't know how to structure. Your characters need depth. You need to compress time and space. Your coupling of words on the page looks great, but writing is not a bunch of adverbs that dress up the verb, or impressive vocabulary, or how pretty something sounds. And besides, when you send your work out to some anonymous agent or producer, you're not going to be there with your baby blues to explain what you really meant by this or that. It ain't the classroom out there. You have to enter that world a fully rounded talent, or with a huge potential talent, or you'll fail."

You'll fail anyway, for a while. Hard work and paying attention will get you through the jungle. Think of this book as a machete, hacking through the debris.

Hot Property is about writing the screenplay in the New Hollywood *and* learning what to expect once your script leaves your hands and plows into the marketplace.

It's the most frustrating and satisfying journey you'll ever make. If you stick with it, if you take the lessons and apply them, and if I've done my job right, you'll learn what it takes to put your vision down on paper and eventually up on the screen.

CLASS ONE

You Liked WHAT??!!

I ask, "Seen any bad movies lately?" Hands shoot up. "*Harry Potter!* Dull and stupid." "*Vanilla Sky.* Incomprehensible, with egomaniacs for characters." "*The Majestic.* Phony and sentimental." "*A.I.* The kid wanted to go home to that woman, his mother, who threw him out? I don't think so."

Other reasons for loathing these dogs: Predictability. Stupidity. Pandering to the audience's lowest common denominator. Ridiculous dialogue. No story. Unbelievable. Logic holes an entire fleet of trucks could roll through. Insipid. Confusing. *What* plot? Derivative. Self-conscious. Precious. Too slow. Too long. Too loud. No depth. Dumb!

On and on they go about all the things wrong with movies. When you plunk down $20 for two tickets, another $20 for popcorn, drinks, etc.—well, for that much you expect your money's worth.

Whose fault is it? The studios who pump up their trailers by gathering all the wicked glances and car chases and hot music to tease you and seduce you into spending that $40, only to have you discover that the trailer *is* the movie?

Or is it the producers and studio execs who, by trying to keep their jobs, aim for that lowest common denominator: mediocre, supposedly inoffensive crap over which focus groups have the final say?

Or what about the director who is under the studio's financial gun? After fighting for months over "creative differences" with actors and producers, he has given up and let them have their way. The director wants to work again and does not want that kiss-of-death "too difficult" rep shadowing him or her around town.

Take *Harry Potter and the Sorceror's Stone,* a mediocre movie at best. Why did Warner Brothers choose workmanlike director Chris Columbus (*Home Alone, Mrs. Doubtfire*) when they could have had a visionary like Tim Burner or Spike Jonze? They had a guaranteed $250 million domestic box office, giant foreign sales, and a forever video life. A squirrel could have directed it and the fans would have come.

Does blame fall on J.K. Rowling, the author, who had, they say, control over director and cast? Or did Warner Brothers, who has four more *Harry*'s in the works, not want to depart from the book, disappointing the fans, thus killing the franchise?

Chris Columbus's *Harry Potter* is like the fancy bistro that spends all its money on décor and none on the chef, serving a flat, insubstantial meal. Those restaurants go under. Fast. Franchise or no franchise.

Why *are* bad movies made? Some are made to satisfy the fiscal budget. On the studio docket are four or five films with similar budgets, any one of which can be made so the studio will not have next year's budget cut back by its parent company.

Sometimes producers, directors, and other studio people get so caught up in that insulated world of movie and money making that they can't see (or don't want to see) the piece of dreck unspooling before them.

Then they realize after it's too late that the movie *was* a dumb idea to begin with, a misconception from the get-go. So they hope the thing will somehow miraculously turn into a masterpiece or at least turn a profit. They can't scrap the movie. There's too much invested.

Vanilla Sky, for instance, is an ill-conceived piece of high-falutin' extract that made little sense. But Tom Cruise starred and, after many false starts, Cameron Crowe came aboard. This is an element picture (the elements, like Cruise and Cruz, were attached), originally shot as a Spanish picture, a story about an egomaniacal, narcissistic rich guy who has acrophobia and a rich daddy who left him control of a publishing empire. By the end of the picture, the Cruise character's ego is intact. He'd been living a nightmare contrived by a cryogenic company. He throws himself off a building to cure his fear of heights. And his message is, don't dream when you can live life without worrying about not looking handsome. Huh? In the theater where I saw it, half the audience left during the first thirty minutes.

As somebody put it, did Tom Cruise need to make a $60 million movie to tell the world that he's losing his looks?

Somebody at the studio level championed it and developed it—to the tune of millions. The studio was in so deep that it needed to make the movie. They had guaranteed deals with talent. They couldn't afford *not* to make it.

This dog scampered up on the screen, wagged its scraggly tail, and was carted off to the video kennel where it belonged in the first place.

When all is said and done, this and many other marginal films like it should never have been made. Writers hit a concept; agents get on the bandwagon; and stars, directors, and producers get lathered up. Even with a fundamentally weak concept, everybody can buffalo the studio into ponying up millions on a dumb idea.

Business as usual. The concept got the ball rolling so fast that the deal outpaced it and became the only thing that mattered. As George Lucas once put it, "In Hollywood they don't make movies, they make deals."

Now everybody has to pay, starting with the writer, without whose idea this never would have happened. But the writer got paid, and got paid more, at this stage, than anyone else. The writer always gets paid, whether the movie is made or not. The big payoff is if the movie goes before the cameras, but the writer always gets something up front.

So when a movie like this fails, it's no wonder the writer is vilified. *The Player* had it right. Shoot the writer.

In this most collaborative of all businesses, everyone stands on the sidelines as a project moves toward fruition. If the movie is made, or is in production, and looks as if it will tank, people all over town disassociate themselves, disavowing this or that, pointing fingers. If, on the other hand, that smell of success wafts in, you can't beat back the people who are jumping in to take responsibility.

Business as usual.

It's like the caddy and the golf pro. When the pro hits a lousy shot, the caddy says, "You blew it." When the pro hits one close to the stick, the caddy, head perked up, says, "We nailed that one, didn't we?"

So, have you see any bad movies lately?

In movies, everybody is a critic. All the good reasons you use to criticize a movie should also be applied to your own work.

* * *

I always point out to my students that the movies they criticize are
movies they have chosen to watch in the first place. For whatever reason,
they have gone to the theater and plunked down $10. Was there something
about the concept of the picture, or love of the star, that compelled them
to spend two hours of their time?

Pay attention to the reasons why you see certain movies and avoid
others. In that choice lies the subject matter or genre of the kind of
movies you should, or should not, be writing.

Make a list of the last ten movies you have gone to see. Think about
those flicks. You will notice patterns forming. Types of pictures emerge—
thrillers, romantic comedies, outright comedies, and oddball independents.

From these insights you will discover other things about the nature of
your likes and dislikes. If you had a choice for tonight, would you rather
see *Fight Club* or *Shallow Hal* or *The Man Who Wasn't There*? Why?

By answering this question candidly, you're drawing closer to the
genre. You have an affinity for this type of movie. You instinctively know
what the mechanics are. Your guts cry out in joy or criticism. Your
organs grind with the ebb and flow of pictures like these.

You know you can do better than this, you say, and you are probably
right. You know this genre, and you know this type of flick because
you've seen a million of them. When you hear about this type of movie
opening, something goes *ka-wang!* in you and tells you that you WILL
SEE this movie as soon as it comes out.

What *is* that *ka-wang?!* It's a tip-off to the kind of movie you love, a
genre you should be exploring in your writing, the type of movie you
want to master.

DRILL: *Make a list of movies that gave you your own ka-wang!*
Those movies you tracked for months, waiting for them to come out.
What was behind the ka-wang? What was that itch to see it all about?
If you can make a short list of those movies and the ones you're now
looking forward to seeing, you'll be a long way toward discovering
what kind of movie you should be writing.

Going Around the Room

There's nothing quite so revealing as first-day students talking about themselves, opening themselves up to total strangers. Call it lower-level group therapy.

It's the first step in the writing process: letting things out of the bag by speaking your mind and revealing what you feel.

It's not easy. Not many of us like to open up to strangers. But that's what writing is. Just because a page and a piece of celluloid and many miles separate the writer from the eventual moviegoer, it's what the writer puts on the page that reveals the source.

If you back off, or hedge, or try to cover up true feelings, people will not want to read you. They will pull up after ten facile, insubstantial pages and pass.

I used to worry what people would think of me if they read my stuff, and so I would only deliver half-truths. I paid the price by eliciting their vast disinterest in reading on.

The truth is that readers are interested in your characters, not in you. This is not a popularity contest.

If you're guarded in the first place, as we all are, the process will take time. In writing, you've got to climb out of yourself and give the story over to your characters.

In Week One, I ask the students four questions:

1. Where are you from?

2. Why are you interested in writing in this strange form—screenwriting—when most of you have never even read a screenplay?

3. What movie influenced you the most?

4. Tell us about your darkest childhood memory.

I answer these questions, too—sometimes right up front to let everybody know that in my class very little is taboo.

These questions all have to do with *back story*, with influences, with the reasons behind what brought them here at this time in their lives. The questions can be intimidating. They're meant to be.

They all address character. Your characters will have a life before we meet them on the page. They have pasts and influences and dark childhood memories, just like you.

The answers to these questions will fuel you through the writing process. They compel you to re-create your past, to discover the movies that formed you and the type of movie you now want to write (your source of your creative urges), and to reveal the dark childhood moments that struck at or formed your fears.

If you can ask hard questions about yourself, you will get closer to the crux of your characters. By continuing to ask yourself these questions you will find paths to the fears, needs, and motivations of your characters. You will be able to tap inner resources leading to problem-solving of character and story. The answer will reveal to you the writer and creator within, the reasons behind your decisions, and the mistakes that might have plagued you as a writer and perhaps a human being.

DRILL: *Get on the computer and type in the questions. Think about them. The students in class don't have your luxury; they have to blurt out their answers in front of strangers.*

When you answer them, be utterly honest. Forget about wonderful style or complete sentences. Just do it, from your heart or your soul or your gut. Let it spill or pour out of you. This pouring or spilling is the best way to get unstuck in writing.

1. WHERE ARE YOU FROM?

This goes to the core of how you define yourself and implies so much more than the question suggests. Your answer *is* the essence of you and determines all the choices you make. This is autobiography; be honest about it. *Where are you from?* addresses heart of character.

In class I ask everyone to close his or her eyes, verbally ask themselves the question, and visually see the answer. That won't work here. Here on the page I'll ask you to do it another way.

Sit in front of your computer and type in the answers (the best method) or if you hunt and peck after each question, close your eyes and *see, then write.* Then go on to the next more specific question.

Where were you born? See the house, the apartment. Rural or suburban or urban? Parents? See them. Both there? What did they do during the day?

With whom did you get along with better? Worse? Why? How did this affect your relationship with men? Women? Which parent did you trust more? Did they get along? Did they not? Why? Did you have only one parent?

Did they divorce? Ugly relationship? Loving? Silent anger? Re-create a moment from their relationship that says it all. Go ahead. Visualize it. Write it down.

How does their relationship affect your relationships today? Are you argumentative? Are you easygoing? Do you appear placid but underneath are you filled with resentment or rage?

You're going to have to know these things about your main characters; might as well use yourself as the template.

Did your family struggle financially? How emotional were the economics? Tight-fisted? Free spending? What are you now? How do you see money now?

Are you an only child? Oldest? Youngest? Were great expectations foisted upon you? Have you met them? Were you ignored?

I blocked out nearly my entire life until I was fifteen, which through therapy and some self-exploration, I am still trying to figure out.

Who was the most influential person of your childhood, negatively *and* positively? Who did you love and trust? Who did you fear? See that person. Paint a mental picture. Write down the description of this person. Fear drives us. How has that relationship affected your life up until now?

There was this guy in my family. He terrified me. He drank and he fought and he was a giant. I loved him and feared him. I never knew where he was coming from. I blocked out almost all of him, but I remember the feeling. He had a name. Dad.

This is autobiography. It's a prelude to creating vivid characters. If you are able to be utterly honest about your own past, your chances of driving to the center of your characters are that much better.

In school were you a leader or follower? Did you have friends, or were you mainly a loner? How so? How has this affected your later life? Are you a loner now? Are you comfortable alone?

I have a friend who, before he goes to bed at night, offers to pay people to stay in the house so he can go to sleep. He can't stand to be alone, even with himself.

As a kid, were you a good student? Were you loved for it? Who was your best friend? Close your eyes. See her or him. What did you admire or like about this person? What did you not like about him or her?

As a child, what was the worst thing you did? The worst! The thing you are most ashamed of. Be honest.

Now you're around twelve. Close your eyes. You're leaving grade school and moving up into another world. Middle school. Puberty enters. What about those hormones and sexual urges? How did you handle that? Were you afraid of them, or wild? How are you now? Gay? Straight? Bi?

I ate a lot. I gained lots of weight. I was a very fat kid, ashamed of my fat. I wore big cardigan sweaters to hide my fat. I was a fat, depressed kid who spent most of his time alone. I wanted desperately to belong. I didn't even have my first kiss until I was sixteen, and I kissed the fullback's girl—which ushered me into a world of hell.

When was your first sexual experience? How was it? With whom? How did you feel about it? What did you think about sex? What do you think about it now? Close your eyes. Think. See.

As a Catholic, I was brought up on a healthy dose of shame. Catholics have shame. Jews have guilt. What do you have? I have lost religion, and I lost my virginity at eighteen to a prostitute in a hotel room in Columbia, South Carolina.

Close your eyes. When did it happen for you? How did you feel?

You have to know this experience with your main character. In order to know your characters on the page, in your present story, you have to know what drives them, where their urges began. You cannot know them now without knowing them then. If you don't know what happened to them before we meet them on the first page of the script, you won't know them at all, and the script will show that.

You're in high school. Close your eyes. Where is that place? Paint a picture. Were you popular? Shunned? Ridiculed? Who were your friends? Close your eyes. See them. Why did you hang around with them?

There was Belinda, a beautiful girl who lived across the street. The first love of my life. Long, dark hair, dark eyes, she was the daughter of the woman I think my father loved. I was always jealous of the handsome twins Linda said she adored. Back and forth she went between them. She told me I was always steady at number three.

There was Jenna, my true pal, who I told everything to, no secrets.

Total trust. Jenna was, as have other women just like her throughout my life, my best friend. Having been brought up by women, I trust women more than I do men. I get along with women better.

Do you read? Are you a DVD-challenged video freak? What do you do when you're alone? What are your secrets? Name two. See them. See yourself doing them. Close your eyes. Write them down.

Your characters will close their eyes and see these things and you will write them down for them. Not what *you* did for the first twenty-five years of your life, but what *they* did.

A fatal error writers commit during the course of writing a screenplay is in asking what they, the screenwriters, would do under this or that given set of circumstances.

Never ask what you would do, but instead ask what your characters would do. Asking yourself ends up with a flat screenplay where every character thinks and speaks the same. Huge mistake. What would THEY do? The characters. Readers don't care what you would do. We all care, however, what your characters would do. Characters are the masters of the story. You are their servant.

Your first real crime, what was it? And your second? Theft? Worse?

Where are you from? means a lot more than place.

One of my students, Ted C., whose father was a dentist, wrote about a crazy dentist who did too much of his own nitrous oxide and lured young patients into his office for sex and other situations, thereby destroying his family and ruining the life of his son, who looked up to him, remote as he was.

Ted's script is odd, quirky, and very funny, with a strong family dynamic—a dark comedy pulled from the annals of Ted's life. It turned out that Ted wrote this for other reasons. His father *was* remote and stayed by himself most of the time, in his office, which was in the house. Ted carried a big resentment against his dad, who cared little for his family and eventually ran away with one of his patients.

Ted not only had an attention-grabbing world from which to draw, he also had a emotional attitude toward it, which compelled him to keep writing. He wrote a lot of the script, he told me, out of anger against and resentment for his father.

He was attached to the story, invested in it. He knew the world well, and he was pissed at Pop. All these things contributed to the writing of a good script.

Ted had had this idea for a while but didn't know how to put it down. In class he discovered structure, dramatic build, character development, *story*. In six months he had a workable first draft.

Ted went back into his childhood to rediscover feelings for his father and mother, the memories of solitude and loneliness, and the awful discoveries he made about his father. He spent a number of weeks before he felt equipped to write, before he felt comfortable enough sort out the painful moments and fashion them into a story worthy of a screenplay.

He got honest with himself, wrote down what he had imagined and told friends, and compared these to what he remembered as having really happened, the sham and the resentments he could not bear to tell anyone.

With a screenplay he had found a vehicle he could use to reveal the truth, with a character—the young man—with whom he could identify even though the young man was more or less himself. Plus he had a purpose—to write and perhaps find a profession. This made the experience more palatable, more purposeful.

In the end, he also acknowledged that writing a screenplay was like therapy. He realized things about his father and himself that he might not have discovered otherwise.

Merri L., twenty-five, is tall, thin, and from Oregon. Her black hair has the texture of velvet seaweed rolling in off the Pacific. Merri is mellow on the outside and fiercely emotional on the inside.

When her grandmother died, she nearly lost her mind. She was the only person who meant anything to Merri. The grandmother's wish was to have her ashes tossed into a lake in Missouri, where she was born.

And so Merri, who was also born near that lake, got in her car, in Oregon, and headed for Missouri with a canister filled with her grandmother's ashes. This journey, which started in sorrow, proved to be the most extraordinary journey Merri had ever taken.

Her journey is based on truth. For the screenplay, Merri took the events of the journey, shaved away the stuff she didn't need, and kept the stuff she did need. She strung the events together, sometimes fiddling with chronology, and turned them into a picaresque story of a young woman and a promise she made to herself and to her grandmother.

On Merri's journey she encountered people, places, and things that got in the way of her mission, big time. These made her stronger. They scared her. She wanted to turn around and go home, but in the end, these hurdles gave her courage and changed her life. She started out to accomplish something and along the way found something phenomenal she never expected—herself.

Merri came from Oregon, but mainly she came from emotion, drive, and need. She had a story to tell that changed her significantly, but only after going through trials by fire, physically and emotionally. As a writer she did not rivet herself to the details of the story, but she remained true to the *essence* of it. She paid attention to that old adage—don't let the facts get in the way of a good story.

Her story, in reality, is an adaptation. She adapted to the screen a story in her life, weeding out the dull and inserting the dramatic and the conflicted. She did not have to go to unfamiliar territory, or places she hadn't experienced, to write about characters she knew nothing about. She told the story of a time in her life that mattered.

In the process of going back and then writing their screenplays, both Ted and Merri understood what character is, how character gets motivated, and how fear drives most action in life and in screenplays. Their characters, loosely based on real people, were fuller.

The questions they put to themselves they also put to their main characters—protagonists and antagonists alike.

When you track back through your own life—as you have done, or will do, using the question *where are you from?*—you should discover gobs of fresh storytelling material. All you have to do is stay tuned.

You do not have to cast yourself as the main character. If you do, you could run into the problem that everyone else runs into: By using yourself as the main character, you will tend not to be as honest as you would be with a character NOT based on you.

Although their screenplays were based on the familiar, both Ted and Merri got stuck. To unstick themselves they found photos of people who they imagined their characters to look like. This enabled them to wean the characters away from themselves, freeing them of the self-consciousness associated with writing a story with the writer as main character.

You've met people who have gone through critical moments in their own lives that far out-dramatize anything you've seen on the screen. It's a matter of seeing life's turning points and recognizing their story potential.

As you go back, keep a lookout for stories you've heard, people you've met, relatives who have gone through hell, who make good drama, and who have stayed with you. Takes notes. I guarantee you'll come back later.

Writers work out of their own experiences. It's a matter of seeing.

The person who carries a camera with him will see photo ops he would never see if he left his camera home. Take your sense of story with you.

Above all, look for big emotional bombs and their big dramatic results.

Where are you from? means, to a writer, *how do I build a past for my main characters?*

DRILL: *Where are you from? There's no right or wrong answer. It's a simple question with a lot of possible, and complex, answers. Get on the machine or pad and let it rip.*

---

2. WHAT MADE YOU DECIDE TO SEEK OUT THIS STRANGE FORM—SCREENWRITING—WHEN YOU'VE PROBABLY NEVER EVEN READ A SCREENPLAY?

This question nets a wide variety of answers. *"I needed one more class to graduate and thought I'd take a look at screenwriting, but I've got two backups in case I don't like it."* I love the honesty.

"I'm crazy about movies. That's what I do when I'm not doing anything else. And I'm hardly ever doing anything else."

I've had students who have seen just about every movie ever made. With this group of people, who must have spent 40 percent of their lives watching movies, it's like having a living, breathing human resource in class. They know plots, characters, and truckloads of arcane information.

One thing about teaching screenwriting that you never get with novel or short story is total context, complete frame of reference. You mention a movie title in class and everybody has seen it or knows something about it. Everybody has heard about it and can give you plot details or even dirt on cast members. The frame of reference is immediate and huge. Not so in books. Hardly ever in short stories. Rarely in poetry.

For some people, to attempt a novel is like facing a mountain they do not want to climb. Short stories are satisfying, but can you make a living writing short stories? Or poetry? Everybody should read poetry, wherein lives the soul of our language.

Screenwriting is the new manna from heaven. One hundred seven pages. Doable. If you write three pages a day for forty days, you have a first draft.

This is attractive to people who have wanted to tell a story but could not find the medium with which to tell it. Screenwriting is all about character and action. Character *is* action. In movies, what one does is what one is.

If you can't see it, it doesn't belong on the page. It's all visual. Screenwriting takes place first and foremost in a visible and visual world. You have to see it. You can't see thought, for instance. Action replaces thought, dialogue replaces thought.

Watching a movie is a passive experience. Reading, on the other hand, is active. The reader controls the environment and can pick up and put down the book at will. In a theater, there is not this option. What does this say about the different audiences? Books take time to read. Watching a movie takes two hours. Besides, they say, who has time to slog through a four hundred-page novel these days?

I don't like it, but this is the thinking.

For me, books are lifeblood. They belong to you. In a book *you* set the pace. Why would you want to write for the movies? After you finish your masterpiece and hand it in, all they want to do is change it.

Let's say your script garners interest from agents, managers, producers, stars, and directors, and looks as if it's got a shot at the big screen. The first thing they do is fire you and hand your baby to fifty foster parents, all of whom are convinced they have striking ideas on how to improve it.

Then, let's say it's produced. It comes out in a totally different medium. You write it on paper and it appears on celluloid or tape. The story has changed shape, and look what they did to your characters! And what about that great dark ending you put on it, which is now light and airy and everybody gets what they want? You want to kill yourself. Is this the writing life you want?

And then, the final insult: It might not even have your name on it because the first thing they did when they fired you was to hire another writer, then another, then four others, none of whom you've ever met. The actors and producers and directors added their changes to it, without consulting you. The Writers Guild's arbitration board gathered all drafts and awarded credit to another writer, someone you have never met or even heard of.

But, hey, you have a picture on, sort of, and people are willing to meet you, to hear your new ideas and pitches. All so you can go through that awful process again. Come *on!* What are you, a masochist?

Why would you want to work in a medium whose writers Louis B. Mayer once called "Schmucks with Underwoods," a perception that has changed little in the last fifty years?

Ah, because you want to write. You need to write. And you love movies. And this is *your* manna from heaven. You're determined, huh? You have a story burning in you, or fifty stories burning in you, and you need to let them out of their cages. And writing movies is the only way you can do it. This is the only way you think you'll be ABLE to do it. You believe this.

Okay, if that's what you want, give it a shot. You already connect with movies in ways you have never connected with books or short stories or poetry. Celluloid veins snake through your body. Your blood runs in frames per second. Your eyes are projectors.

Okay. It's your manna, your heaven.

DRILL: *There is something you love about movies and something else that makes you want to write them. If you're going to write, what is it about movies (as opposed to books, short stories, etc.) that gives you this urge? Misspell everything, who cares! Forget about sentence structure or logic. Just get it down.*

CLASS TWO
Big Movies, Dark Memories, and Healing the Writer's Wound

3. WHAT MOVIE INFLUENCED YOU THE MOST?

What's the movie that influenced you the most? Not the one you liked the best or loved the least, but the one that *affected* you like no other?

Citizen Kane? Miller's Crossing? Lawrence of Arabia? Goonies? You never know how a particular movie is going to grab you.

Here's Scott Sand, a student from Pittsburgh, who is writing a character-driven movie about male bonding, revenge, and betrayal: "*Miller's Crossing* moved me with its loneliness, with the overwhelming sense of being alone in the world, enacted through heartbreaking betrayals and reversals. Eddie Reagan (Gabriel Byrne) doesn't fit in. He is loyal to his boss but is secretly dating his girlfriend. In the end Eddie betrays his boss to save his friend, Bernie, who later betrays Eddie.

"I have always put loyalty above obligation, and sometimes it's hard, so I responded to this. It's not a caper movie but a character story; the complexity is in the hard decisions the characters are forced to make.

"For my computer desktop I've chosen the image of Bernie pleading to Eddie for his life, trying to convince him that they are different from the people they work for. But they're trapped, too, by the things they do.

"It's sad, dark, and lonely. For me, the image of that hat blowing through the woods sums up the picture. And the line: 'There's nothing sadder than a man chasing after his hat.' "

Here's Allison Elliot, a student who writes about herself in the third person: "Allison Elliot was born prematurely in Rochester, New York, April 10, 1978. The jaundiced infant was placed in an incubator and stored in a room away from the other babies for being yellow and strange looking. This pattern would repeat itself in various guises for the rest of her life."

Here's what Allison says about the movie that most affected her: "When I was ten or eleven I saw *Amadeus*. My intense reaction focused on the character of Salieri, the court musician, and his complicated feelings for Mozart.

"He befriends Mozart and proceeds over time to destroy him. In so doing, the calculating and vicious Salieri engineers his own demise. As much as I marveled at how low he could sink, I could not get rid of strong feelings of sympathy for him.

"The tragedy of Salieri's life is this: God gave him the desire to be a great composer but not the ability. Salieri had been living under the impression that he was a success. He had royal commissions and the love of his audience and critics. He was upright and religious and he devoted his music to God. All of this came crashing down when he meets Wolfgang Amadeus Mozart.

"When he hears Mozart's music, Salieri recognizes his own inadequacy. He comes face to face with true genius and knows he is incapable of such beauty. This might have been bearable if Mozart were a great man. Instead, he's a silly, immature, whiny, oversensitive libertine.

"For me, the movie abolishes every notion about justice and fairness. *Amadeus* is about the mystery of genius and the mystery of hate and, following that line, the mystery of God. No matter how much one tries to criticize or explain away Salieri's behavior, you can't get past the feeling that he's been wronged.

"Salieri can no longer make sense of his own life and neither can the audience. The idea that the bestowal of genius or talent is as random and undeserved as the bestowal of, say, Down's syndrome, is a hard pill to swallow at any age. Salieri chokes on it and the result thrilled and terrified me."

Will Oakley, a tall, gangly grad student from Alabama, has this story to tell about how *Pee-Wee's Big Adventure* changed his life: "It was the funniest movie my six-year-old eyes had ever beheld. At a Chinese restaurant afterward, while my mother and sister ate Mongolian beef, I performed Pee-Wee's greatest scenes.

"That fall I returned to school. I hated it there. I was no good at sports, and in Alabama, if you're no good at sports, all you're good for is getting your ass kicked.

"One day the teacher was called out of the room, and the class bully started making his rounds, pounding us athletically challenged kids. When he came to me and was about to sock me one, for some reason I let out Pee Wee's weak, apprehensive high-pitched laugh.

"In that moment everything changed. The bully said, 'Do that again.' I did. The class went into hysterics. When the teacher came in she found me reciting the line from the movie: 'I know you are, but what am I?'

"I got my name on the Frowning Face list that day, but I didn't care. The other students liked me. I started checking out joke books from the library and using my allowance on whoopee cushions and peanut brittle cans filled with spring snakes.

"I stayed up late watching Johnny Carson's monologue and next day did his jokes in class. Humor became my shield, how I made it day to day in the vicious world of the Alabama educational system.

"I was one of only two boys in the school who didn't play football, but I was allowed to live a wedgie-free life. The other boy, a Trekie, disappeared a month later."

The question I put to these students—What's the movie that influenced you the most?—goes to the heart of your creative and emotional impulses. You will probably key in on the genre you should be in. In Will's case, it's a kind of David vs. Goliath comedy.

The next question to ask yourself: *What kind of movie should I be writing?*

Some people answer, "Oh, I like all types of movies. I'm not particular." I hate that answer because it inevitably leads to the writer running through a bunch of story lines, crisscrossing genres, unable to make up his or her mind, and finally meeting that big wall: utter frustration.

What kinds of movies make you shudder with anticipation? Todd Solenz movies? Arnold's action extravaganzas? The Coen brothers? The Farrelly brothers? What's *with* all these brother teams?

Is it the tone that moves you? The oddball story lines?

What *is* it about that tingle that says, "I can't *wait* to see this movie!" Familiarity and great expectation joining forces? A signal that this is where you truly love to be?

What a tip-off. There's none stronger. This is the area or genre you should be writing in.

And while you're thinking about that, I'll tell you about an experience I had, which in my creative life could have been the worst thing that ever happened to me—and was for a while. It could have stopped my writing career dead, and it almost did.

During my first year or so in this writing business, when I was just getting my feet wet, I had finished a novel and was scouting around for another idea. My agent and I were sitting in his office in New York one day when he said to me, "I have the next book you're going to write."

"You do?"

"It's about the fur industry," he announced.

"The fur industry?" I said. A bell went off; one of those dull bells that indicates minimal interest.

"The time is 1600," he says. "We're in Canada, in Thunder Bay. Fur trappers send their pelts down river to St. Louis, where they're bought by traders, who sell them to manufacturers, to rich consumers, who wear these magnificent, elegant warm coats. John Jacob Astor made his fortune in the fur business, along with a thousand other hungry capitalists. The history of America is the history of the fur business, in every aspect. Struggle, opening of the West, glamour, politics, billions of dollars, from dreary Minnesota woods to the great salons in every major city of the world.

"You follow a couple families over a four-hundred-year period, using the fur business as a metaphor for America rising and changing with the times. Take these two families, always at war with one another, through the centuries. Take them to St. Louis, the gateway to the West. Take them to Russia and the pricey fur business, to the murder and mayhem of the people willing to kill over the this furry goddess."

Furry goddess? I'm thinking.

"To the ultraglamorous fur industry, the rise of the Communist party, the beginnings of the American mobster. Glamorous on the outside, exploitative and murderous below."

I'm on the edge of my seat, watching my agent/storyteller spin this yarn of epic proportions.

"You take us to the grand international salons. You take us through the sweatshops, through the Communist party scandals of the 1920s and 1930s, through HUAC and Congressional subcommittees. You lead us into the multibillion dollar stolen pelt business, to the veldt of South African exotic hides. And through the war against fur, the animal rights groups.

"You've got the whole world to tell your story, but specifically through the multibillion-per-year fur industry for which thousands of people have died, and others made their fortunes, seen through the eyes of two warring families."

"Okay," I'm saying, my head pumping up and down.

"And I even have your title," the agent said. "Call it *Mink!*"

Oh my God. I was breathless, flabbergasted at the immensity of it all. But I could see it; a big, rambling epic moving across time, driven by destiny. The history of the world through animal pelts. *Mink!*

So I gathered up my ambition and wits and spent the next four years, off and on, in library stacks, interviewing furriers, charting family ancestries, planning big moments over time, finding anchors or turning points by which to tell the story, jumping sometimes seventy-five years at a clip.

I talked about it to friends. In my mind I made this an event of monumental proportions. But the truth was, I was failing. I knew it but I didn't stop or step back. I was determined to see it through, no matter what. But deep down I was panicking.

I had mountains of research; I devoted an entire room in my small apartment to this monster. I filed and arranged, refiled and rearranged. I had note cards about note cards. Red, yellow, orange, white.

I built a giant corkboard against one wall to see what I had. What I had was overpowering and growing out of control. I would sit for hours looking at the movement of my two families, over time and space, intersecting. Fur and melodrama. Fortunes rose, lives were lost. The migraines began; I fell into a dark stupor.

I pretended to everyone that I was doing fine, but they knew better. Yet they kept encouraging me because they loved the idea. *They* loved it. *I* loathed it. I wished I had never gotten in, and now I didn't think I would ever get out. My Frankenstein was eating his creator.

My first real breakthrough—let's call it break out—came when a friend who saw my dilemma asked me a question I wished I had asked myself. She said, "Hey, Chris, do you even like to read this kind of book?"

The question was like a tsunami crashing over me. She said she had never seen me more dumbfounded. My jaw hung open. I blubbered something.

"No," I managed to say, "I hate to read these kinds of books."

"Why is that?"

"I can never keep anything straight. I lose control of the situation. I lose interest. I like stories that take place in short periods of time, all revolving around one central event, with characters in conflict and utter turmoil, with a ticking clock."

"Then what in the hell are you doing trying to write this book?"

"Committing suicide?" I said.

"Exactly."

What a revelation! I had suspected as much before, but I buried the thought under those mountains of research and denial.

What a hard lesson to learn, but that's how I seem to learn all my lessons. I keep making mistakes until they pile up and then one day—KABOOM!—the revelation whacks me up side the head and I finally get it.

I abandoned this dead horse, uh, mink, and got the mink off my back. Yet even today, years later, I sometimes wonder if I had just pulled the truck a little farther . . . After which the reality of that situation clobbers me, as it did then, and I know I made the wise choice.

These days, one of the first things I tell anybody who asks me what they should write, is this: "If it's a novel, tell me where you go when you first enter a bookstore, when you're looking for something to read. Mystery? Women's fiction? Romance? Sci-Fi? Literary fiction? Where do you go? What draws you to that section? That's the area in which you should be writing your book."

In movies, it's the same thing. You know what grabs you. You know how you feel when that certain movie is out and you *have* to see it.

You know the genre. You love it. You live for it. It's in you and has been since the beginning. You've had a love affair with it without even knowing it.

That's where you should be. Your instinct lives there. Your passion thrives there. Your anticipation boils over there. You can analyze it. You're confident talking about it. Your subconscious takes baths in it.

When you want to write a movie, you have to ask yourself that question. *Where do I gravitate? What kind of movie really turns me on?*

Thank God the *Mink!* cautionary tale made itself known to me. I would still be sailing down the river of no return with those two families. After investing in generation after generation for four hundred years, having to kill them off and start again with a whole new bunch of characters every seventy-five pages, always keeping in mind where each of them had come from and where they were going, I had had it. I carry a Palm Pilot because I can't remember what I'm supposed to do at 3 o'clock. Or what I did at 7 A.M. this morning. How in the hell was I supposed to remember every family member from two clans, and what they did—along with their friends, acquaintances, and enemies—over four centuries?

If the book didn't kill me, the migraines, and the frustration, would have.

Write what you know also means write what you *want* to know, or what you want to know *more about*. It goes back to why you like story-telling in the first place. What *kind* of storytelling? What kind of tone? Voice? Does the story take place in four hours, four days, or over four centuries? What attracts you?

What do you like to read? To see? Do you love epics? I'm not wild about epics, except David Lean's (*Lawrence of Arabia; Dr. Zhivago*), and I sure as hell don't want to write one.

When you go to the web, or to the school library, or to the bookstore to pick up a screenplay, when you're there looking at titles, what stops you? What about that movie sitting on the Blockbuster shelf makes you want to read the screenplay?

What movie has influenced or affected you the most? If you're not able to answer this question, you might spend an exasperated lifetime writing against the grain and wondering why you're not loving what you do. Your own *Mink!* could smother you!

In fact, you will most likely go through your own *Mink!* fiascoes to understand the nature of that beast. Even though experience is the best teacher, I wouldn't wish it on anybody. It's enough that one of us had to go through it. The least I can do, by telling you my sad tale of woe, is to try to steer you away from that pit.

If you're going to fail and learn lessons from it, do it in your own genre, not somebody else's.

I wish I had read something like this, from someone like me who had been through this, before I took off on that extravagant, time-consuming, migraine-begetting bad acid trip of an experience.

But the truth is, I had to go through it in order to recognize it and to pass it on later.

Search in your past for the key to your likes and dislikes. There is no reason for you to go through years of struggle when all you have to ask yourself is one question: *Do I even like to read that stuff? Or in this case, see that stuff?*

Here's Asa Pittman, who moved to Boston from St. Louis where she got her B.S. in pre-med:

"Steven Speilberg's *Empire of the Sun* terrified and inspired me. As a shy, overprotected kid, I first saw the movie at ten. It disturbed me to think that kid could be left alone in the world. How could James survive without his parents? How could I survive without my parents? It was the first time a movie moved me that way.

"I watched the movie several times over the years, in horrified fascination, hoping to feel the same emotional tug. Instead, I saw how James dealt with adversity.

"He not only survived without his parents, he thrived when most adults perished. I learned from James that who you are is not always who you have to be.

"James the sniveling British brat became Jim the thrifty POW and honorary American. When I feel that I have failed or have not been as courageous as I should, I think of James and his capacity for change.

"For five years I have lived in another part of the country from my parents. I spent last year alone in a foreign county against my parents' wishes. I feel I have Jim and *Empire of the Sun* to thank for that."

DRILL: *What about that movie made you stand up and take notice? What was it? What did it do to you? What was the fever? Get it down on paper. Get it down on the machine and save it. When you're writing your screenplay and you're stuck, you'll come back to it and get unstuck.*

4. WHAT *ABOUT* THAT DARK CHILDHOOD MEMORY OF YOURS?

My earliest dark childhood memory begins with me sitting on the upstairs landing of our home. It's midnight. I'm in my jammies. I peek down through the slats in the railing and watch my parents and their friends party.

I see people drinking and arguing. I see husbands and wives signal to other husbands and wives. I see hands flit across backsides and over shoulders, and secret looks. And even sometimes one husband and another wife slip off through separate exits and rendezvous in other parts of the house, then return to the party as if nothing happened.

I listen to very bright, drunk people arguing. The later it gets, the more the arguments heat up. I hear a lot of repetition, loud repetition, as if nobody is listening to anybody, including themselves.

I see my mother and father involved in all this. They are the young darlings of this community. Successful, smart, a beautiful couple. I notice how through manipulation—intellectual and physical—and fueled by alcohol, these people seek pleasure.

The things they say are funny and angry and wicked. Outrageous. I sit up there on the second floor, in the shadows, once, twice, three times a week, month after month, year after year, watching. Listening.

It's *Who's Afraid of Virginia Woolf* from a balcony seat. I see double-dealing, deceit, sadness, joy, and heart-wrenching pain. I know these people. They're my parents' friends. I go the school with their children. What I see from my balcony seat are very different people from the responsible parents I meet during the day. Through my young eyes I see this dichotomy and it puzzles me.

Things are not what they seem.

I see my father's best friend grab my mother's best friend's butt and the best friend slide toward him. I see my Mr. Tyler slide his hand around the waist of Mrs. Petrie and the looks they give to each other. And then they slip out of the room, to a secret place, in the dark. And they don't come back for a long time.

My imagination makes me strangely ill. But can I tear my eyes away? No. I want more. I love being this voyeur in the dark at the top of the stairs—with my future forming before my eyes, molded by what I see below.

How dark is this childhood memory? Dark enough.

These nights became the basis for what I do now. Write. The future writer watches, unseen, inspecting his future characters.

By ten years old I had started to write plays, and for the next ten years I wrote dozens, hundreds of them. Snippets of plays about people who use deceit, chicanery, verbal manipulation, and liquor to take from others what will satisfy themselves.

People deceive one another; husbands deceive wives, wives deceive husbands. I am deluged by the absence of trust, a theme that will later saturate my work, as well as my life.

It's not just the childhood memories themselves that I ask my students to bring into the open, but what the memories *mean*. How they worked their way into their lives.

How, I ask them, would you feel if you saw extramarital affairs blossom on a daily basis, watching this nocturnal soap opera unfold? How would you develop a character in adulthood who spent much of his childhood watching this behavior?

Did the young recorder of these events later become a participant in them, slipping from the observer to the (self-) observed? Did I climb down from the balcony seat to the field, from the fan to the player?

By asking these questions, you draw closer to yourself: *Why do I do what I do?* And, therefore, closer to the characters you create: *Why do they do what they do?*

You have to begin somewhere. Why not with yourself? Not your superficial self, the one you paint for others to see, but the one you know, warts and all. You have to be willing to own up to yourself before you're able to peel away the layers of your characters.

Dark childhood memories are a good starting point.

I remember one student who said he used to physically brutalize his brother and sister, then demand that they make up lies to tell their parents that some strange kids mauled them. Eventually, the student began mutilating himself. In this way it would seem that (a) he would also appear to be a victim and (b) out of guilt, he felt he needed to experience the pain he was inflicting.

By age twelve, he grew out of this behavior. In his early twenties now, he has no contact with his siblings, who want nothing to do with him. They have moved away and will not forgive him.

It's a source of great anguish for him. Nightmares haunt him. Drugs and psychiatry have not helped. He has decided to try to write himself to the source and perhaps by doing so will be able to forgive himself.

Dark childhood memories. They themselves can begin a quest suitable for a movie. This student is writing a story about a man who will do anything to get back into the graces of his battered family.

His working title: *What Comes Around . . .*

Once you extract one fully developed childhood memory, others invariably follow, as if they're all lined up back there in your subconscious, waiting to be urged into the light.

A handful of them will make a huge impact. Dorothy Allison, in her remarkable memoir, *Bastard Out of Carolina* (which became a movie directed by Angelica Huston), focuses on one moment in time, the pivotal moment, as it turned out, that established all her significant behavior later on.

When she was ten years old, her mother had a relationship with an abusive boyfriend. The boyfriend was so abusive, to both the mother and to Dorothy, that Dorothy begged her mother to leave him. Her mother had to make a choice between the boyfriend and her daughter.

She chose the boyfriend because she was afraid she would never find anyone like him again (and everything *that* implies). Her daughter, on the other hand, had her whole life in front of her and would make her way.

So the child Dorothy was sent off and the mother remained with the pain. And this, Dorothy Allison tells us, impacted her life like no other event. Read the book. It's amazing. Then see the movie.

In your screenplay you'll be focusing on the most critical moment of your character's life—a moment at a juncture of life and death, figuratively and literally.

It can be no other way or the story will not be worth telling. The stakes have to be at their highest. There will be no turning back by your main character, even though she might want to, because as the story progresses that door to the past closes, forcing your character to face the present, and the future. You will now discover what she is made of. Your *character* will discover what she is made of.

Consider Will Hunting when he is forced by circumstances to face his fear centers: his heart, his genius, and his psyche. He tries to run and hide from the confrontations with his girlfriend, played by Minnie Driver, and Robin Williams's character, the MIT professor, but there is no place to go. The world keeps intruding. Eventually, even his friends tell him he can't stay with them. Will Hunting has to turn and face the harsh light of the world and of himself. The writers are relentless. They attack these fear centers and pull Will, screaming and yelling, into the harsh light of day.

The writers closed the door to his prison of fears. There is no place for him to go finally but forward. So what is Will going to do now that he has entered another cage, that of the world at large?

Assailed in the heart, mind, and psyche, he is pushed out of his self-imposed darkness. His genius, his love, and his dark childhood memories are yanked from the shadows and cast down before him.

He fights. He resists. He tries to crawl back to his life in South Boston. Good luck, Will. South Boston sank into the sea. You're on your own now. Deal with it.

When you look back at your own childhood, there are moments—big moments—that slammed you up against the wall of experience. When you came to and climbed to your feet, you were about to become somebody else, or at least felt like someone who had just been through the most extraordinary moment of his life, as if you had been through the wringer.

Childhood memories boost the critical aspects of story. You give credence to the bomb exploding in your character's life and the ensuing fallout. The bomb illuminates the action your character will take to restore order to his shattered world.

When she was five, Robin C.'s father left home with the next-door neighbor, his best friend's wife. Robin hasn't seen him since. She's twenty now and thinks about him and what he did. She's no longer as angry as she was, or confused. She gets it now, more or less.

Her parents had a rotten marriage. They fought all the time, although they never raised their voices. They carried silent resentments that sounded like avalanches in Robin's mind. They were always avoiding or turning away from each other, yet always crashing into each other because of the circumstances.

When her father left, Robin went into a deep trance, an excruciatingly painful stupor from which she didn't emerge for ten years. The separation also devastated her mother, who now lives alone, blaming everybody else for what happened.

Robin embraces loneliness. She wants to be a writer partially out of her need for solitude. She's agoraphobic but admits that agoraphobia might be an excuse for her need to stay away from people. She trusts no one.

But boy, can she write. She writes about couples splitting up and the impact on their kids. Robin says she has written a thousand variations on that theme and will write a thousand more. It's become the linchpin of her oeuvre. She's getting better and better, and when she's able to put her characters in more active verbal conflict, she will be there.

Gary N. is from Minnesota, Viking stock. He can relate to *Fargo*, all the Coen brothers' movies, he says, except *Miller's Crossing*. He is convinced that somewhere in the making of that movie the Coen brothers had been on the verge of splitting up.

Gary is a very funny guy. He was brought up on comic books. Action heroes are his soul mates. He hated *X-Men*, the movie: "Too dull. Wooden characters. The action is predictable. I wanted X-Men as written by the Coen brothers."

Gary has read all the Coen brothers' scripts and all the action heroes created by legendary Stan Lee's work, from his Incredible Hulk to the pantheon of Marvel Comics marauders. In his writing he wants to humanize, and stylize, action stars.

When I asked Gary how he came to fall in love with these characters in the first place, he said, "Look at me. I'm thin and edgy, very un-Vikinglike. In my Minnesota town I was the kid they vilified."

They put small, furry animals in his lunch box. The girls laughed at his skinny, hairy body. They broke his glasses. They called him Fairy Gary and other names.

Like the kid in those ancient muscle mags who got sand kicked in his face, Gary dreamed of being someone other than who he was. He latched on to (Spider-Man, The Hulk, X-Men creator) Stan Lee's work.

Gary spent most of his childhood alone, buried in Stan Lee's heroes. From them he created his own, adapting the heroes of his youth into the heroes of his imagination.

From his parents, two other non-Viking types who had to fight their way out of an abyss or two, he learned humor as a defensive weapon. Oddball humor. They were Jews among Presbyterian warriors. They *had* to develop wit.

From early on, Gary, pen in one hand and pencil in another, wrote and sketched his way into adulthood. His themes are modern David and Goliath melodramas; thoroughly unpredictable, riotously funny, and loaded with suspense.

Until he turns things around, Gary's David will get the shit beat out of him by Goliath. It's classic storytelling. The more interesting scenario: Until he turns things around, a complex David will always get the shit beat out of him by a complex Goliath.

Gary believes he will spin dark childhood memories into gold.

The message is: Write what you know, but don't stop there.

Cameron Crowe wrote *Almost Famous* from his experiences as a sixteen-year-old journalist for *Rolling Stone* magazine. Crowe hauled his central character into the world of the movie as a wide-eyed kid about to journey across the bridge from innocence to experience.

Cameron Crowe didn't arbitrarily choose that moment in time. It was a moment of great transformation for him, one of his life's turning points. Big change was the result, along with wisdom and hard-earned badges of courage and the loss of that innocence we all must shed. I could relate. Could you?

It matters that you want to put your main character through the wringer. It matters just as much or more who this character is. Who is this poor slob you're going to send through hell, and where does he come from and what baggage is he hauling with him that he deserves this transformational journey? Childhood memories, dark or light, make good starting points.

From these memories, a real human being starts to emerge. He is about to enter a world he or she has never seen before and is ill prepared to face.

By endowing your character with vulnerability and fear, you establish someone ready for change, and not some pasteboard cut-out the reader doesn't care about.

What's the worst thing you can ever hear about your character? "I didn't care about him, so the story didn't matter." See *Vanilla Sky* and *Harry Potter*. The filmmakers made a mistake. They gave us a couple duds for main characters.

Your process begins by tracking back through time and finding the building blocks to construct a human being we can relate to, care about, root for, and fear for.

DRILL: *Take a moment. Think back. That thing that happened to you long ago, the thing that made you feel guilty or shameful, or gave you a phenomenal sense of well-being, or sent you hurtling toward despair. What was that thing? Write it down. See it. Make it a scene. Who was there? What happened? How did it make you feel? How does it make you feel now? Can you give this feeling to one of your characters? Dark childhood memories. You gotta luv 'em.*

When Did You First Start to Write, and Why?

As a kid, my parents read to me from Dickens. They did this because, they later told me, they could not bear to spend time reading to me from *Goo Goo Goes to the Garage* or *What Lydia Felt When She Saw a Dead Flower*. They read Dickens because they liked to read Dickens. He told wondrous stories, with remarkable characters, dramatic as hell, many of them about kids.

I went through adolescence longing for a Dickensian childhood. What does that tell you?

My first memory of my own writing? Bread-and-butter notes, little thank you notes I would write to the neighbors after my mother would take me to lunch at their homes.

A couple of lines would have sufficed, but I wrote essays on how lovely the food was, how much I enjoyed the décor, why I thought their dog was an ideal pet, why I thought their children were first rate, and on and on. Everyone thought they were so charming, so funny. I had an audience who wanted more; always a good sign.

My next big writing moment came at fifteen. I had been writing love letters to a girl; big, mushy purple-prose testaments to my deep-seeded love for her. Reading these things after many years, I believe I was in love with my prose as much as I was in love with her.

One day I picked up the phone in the living room and heard the mother of the girl to whom I had written the love letters reading the latest to my mother, who was on the extension in the kitchen.

I was of two minds. One, I felt horribly betrayed by the girl's mother chortling about my heartfelt yearnings for her daughter—to *my* mother!

Two, they were *loving* what I wrote. Ecstatic. *Hmmm,* I remember thinking. As her mother read along, pausing in places, dramatizing moments, my mother laughed out loud, got deadly silent, said things like, "Just wonderful. Read that one again."

So at this moment, at age fifteen, I was given the opportunity to watch two trains—one of art, the other commerce—crashing into each other. On one hand, my deeply personal thoughts were being thrown haphazardly into public view. On the other, I was able to experience that extraordinary sensation of listening to my own work being read aloud by an audience who *loved* it.

What did this mean? The more personal your stuff is, the more the public will gobble it up? Who knew? I did, however, know that Mom and Mrs. Bundy were having a ball.

I never thought of myself, or identified myself, as a writer. When people have asked me when I realized I wanted to be a writer, my answer has always been, "I didn't." I never thought of myself as a writer and felt that calling myself one would be pretentious beyond words.

I point to these two early episodes as benchmark moments that lighted a path for me. I just wrote. All the time. In high school, influenced by the French absurdist theater, I wrote French absurdist plays. In college, influenced by Sam Shepherd, I wrote American Sam Shepherd–like plays.

My uncle told me to read Saul Bellow. I did and saw what language and character could do to a story. I kept reading and writing. I couldn't help myself.

And I went to movies.

I never read scripts. Like a lot of people, it never occurred to me that there were hundreds, *thousands* of screenwriters in Hollywood who toiled every day trying to make art out of their craft.

My first experience with screenwriting came when Paramount bought my book, *The Hunter*, for the big screen. After two other screenwriters couldn't get the job done, the producer asked me if I thought I could do it. I said absolutely and went off to find out what a screenplay was.

That was the beginning.

And here you are now.

Were you a lonely kid, as I was, needing something to do when you were alone? For me it was writing and golf. My parents handed me a book and a seven iron and sent me off. The perfect pastime and the perfect sport for a solo individual. With books and golf I didn't have to deal with people that much, if at all. I didn't have to be on. When I went out of the house into public, I didn't have to be the dancing pony, an awful burden that made me, ultimately, want to stay at home. An insatiable aim to please, if handled improperly, can be a mighty burden.

DRILL: *In a couple of pages, write down what you can remember of your early writing experiences. Notes to yourself. Little scenarios in which you wrote these things, short pieces. Stories, poems, or letters. Take the time to recapture some of the early feelings that led you to want to write. What leads you today to express yourself on paper? What drives you to tell and retell, in stories, the history of your life—as if trying to resolve some mystery or heal some wound that has dogged you for as long as you can remember?*

Sometimes you don't have to write down all the stuff right away. Often you can sit back and close your eyes and let the memory flood through you. Then commit it to paper.

CLASS THREE

The Three Horsemen of the screenplay: situation. Concept. Story.

1. Situation

John le Carré once defined the difference between a situation and a story as this: A situation is a cat sitting on a blanket. A story (at least the beginning of one) is a cat sitting on a *dog's* blanket. By adding conflict, a story can begin to be told.

Nothing moves forward in any screenplay except through CONFLICT.

Hamlet going home for the weekend to see his mother and stepfather is a situation. Hamlet going home and discovering that his mother and stepfather had been having an affair long before his father's death, and that they conspired to kill his father, then *did* kill him, is the beginning of a story.

For Hamlet, a twenty-eight-year-old perpetual student and rich kid, going home has never been a picnic. Something has been troubling him for some time now. He doesn't know what, but it's been making him miserable.

Going home this time, when he learns the awful truth, finally makes his life worthwhile. *He has something to do.*

By putting your character in emotional and physical hell, the story becomes your character doing whatever she can do to rid herself of the problem, thus showing what she's made of: *character*.

In the Coen brothers' *The Man Who Wasn't There*, the situation is Billy Bob Thornton as a barber finding out that his wife is having an affair with her boss, adding to the barber's already pathetic life. The story kicks into gear when the barber, seeing an opportunity, anonymously blackmails the boss (as payment for having an affair with his wife), thus sending everyone's life spiraling out of control.

At the beginning of each story, the main character is unsettled, wanting more out of life than he's getting. The character feels that something is drastically wrong with life as it is and wants to change but doesn't know how. And often he only vaguely knows why.

You, the writer, provide motive and opportunity to your character's need for change. The question you pose to yourself: *How can I screw up my main character's already screwed-up life, turning a situation into a story?*

Here are big-budget and small-budget movies, all following the same rules:

Planet of the Apes. **Situation:** Mark Wahlberg and his favorite ape travel through space. The ape flies a mini-module into an electrical storm, Wahlberg goes after him. **Story:** Wahlberg hits the storm, is thrust ahead in time, loses control, and crash lands becoming a prisoner on "The Planet of the Apes."

The Business of Strangers. **Situation:** An unhappy business executive (Stockard Channing) fires an employee (Julia Stiles). **Story:** That night they commiserate over drinks and hatch a plan to humiliate a corporate headhunter to get back at corporate men in general.

In the Bedroom. **Situation:** In small-town Maine, a college student is having an affair with a woman (Marisa Tomei) who is estranged from her husband, son of a local prominent family. **Story:** The husband kills the college student and gets away with it. The college student's parents (Sissy Spacek and Tom Wilkinson) plot vengeance as a way to handle grief and save their own crumbling marriage.

Notice in all of these that life is going along on its own even (or uneven) keel, until you the writer drop a bomb into it to see what falls out. This is storytelling.

DRILL: *Make a list of movies you've seen recently. Strip away story and concept. Eliminate conflict. Then see the situation for what it is. Then restore the conflict. This is how situations become stories.* See *what's there. These are building blocks.*

2. Concept

You've heard it before. Eighty percent of all screenplays are bought on concept. When a script comes in, it matters how well it's written, but it's the concept that sells it. The producers can always hire another writer to clean it up.

Studios buy a book or a magazine article or somebody's life story because it will make a movie that people will want to see—the more people the better. They hire an established writer to make movie sense of it and hope that it reaches the screen through the laborious development process.

Cold Mountain, a very well-written book, spent a lot of time in development and had many big actors attached to it, all of whom fell away. It had a weak concept, and the studios couldn't get a good screenplay—until after many writers and a significant change of cast. The concept stayed alive because the producers continued to believe in it and the book had won so many awards.

There are two messages here. *Cold Mountain* does not have a high concept. A "high concept" is an idea that a studio or producer can grasp in one sentence that says, "This is a movie!" In this one sentence you get the whole idea of the movie—beginning, middle, and end.

Cold Mountain is about a lot of things, but on the surface it's about a soldier returning from the Civil War and fighting his way through all sorts of obstacles to reach home. Not a bad concept. But it's a period piece. It's beautifully written, but so what? When a studio buys a book it buys the story, not the writer's voice. The writer's voice does not travel well to the screen. Witness *Bonfire of the Vanities* and other book-to-movie disasters.

The second message: If the story is good enough, or hot enough, or if a star says he or she wants to do it, it will probably get made. "There's no accounting for good or bad taste" and "Nobody knows anything" are two of the most often repeated lines in Hollywood.

So what is concept?

The short version:

Speed: *Diehard* on a bus. *Star Wars*: *Wagon Train* in the sky. *The Car* (a car that eats people): *Jaws* on wheels.

The concept behind *Shallow Hal*: What if a guy spent his life seeing only the inner beauty of women, never the outer blemishes—in this case, extra weight. The problem: He's the only one who does see the inner beauty. Everyone else, seeing the weight, remains his or her same, superficial self.

The object of affection in *Shallow Hal* is played by a Rubenesque Gwyneth Paltrow, the point here being that beauty is skin deep and, therefore, you almost never get to the good stuff beneath—to a world where inner beauty is the only beauty that matters. A big reversal on the norm.

Good concept. Makes you think. We can all relate.

For his good idea, along with his story, characters, and execution, the writer, in this—his first screenplay—made $1.6 million and launched his career.

What got the ball rolling? Concept. Situation becomes story becomes concept. Eighty percent of all screenplays are bought on concept.

Good writing sells the writer. Concept sells the movie.

From the moment you start to conceive of your idea, start thinking about the one line that will sell your movie.

A *lot* of people need to buy your concept before it reaches the screen: agents, producers, studio mavens, director, actors. *You* need to buy it. If you're fuzzy about what your script is about, how do you think everybody else feels?

You've got this idea. Somebody asks: "What's it about?" Your answer: "Well, there are these two guys, a CEO and his number one. The CEO is great and powerful, but he's got a problem. He's got a girlfriend or wife he's crazy about. His number one wants to take down the CEO, so he fans the fire. He whispers to the CEO that his wife is fooling around with another guy in the company. The CEO's jealousy drives him mad. Everything crumbles around him. As he falls, the number one rises up to take his place of power."

Not bad. Good general idea. Wordy. How about *Othello* meets *Bad Lieutenant?*

Strong concept + audience attraction = box office.

What does *Othello* meets *Bad Lieutenant* have going for it? And what does it *not* have going for it?

1. *Do we get it?* What's not to get? A tenth-grader can get it. A giant among men is taken down by his own fatal flaw: insecurity. Specifically, jealousy.

2. *Strong enough to attract a big star?* A modern-day *Othello?* Denzel Washington? The original *Othello* has a strong but

downbeat ending. Hollywood might try to dress it up by having the main character turn things around.

On one level, this is a workplace movie about a disgruntled employee and his need for revenge. Iago is passed over for promotion. He suspects that Othello might have had an affair with his own wife. He plots revenge on his boss and carries it out by exploiting his boss's fatal flaw.

It's a plum role, a star turn. Three star turns: Othello, Iago, and Desdemona. A modern-day Othello in a corporate environment? Sex with an interracial couple: Desdemona, the white woman, and Othello, the black titan. And Iago the white lieutenant, who himself might even lust after Desdemona or have hidden loathing for blacks in general and Othello in particular. Iago believes he deserves to be on top and has been waiting for the right time to make his move.

Iago chooses this moment to whisper in Othello's cuckolded ear—Desdemona is screwing around. With whom? The guy who got Iago's job, the guy Othello chose over him. How perfect can revenge be?

You the writer (or in this case, Shakespeare the writer) have chosen the most critical moments in all three lives to tell the story. The stakes will never be higher. People will die; fortunes will change.

3. *Sequel possibilities?* Maybe in the end Iago escapes and runs off somewhere, but he'll be back.

4. *Emotional and dramatic hot buttons?* Lust, power struggles, a fallen hero who rises up out of his own ashes to slay his former friend and comrade, now betrayer—what else do you need?

Shakespeare knew what he was doing. I'm getting so lathered up with this, I ought to go out and write it myself. This concept has legs.

Many less-appealing concepts, often tired and cliché-ridden, still manage to crawl out of the lame barrel.

Here's one: "the old pro called back to do one last job."

Hollywood is forever putting new spins on ones like this because there are old pro actors out there who can still draw, especially if they are teamed with a younger actor with rising or established star power. As an extremely conservative business (conserving one's own job), studios rely on so-called "safe" concepts, which often backfire and lose money.

Redford and Pitt in *Spy Game*. Hackman and company in *Heist*.

But how many times can you go to this well? Never too many, apparently. Hackman carried *Heist*. "The old pro called on one last time" is a concept that will be around forever. Robert DeNiro, a fine actor, has opted for this sub-genre so many times he probably has lost count. I have.

This doesn't mean you shouldn't write for this genre. If you're convinced you've got a new twist and love this kind of movie, write it. But know going in that ten thousand people just like you, along with A-list scribes, are building the same derivative house.

DRILL: *Call it "The Tweak Factor." Take your idea and meld it with another idea; construct a bridge between them. For instance, in a film I recently finished: For five years I had carried the idea of two pilots I had met who repossessed airplanes for a living. One day while in Manhattan, I heard a lecture about robotics and artificial intelligence. I felt the spark. The repo guys grab a plane and in the plane is a beautiful woman, the niece of a powerful man, who wants her back desperately. But she ran away. Why? The repo guys fall in love with her, and the chase is on. The woman, it turns out, is a highly developed android.*

I tried to meld many ideas with those two repo men; none worked, until now. And even this idea needed a lot of work.

Sometimes you start off with an idea, as you often do when adapting a book to film, but in the course of the rewrite you realize that the small idea is wonderful while the large one you can lose. Good Will Hunting started out as a high-tech thriller about a lonely genius. They dropped the high-tech idea and went smaller with the genius—which turned out to be the bigger idea after all.

Remember: There is something in your original idea that's on solid ground. It might only need another element to turn it into a strong concept. Take your time. Remember this, too: Impatience kills.

3. Story

You discover stories in the strangest places.

I discovered this one in my school mailbox: "Dear Mr. Christopher Keane. I attended your script-writing workshop last Wed. when there were 10 extra kids that showed up. I'm gonna show up again tomorrow. Hopefully someone dropped the course, or you might be willing to let in one extra kid (that would be me). I NEED this class. If you don't let me in I'll go crazy. *PLEASE*. If you do, you won't be sorry. I promise. Thank you." (signed) Andrea Portnoy.

Andrea said she would "go crazy" if she didn't get into my class. Here's what I did: I let her in.

And then, in my imagination, over the next several weeks, I concocted a story.

In my **Story,** based on a **Situation,** I turn Andrea into a mentally disturbed stalker-student. In this **Concept,** I am a teacher, married with a kid, and Andrea is a younger, crazier version of Glenn Close in *Fatal Attraction.*

Eventually the teacher, who fears being punished for bad behavior—getting too close to Andrea's craziness—tries to pull away. But does he? He senses this woman's power and he *still* lets her into his class. What's that all about? Testing fear? Maybe he wants to get close to the flame but not get burned? He wants to test his resolve? He has an inflated sense of his ability to say no? Maybe he wants to hook up? Oh boy. What does this say about his relationship with his family, or about himself?

What about her? She has her own issues with authority figures. There is something about the teacher that ignites dark and dangerous images from her past. Somehow she wants to get back at the teacher. But not just any teacher. One who reminds her of something bad that happened to her long ago. We will later learn that this is not the first time Andrea has played out this scenario.

As is, this is too close to *Fatal Attraction,* so do we throw in a little *Something Wild* into the mix?

Notice that Andrea and the teacher are now drifting away from the real Andrea and the real me. Andrea's wires get crossed (they've been crossed for a while), and she becomes dangerously aggressive. She wants revenge. But she's smart and canny and manipulative and bright and good-looking, and she has spent twenty years of her life going after and getting what she wants, all driven by fear and a hunger for retribution.

The teacher is about to become her next target. But the audience doesn't know any of this yet because one of your obligations as a writer is to *never give the audience any information until the audience needs to know it*.

Keep the reader in suspense. Let the story unfold naturally. Andrea's past is back-story, which should be revealed in drips and drabs throughout the story to create suspense, shock, and tension.

The **Situation** is that Andrea writes a note, a funny note, an innocent-seeming note. The note might have a sort of sinister twist to it, but not if the teacher doesn't see it that way.

The teacher, in any case, thinks it's charming and aggressive, and he likes women who are aggressive. His mother is aggressive; the woman he married is aggressive.

Now you start building toward tension points, searching for the major dramatic beats of the story.

Your main objective is to keep the reader interested—interested, fascinated, on the edge of their seats, wanting more. Don't ever dump information on the reader; *dramatize* it.

Bad example:

```
                    TEACH
        Andrea, how'd you find out I'm a big
        collector of goldfish? I started
        collecting my fish when, as a
        child, I had no friends.


                    ANDREA
        Oh, gee, Teach, I love fish. I was
        a lonely kid, too, and I'm also a
        collector.
```

I'm nodding out writing this. You must be comatose by now. Let's try again:

```
                    ANDREA
        Hey, Teach, I hear you collect
        fish. Could I see them?


                    TEACH
        I have some in my apartment.
```

ANDREA

Big?

TEACH

Huh?

ANDREA

How big is your equipment?

TEACH

Equipment?

ANDREA
                (smiling)
How big are you, Teach?

TEACH

Big? I mean, I collect fish. I'm not
SeaWorld.

ANDREA

What about your wife?

TEACH

What about her? She's knows about
my fish.

ANDREA

I'll bet she does. Do you invite
other students up to see your big
fish? I would love to swim with
your big fish. How about today?

TEACH

Today?

ANDREA

Now.

TEACH

You wanna see my fish, now?

                              ANDREA
             Have you got a big, eager fish or a
             shy fish that needs coaxing?

                              TEACH
             Ahhhh . . .

                              ANDREA
             I live right near your apartment.
             And I adore big fish.

                              TEACH
             You know where I live?

It ain't Shakespeare, but at least it's got some energy, some meat on
its bones. Who knows if Andrea will like swimming in these metaphorical waters with Teach's big fish, or will he be, at night's end, as they
say, *swimming with the fishes?*

What have we got here? Sexual innuendo, anticipation. A married
guy. Danger. We are working this concept and story. Is this more of a
very black comedy? Does this distance it from *Fatal Attraction?*

You have created potential. You have started to build drama and the
anticipation of more drama.

Flat writing is dead writing. The reader tunes out.

Back to the **Concept:** What happens when a young, twisted student
exacts revenge on her teacher for reasons that neither one of them understands—until it is too late? Sound promising?

This concept can also be used as the **Log Line,** a one- or two-line tit-
illating pitch or hook that gets the agent, producer, and studio exec
excited. The log line is also for the sales department.

This log line, after it's developed and spun into fine gold, will become
the pitch your agents feed to the rest of the industry, selling it up the
movie food chain until it reaches a big studio cheese who can say yes.

Your intention with this pitch is to get the food chain salivating.
Other movies will come to their minds. Stalker movies. Movies about
secret intentions. Glenn Close/Michael Douglas in *Fatal Attraction. Play
Misty for Me,* Clint Eastwood's first directorial effort. The Michael
Creighton/Demi Moore/Michael Douglas sex-in-the-marketplace feature,

Disclosure. Harrison Ford and Michelle Pfeiffer in *What Lies Beneath*. Movies that made money and got strong notices.

Now you're starting to get savvy. You focus on the simplicity of story: the stalker and her target. This is the axis, or spine, around which the story will spin. Don't spin off it. *Stay on the axis*. Camp on the spine. Most scripts fail when the writer wanders or spins off in another direction, forgetting the core of the story.

Three-quarters of the way through the story, you know that the teacher will have to turn the tables and go from the stalked to the stalker. His life is nearly ruined, and he's got to somehow resolve the **Problem**. He can't run; he can't hide. His only alternative, he believes, is to turn and face the enemy.

At this point, though, it doesn't look as if he will ever be able to get out of this jam. What can he do? He will have to start thinking, in significant ways, just like her.

Like any good sociopath, the stalker (Andrea) has separated the target from the rest of the world, leaving him alone out there, so she can have control over him and manipulate him in the web she's created.

Let's back up for a second. A key element here is that there's something missing from the teacher's life, some *internal demon* that has been stalking him forever, which has allowed this to happen in the first place. This is the main character's *fatal flaw*, which he has to face up to if he's going to move on.

Without this fatal flaw, none of this would have happened in the first place. Remember: Without Othello's jealousy, when Iago says, "Hey, Othello, I saw Desdemona downtown making out with your Captain," Othello says, "Oh she does that. Means nothing." That's the end of the story of Othello. Jealousy drives Othello, Iago knows, and this, in turn, drives the story. Your main character's fatal flaw drives the story.

Close your eyes. Think. What fatal flaw drives *your* main character?

Make a list: five movies that grabbed you. What drove each of the main characters? One of the seven deadly sins? What was his or her fatal flaw?

In this story, a fatal flaw dogs our teacher, and always has. He's got to face up to it, whatever it is. Insecurity? Fear? Your character eventually has to face the terror, head on, which will be the hardest thing he has ever had to do.

Fatal flaws often become comforts. Even though flaws make our lives miserable, even though they blot what goodness we might possess, they become security blankets to us. The familiar is never as terrifying as the unknown, and so we embrace them, thinking they are not as bad as they could be. Wrong. They are our worst nightmares, under the guise of comfort.

We stay in a relationship or marriage because it's familiar, because at least we're secure in our grief. It becomes a hedge against the unknown. But we wonder why we're not getting on with life, getting joy *from* life, or why we're always in a rut.

Your main character has a suicidal attachment to a fatal flaw. In this story, the teacher does. The student does. The story is about the one last chance the teacher has to break the chains, to face this *thing* and get rid of it once and for all. Or, failing that, to live with it forever, *because there will never be another chance like this.*

Back to Henry James's comment: Your story must take place at the most critical moment of your main character's life, or your story is not worth telling.

In *Fight Club*, the Ed Norton character has for a long time been dogged by the ordinary life he leads, so what does he do? He creates Brad Pitt to give him some excitement—the Mr. Hyde to his Dr. Jekyll. Look where Hyde leads him, and see how hard it is for Jekyll, once he brings out Hyde, to get rid of him.

In almost all stories, your main character needs to change the shitty life he's leading but can't because he's locked into the prison his life has become.

So you, the writer, bring in a stranger to shake things up. This stranger represents the personification of all your main character's fears—often under the guise of his hopes, wishes, and dreams.

What can this stranger be? A person, a disease, an accident, a disaster. It will take a big disaster to dislodge your character from his or her routine life, to break the chains.

Your character thinks the disaster is the worst thing possible. But it's not. It's the cure. The antidote to the fatal flaw. Screenwriting is, in large part, the act of turning the worst possible situation into the best possible situation.

Let's go back to *Fight Club*. The Brad Pitt character looks like the best thing that could ever happen to Edward Norton's character. As the story progresses, Brad Pitt starts taking over—literally everything—until Edward Norton's life becomes totally unmanageable.

Edward Norton now must act. He battles this creature he has created and defeats him. And his life improves. But what a journey!

What does it takes to make a good story? For one, putting the character at the most dangerous, wild, terrifying moment of his or her life and seeing what happens. Have some fun! Put the "fun" back in dysfunctional.

What will your character do when the stranger comes to town? Force your character to face his demons and to eventually escape from his strangulated existence.

There's your story.

For two-thirds of the story, you throw everything you can at your character, until your character says "*Enough!*" and begins to fight back. Edward Norton goes after Brad Pitt, who represents, literally, all of Edward Norton's worst intentions.

In our story, this is the moment in our teacher's life when that internal demon will rear its ugly head again—that demon-based flaw. He will have to confront and slay the dragon to stop the evil student.

Never be too easy on your main character. He has to earn the change you put him through.

In Act III, the characters take on huge, startling, fascinating dimensions. Mano a mano. Fight to the death.

As the reader, and later the viewer, I should not be able to tear my eyes away from the battle. I *need* to find out what happens. And so I turn the pages, breathlessly.

Even with all this tension and conflict you've created, as the writer you must always up the stakes. Borrow from your past, from research, from any source you can, to jeopardize your protagonist and make the stakes higher than they have ever been for him.

Your characters need faces. They begin to take shape. They posses motives (murky), and pasts (sketchy). In this case, the teacher is insecure about his relationship with his wife, but not because his wife has given him any reason to be. He's insecure to begin with, from way back, let's say from a debilitating relationship with his parents. He has, I'm thinking, abandonment issues.

He's never worked out these issues (the inner demon), but he's about to. Does he learn some hard-won lessons? Does he ever!

See how a simple note from a student who wanted to get into my class has progressed to this? So far, we have merely scratched the surface. But it's fun. You get lost in the swirl of creativity.

When working on your screenplay, ask yourself these questions: *What's the concept? The idea or notion behind the story? What gives the story focus?*

In Hollywood, they ask *what* it's about, not *who* it's about. The concept gets you in the door, the story will find you a seat, and the characters will keep you in the room.

Stories are the meat on the bones of the concept. Stories take great effort. They're like relationships. They don't come fully realized. You have to develop them; participate in them; create, manipulate, seduce, and love them; and do all the things you would to form a dynamic, satisfying, passion-and-drama-filled relationship.

What about that moment when a great idea strikes you, or when a concept is suddenly fully formed? When you've hit upon something and can run with it, all the way to picture? You've never seen this concept onscreen. Nobody has. You *know* it's unique. It's got chops, as they say in the business.

Time passes. You begin to wonder why you keep this idea or concept close to you for so long, why you haven't started developing it more thoroughly. Days go by, even weeks, without you adding to or subtracting from it. Why is that? You want to savor the brilliance of it?

Most likely it's because you have the sneaking suspicion that this concept or situation, or idea, has many miles to go before it reaches home. Too many miles. You refer to this brilliant idea as a story, but it's not a story. It's barely a concept. Maybe it's no more than a situation.

At some point you can't stand to let this thing fester any longer; it's time to take it out of the jewel box. Get on your computer, or on your pad, and start to write. Start with the big dramatic beats, the highs and lows, the turning points. In other words, you start to structure.

Almost immediately you run into trouble. Trouble in the sense of problems. Problems you hadn't seen before. This brilliant idea is unraveling before your eyes. Context creeps in, and behind context, content lurks. The thing—and that's what it's becoming, no longer the brilliant story but the THING—has become that festering, out-of-control sore. It's in your brain, and it's giving you a migraine.

You want to drive it out, but your brain tells you that it's not yet time. You've had this THING in your cerebral womb for some time now. It *must* be good. All it needs is a little oxygen to breathe.

Like any potentially brilliant child, it's developing growing pains. Appendages, limbs, body parts—call them what you will—are sprouting up all over the place. The core idea is changing, transforming before your widening, shocked-stupid eyes.

Remember the old days—just weeks or months ago—when you were so happy with it? When you dreamed of this love child becoming your grand gesture to the world, an emblem of your personal testament, the incredible story that would make it to the silver screen, with your name up there attached to it. Your creation.

But look what it's become—a virus. I get this virus every time I begin a project. It's as if I'm caught in a bipolar swing, traveling at supersonic speed from absolute ecstasy to utter despair. Call it creative postpartum depression.

Everybody gets it. *There is no perfection,* the voices keep reminding me, *it's all a progression toward something.* Nothing ever comes out fully or perfectly formed, no matter how strong we will it to.

Take it easy! Step back, look at it, and see what you've got. Go back to the beginning. It's still there, this brilliant idea. It's taken on new components, but the essence is there.

What's the rush?!

How do you think I felt about *Mink! The Book That Ate Its Author*? I let that idea get way out of control. I dressed it up so quickly and so lavishly that it never had a chance to return to its essential self. I frantically built and built until I had constructed an out-of-control, architecturally untidy heap.

How do you stem the tide? How do you steer this original idea, concept, or situation away from the hell it's heading toward and into a solid story? What tools do you need to make that happen? One of the software tools I use is Storybase at StoryBase.com. Try it. It works. It gives you tools to organize your story and your passion.

DRILL: *This story idea of yours: Where did it come from? Think back. How did you come up with it? With all the story fodder you hear every day, why did this one stick? There's something there for you. What is it? Write down the progression or germination of the idea. Just type for now; you'll edit later. Let it pour out of you.*

Something in there is worthwhile. Go find it. If you do, it'll probably act like tumbleweed, picking up all sorts of stuff along the trail. And little by little, you'll be watching a full-fledged story coming to life.

CLASS FOUR

Where Are Those Stories?

As far as I can tell, stories are not found, they're discovered, revealed through observation and hard work. Often they spring out of the closet and need to be dusted off and studied before they're ready to be written.

A situation, concept, or character begins the process, followed by the plot, the character's motivation, and the dramatic build. All have to be formed, molded, and structured before you can even call it a story.

Good Will Hunting started out as a thriller about a reluctant genius getting embroiled in the high-tech world. The only scene left from the original is where Ben Affleck's character, posing as Matt Damon's character, applies for a job at a high-tech company.

The Miramax producers who read the first draft saw something they liked—the screwed-up genius character. They didn't like that the story was heading into big-budget, high-tech thriller country.

Director Rob Reiner read it and told the guys to tone it down, to avoid high-tech country, but to keep the location, Cambridge, Massachusetts, and Boston's Southie.

Forget about trying to compete with the big studio writers and their thrillers, Reiner told them. It's not that kind of picture. It's a neighborhood movie, about a reluctant genius tormented by his fears.

Miramax sent it to other heavy hitters, like William Goldman, who also saw a more personal story with big implications that audiences could relate to. Damon and Affleck went back to work and wrote another draft.

Now Goldman and other writers had a script they could polish, with the genius aspect intact and the high-tech concept stripped away, making it the personal movie needed. Goldman and the others emphasized university vs. the working class and a main character with a superconductor brain who lives in blue-collar land, straddling two worlds—comfortable with one, slipping into another. The new writers were also conscious of the theater-going public's demographics (eighteen to twenty-six) and decided that driving the story into the high-tech world would be missing a grand opportunity to put the Damon character at risk in a school atmosphere, which the audience had all experienced. They also kept it classy, at Harvard and MIT, where even geniuses have big problems.

Goldman and other uncredited writers built on the foundation established by Damon and Affleck. The rest is history. The reason Damon and Affleck received credit: The Writers Guild of America assigns credit to the original writers if at least half the story that made it to the screen belongs to them, or if no challenge was mounted by subsequent writers. To the best of my knowledge, no challenge was mounted.

That's one way to break in. Don't let Matt Damon and Ben Affleck being already established actors put you off. I can't tell you the number of famous stars who have tried to write screenplays or pitched ideas, and only out of deference were not hustled, like regular folks, out of studio offices.

I'll talk later in the building character section about what Affleck, Damon, and the heavy hitters did with their main character in *Good Will Hunting*, how they pulled him from the prison of his own fears into the harsh light a new freedom.

In your own stories, find the central flawed character and drive him or her into the heart of the story, as these guys did. Affleck and Damon were young scribes with an idea. They were no farther along than anyone else. Just because they had Hollywood access doesn't mean they were guaranteed of anything. They had to fight hard to get cast in their story. In other words, don't let their celebrity prevent you from going after your own story. If they didn't have an excellent idea at the center of their high-tech thriller, they never would have been invited into the room. In fact, you know how producers and directors feel about actors with ideas for movies. Enough said.

In your stories, build through conflict. Throw your main character for a loop every ten pages. Just when the main character looks as if he is going to get the prize, throw a bomb in his path, and then, injured and dizzy, he has to find another route to the prize. These are called reversals. Build your story through a series of reversals that make life hard for your character and demand that he dig deep to find alternate routes.

In this chapter we're going after story:

- How to recognize one

- Finding out what character the story belongs to

- The compression of time, space, and language

- The art of adaptation

- If you haven't lived it, where do you find it?

- Indie love

- Taking smart chances

Look, There's a Story! I'll Write That!

If only it were that easy. Then again, it *is* that easy—if you're tuned to the right station. How do you get tuned?

Like the photographer who carries her camera everywhere, you have to be actively on the lookout. The late Gary Provost, a great friend and one of the best writing teachers on the planet, scoured newspapers and magazines. Some writers go to old movies that did well and try to find an angle to update them. They try to figure out why the movie did well, they read reviews and the script, and they watch the movie and break it down. Then they ask themselves how they would take certain elements of the story and reconfigure them to take place in a present-day setting.

Others go to obscure periodicals or to books such as *The 100 Greatest Crimes in History*.

Look around you. Do you see people in crisis, even among your closest friends or people you know? Surely you've been witness to tragedy and how victims have either fallen before it or shown great courage against it.

A story I like to tell happened to a writer back in the 1970s. She was living with her family in Lake Forest, Illinois, outside of Chicago. She was a writer, then and now, always on the lookout for something to write about.

She had had some success but no breakout work. She could craft sentences and delineate characters, but she didn't have a strong enough vessel—a story and structure—to dump all this talent into.

For quite a long time she lived in a lovely neighborhood with her family. During one stretch of time she noticed that something was going on with the neighbors.

She was witness to a tragedy in the making. Through her kitchen window, across the lawn, and over the low fence that separated her yard from her neighbors', she watched the daily disintegration of a loving, smart, and passionately involved family.

The reason for this disintegration was the older son, who had died in a boating accident at seventeen, tearing the family apart.

The writer saw the toll this tragic death took on the family. The mother, heavily into denial, went catatonic. The victim's younger brother, who was with him in the boat when it capsized, blamed himself for his older brother's (his hero's) death. The father, a professional man, tried to keep the family together, failing at every turn.

This is the real-life story that writer Judith Guest would turn into an international bestseller and Oscar-winning movie, *Ordinary People*.

Judith Guest did not have to go to space or to another city or even down the street to find her story. There it was, unfolding before her eyes, in her backyard.

She witnessed a single awful event, at the center of a family, that nearly destroyed its members. She watched the concentric circle of pain caused by the death of the hero-son sweep through the family and drive them to the brink of madness—with one in particular, the mother, falling over the edge.

She saw a once-strong resilient woman lose her mind. She watched the father, a man who might have faltered when his son died, instead come to the fore and pull what he could together. She saw a loving brother, who blamed himself for the death, who himself teetered at the brink of insanity, fight his way back.

The key here is how the family would react to the tragedy. Who would make it, and who would not? The results are shocking. You never would have guessed. Surprising the reader and upsetting the reader's expectations are fundamental laws of good, dramatic storytelling.

People around the world who face tragedy in their own lives (who hasn't?) relate to *Ordinary People*. Judith Guest told a simple story with characters hurled by circumstance into the most devastating time of their lives, creating a violent tear in the fabric of their family life.

Through her writer's filter, Judith Guest changed the story. She altered characters and she moved events around, all in the service of the story and the characters who inhabit it.

Look around your own family, into your own neighborhood, and you'll find—like the photographer who carries her camera (or Judith Guest)—stories to tell.

One of my best students, Rachel Grissom, a slender, energetic blonde from the South who now lives in Hollywood, doesn't have to look very far to find potential stories.

Part of Rachel's family lives in New Orleans, where her script, about cemetery thieves, takes place.

Here's Rachel's take on finding stories:

"Finding stories is actually very easy for me, and a very unconscious thing. I always write about things that interest me.

"How did I get the idea for my script? I had relatives in New Orleans and found the city fascinating. I have family all over Louisiana, so I grew up with the Southern culture. And I have always found the way a community buried its dead intriguing, its manner toward them (wakes vs. funerals, Judeo-Christian beliefs vs. reincarnation, etc.) fascinating as well.

"So when I saw an article in the newspaper about a ring of cemetery thieves in New Orleans who had been busted, but only after they had stolen and unloaded more than a million dollars worth of stuff, it was an easy jump.

"I see stories everywhere. They usually have to do with what people do to survive. Example: What kind of people, what kind of lives, do you see in the background of your daily existences? What is it like, for instance, to drive a subway? What is it like to work the coatroom of a Boston club?

"I'm currently working on a story about a woman who is a professional eulogist.

"Whenever someone in my family dies, they make me give the eulogy, because few people in my family have a college education (which I do) and none have public speaking experience (which I have). Therefore, up to the podium I go. Sometimes it is difficult to give a eulogy for someone who was a bad person. That can't be uncommon. What do families do if they don't have someone to give that speech?

"A story is born. I think this is easy for me, partly because of my improv experience. Often, to get people comfortable with speaking off-the-cuff, if you will, teachers will make you only tell stories that are true, so you don't have to work at making it up as you go along. Doing that, you quickly learn that everyone has a story. Everyone.

"Each and every story is wonderful, complex, sad, and funny. Every single one. Everyone is afraid of something. Everyone has lost something.

"I can look around at my family, easy. I have a cousin who was dropped on his head, causing brain damage, who now works for Sea-World. My grandmother was offered a basketball scholarship to the University of Missouri but had to give it up because girls in her family did not leave home before marriage. She married a drunk gambler, had three kids, worked her way through college, and taught in inner-city Memphis during integration.

"One of my brothers slept with my other brother's fiancée. My father could've been a golf pro, until his back was damaged by polio. My stepfather raced stock cars and motocross. My other grandmother was reborn (for the better) when her husband of fifty years died.

"When my best friend's father's wife was paralyzed in a car accident, he left her for a prostitute he met doing drugs in Singapore. Another friend of mine has a disease where her collagen is disintegrating (it's worse than hemophilia). A bump would kill her.

"I'm thinking about writing a collection of linked stories all about the way the men on the maternal side of my family have died. Almost every single one of them has died an early, unnatural death. Burning to death. Shot in the back. Falling off a ladder. Suicide. Drunk driving. A friend of mine insists I should warn any man I date.

"Another friend once asked me for advice on how to get started with a story. She had lots of beginnings, lots of characters, but no finished story. She couldn't think of how to move forward.

"I told her, 'Take the character you know the best, the one you've fleshed out the most. Then figure out what the most important thing in the world to that character is. Then take it from him, never to be returned, and see what he does!'"

Is It Classic Storytelling?

A story that made a big impression on me was "Little Red Riding Hood." I was nine and my mother said to me, "Don't worry so much about Red. She's kind of dull. Get interested in the wolf." The wolf is the tale's best character, a potentially complex villain. "Why don't you take a look at the story from the wolf's point of view?" Mom said. "Ask yourself how the wolf feels about all this."

Okay, but why should we care about the evil wolf? All he wants to do is eat Red for dinner.

Not true, I would learn once I got thinking about it.

Here is what my mother explained to me about the story, and what I added to it in the years to come.

We have a wolf, a sad guy who lives in the woods, alone and hungry. One night, through the trees, he sees a light in the woods. He discovers a farmhouse inhabited by an old lady.

The wolf sneaks a closer look. It's homey in there, with a fire, and the old lady seems very nice. The wolf needs companionship, a meal; he's desolate and desperate.

The next day he picks flowers and puts them on the back porch. The old lady finds them, and that night she puts out a dish of something.

The wolf wolfs it down and leaves more flowers, or perhaps something he's carved out of wood. To make a long story short, one night as the wolf is eating the food the old lady has left for him, she appears and invites the wolf in to eat his meal at a proper table.

Thus begins the best relationship the wolf has ever had, and probably the best relationship the old lady has had, too. She likes this wolf; she's also in need of companionship.

A bargain is struck. In return for being fed and housed, the wolf agrees to do handiwork around the house.

This goes on for a few weeks. The wolf has never been happier. Finally, after all his roaming around, he's found a home and an interesting person with whom to while away the evening hours.

One day the old lady asks the wolf to stay in the woods, just for the day. Her granddaughter is visiting and the girl wouldn't understand the nature of her grandma's friendship with a wolf.

The wolf says sure. That day, the wolf, now hiding in the forest, positions himself to see the visitor.

Ohmygoodness! When he gets a load of Red Riding Hood his heart stops. He can barely control his sudden and overwhelming love for this girl. He hyperventilates, he sweats, and his heart pounds.

After Red leaves, the wolf returns and asks questions about her, but not too many because the wolf is no fool. If the old lady ever realized how he really felt about her granddaughter, she would kick him out.

So now the wolf has another thing to be grateful for—anticipating Red's next visit.

But gratitude is not what he's feeling. It's more like obsession. When she visits again, he hides and watches. Later, when he returns to the house, Grandma asks him what the matter is. He says he must have come down with something; maybe he caught cold in the woods.

Time goes on and Red visits again and again. Grandma starts to notice the wolf's erratic behavior before and after her visits.

Grandma is worried.

On Red's most recent visit, Grandma catches the wolf peeking through the window at Red.

Now Grandma has to do something. The wolf's behavior is unacceptable. As much as Grandma likes the wolf, she is now afraid for her granddaughter's safety.

She tells the wolf he has to go.

Now the wolf's obsession for Red enters the hot zone. He cannot stand the idea of not seeing her, or the idea that he will be thrown out of his happy home. And so obsession turns into something else.

It turns to murder.

The poor wolf who had everything—a friend, a place to live happily, food on the table, some joy—has been destroyed by his obsession for a girl.

So what do we have here? "Little Red Riding Hood" from the point of view of this disturbed wolf gives me a greater understanding of the story and its complexities and the role of the villain, whose job it is to drive the story toward catastrophe.

Over the years when I returned to the story, I began to look at this story and others from *all* the characters' points of view. One thing that occurred to me at nine, and was refined later, was that I had better pay attention to *the character through whom the story should be told.*

When I started to write my own stories, I stepped back to see them from the points of view of all the major characters. Often I would realize that the main character I had originally chosen was not the right main character after all. There was another character, through whose eyes the story became much more interesting.

Sometimes the story belongs to another of your characters. At the beginning of your story you might have chosen the character you identified with, rather than the character through whose eyes the more dramatic version of the story should be told. *Give the story to the character who changes the most, who is most affected by the story, the one who has the most at stake.*

What if Robert Towne, writer of *Chinatown,* had decided to make the movie about the incestuous relationship between John Huston and Faye Dunaway instead of focusing on Jack Nicholson? Believe me, he might have. The Huston/Dunaway subplot is edgy and weird. In this scenario, the Nicholson character could have played a small cameo role.

Writers have committed this error in judgment and later wondered why they had to put the brakes on the story because it wasn't going anywhere. The script ended up in a drawer somewhere, all because the writer didn't look around the cast to find another, better character through whom to tell the story.

In the Coen brothers' *The Man Who Wasn't There,* what if the story was taken away from the expressionless Billy Bob Thornton character and given to the actor who walked away with the picture, the high-powered lawyer, played by Tony Shalhoub.

You can do this with almost any picture.

DRILL

- *Take three or four of your favorite movies and climb behind the eyes of the two or three main characters. See the story as they might have seen it. The results might shock you, and it's an excellent drill for your own stories.*

- *Think about your own story from the point of view of each character. Then choose the right character to tell your story by working out each of the characters' points of view. You'll end up with a much fuller story, with characters whose motivations you now understand.*

- *Write a page or two on the backstory and motivations of each of your main characters, as if the story belonged to them all. How does your story change?*

Would You Just Shut Up and Get on with the Story?!

A writer's journey to the heart of a story is filled with obstacles, detours, and reversals. Distilling the story's essence to get the most potent effect requires an understanding of one of screenwriting's flagship concepts—*compression*.

One definition of movies is a rapid acceleration of major events that happen over a short period of time. A chief component of that definition is compression, squeezing things together so there's no flab hanging from the story.

The three elements of compression are time, space, and language.

COMPRESSION OF TIME

When you think about your story, one of the things that will come up is length of time. If your story takes place over a six-month period, ask yourself if it's possible for it to take place over a week or even a weekend.

Take *Three Days of the Condor,* staring Robert Redford and Faye Dunaway. The book upon which the movie was based is called *Six Days of the Condor.* For Hollywood, six days were three too many.

Some movies demand five years or more (*Lawrence of Arabia, A Beautiful Mind*), in which case the writers used compression in other areas.

The key is to eliminate dead time. If, for instance, a character must go through a pregnancy, a weekend won't cut it. The problem might be what to do with those nine months waiting for the pregnancy to unfold, in which case you ask yourself: *Can my character already be pregnant for, say, eight months?* Maybe the story is not the pregnancy in its entirety, but the events leading up to the birth.

COMPRESSION OF SPACE

A rule of thumb: Never separate your characters for long periods of time, no matter what Nora Ephron might tell you. Sure, in Ephron's *Sleepless in Seattle* the characters meet only at the end. That movie is an aberration, a once-in-a-lifetime occurrence. Upon close inspection, you'll notice that the writers had to drag so much extra baggage into that picture, just to keep it alive and kicking, that in truth, although it might have been all fuzzy and warm, and it did make money, it wasn't a very good picture. It's a tribute to Ephron's talent that she was able to sustain the tension for as long as she did.

They say that the best way for turmoil, drama, conflict, and tension to prevail is to throw the characters into a closet and lock the door.

One of the best uses of compression of space is in one of the most popular movies ever made, *The Graduate*.

In this movie, the writers have a situation in which they want to put the main character through a series of life-altering events. They want to make him squirm and sweat bullets so he *earns* the changes he goes through. This will be no walk in the park for Ben Braddock (Dustin Hoffman).

So what do the writers do? The first thing is to put the character in a place he does not want to be, where he will be in constant conflict.

They come up with the only place guaranteed to make him miserable—at home, with his parents, who give him sports cars instead of love and treat him like a stranger. Pressure from the get-go.

In your stories you have to put your character where he is most uncomfortable. In that way, he needs relief, and to get relief, he needs to act.

You never want your character to be comfortable. Or if he is comfortable, make sure it isn't for more than a second or two before the shit hits the fan.

Next the writers says, *Okay, what life-altering experience can we give Ben that he has not had before? How about—sex? Okay, what shall we do? Bring in an old flame from school, or maybe somebody he used to have a crush on?* Too easy.

They look around and their eyes fix on next door, right across the hedge, to the neighbor. Who's living there? It's Mrs. Robinson, an older, wiser women, who smokes like a chimney and drinks like a fish.

Perfect! Older woman, young man. Ben falls into her clutches, right in plain sight of his parents, who also know and disapprove of Mrs. Robinson.

So off Ben stumbles, to have this eye-opening sexual experience with Mrs. Robinson, who can't believe her good luck. Nice, fresh young meat, next door, marching into her clutches. Ben gets an education.

What exquisite pressure. Right next door to his dreaded parents, and he's with a woman old enough to be his mother. Ben gets laid for the first time. Compression of space.

The story doesn't have to veer off somewhere in search of a woman. She's right there, and she's ready. Lesson: Look around before you go traipsing off in search of adventure that might be right under your character's nose.

Now that he's in this awful place with his awful parents, and no longer a virgin, having given it away to the hawklike, booze-swilling Robinson, the writers think: *What else has Ben never experienced?* Ah, love.

The writers start searching for an object of his love. They go through the same drill: What about somebody from college? What about a girl he knew from high school, still in town, maybe across town, or even in the neighborhood?

Wait a minute, they cry. *Doesn't Mrs. Robinson have a daughter?!* Perfect! And so Ben, while boinking Mrs. Robinson or, more appropriately, getting boinked by her, falls in love with her daughter, and *she* falls in love with *him*. Compression.

And all of it right next door, and in just a short period of time. Ben goes through a life-altering experience and in the end heads off with the girl toward an uncertain but more promising future.

COMPRESSION OF LANGUAGE

This is Strunk and White territory. I am not one of those who believes that screenwriting has no author's voice. There's some ridiculous press out there that says that because screenwriting is a bastard art that other people will eventually turn into digital or celluloid, the writing by definition is (and should be) flat and dull.

Hogwash. The voice or style of the writer might not be in evidence as much as in novels, but read some screenplays. Read screenplays by screenwriters and not necessarily by directors with laptops. Not that directors can't write, but it's not usually their primary concern. They want to *make* a movie, not *write* a movie. Screenwriters want to write movies.

I mentioned earlier that some studio people insist that 80 percent of all screenplay options or purchases are due to the concept, not the writing. Fair enough. That's true in publishing, too. You can write up a storm of a story, but if it's not going to entice an audience, it's not going to be bought.

I once read a forty-page short story about a guy watching and cogitating over a rock he found by a riverbed. It was beautiful, profound; it transported me, as all good storytelling should, from one place to another. Would it have made a movie? No. A book? No. A short story in a book with other such well-written, evocative stories? Probably.

How many times have I heard agents and producers say, "Boy, can so-and-so write. All she needs is the right idea." Sometimes if a script is well written an agent will take on a writer and send it as a writing sample to producers or studios with open writing assignments.

But, if you have an idea and the writing stinks, readers at agencies and production companies will toss your script by page ten. Nobody wants to slog through a poorly written script.

Major problems to watch out for:

1. Big, blocky paragraphs chock full of *Architectural Digest* descriptive passages of rooms and lawns.

2. Dialogue that sounds as if it's come out of a law book, or from a crashing bore who can't shut up, or from someone who uses "Really?" or "Totally!" every other sentence.

3. Characters who explain the plot to each other.

4. Herds of characters galloping across the first ten pages.

Things to do to prevent these problems:

1. *Build active sentences.* The ball was not hit by the boy. The boy hit the ball. Use basic active sentence construction. We tend to forget this. A movie is about someone in *active* pursuit of something: a way to get into it or a way to get out of it. The language should reflect that. If you offer dollops of passive sentence construction, you'll interrupt the reading experience, sabotage your characters, and lose story momentum.

2. *Kill all adverbs.* Adverbs are lazy, showy accessories that prevent the writer from utilizing the power of the verb. How many sports announcers, those great saboteurs of the power of the verb, make good writers? None? Right answer. Those "-ly" weasel words ruin more good scripts. They're like vermin. Use a simple noun, a strong active, visual verb, and move on.

3. If you must write a long, descriptive paragraph, write it out and then edit, edit, edit, breaking it down into smaller para-

graphs. Read it aloud. Does it sound too phony or overwritten or purple? This also goes for characters. When they speak, let them go, edit later. In that coal mine of babble there is a diamond hiding. If they talk too much, put a sock in their mouths and condense.

You're not supposed to let the characters explain the plots to each other or, by implication, to the audience. *Show* the damn thing. Don't write to fill space. Don't worry about how long, or short, the script is supposed to be. Keep in mind what each scene itself is about. Don't get the characters jabbering about what we can already see or have already seen. You don't need a Greek chorus to explain action. Compress and distill.

See *Monster's Ball* for compression of language and absence of dialogue. We are inundated by TV, in which people never shut up, even on clever shows like *The West Wing*. On TV, silence is anathema. If we hear silence we think the set is broken or the audio got screwed up.

4. Do you *need* all that description? The essence of the place or object or character will do. Ask yourself this: *If you were looking at a room or a vista you're about to describe, what one or two things would grab your attention first?* There's your description. Get them down and move on.

   Are the character's ears huge? Is her face pasty white below a shock of dreadlocked red hair? Is the house a small, faded blue stucco box on a gravel lawn with orange sprinkler stains running up the walls? Essence.

5. Watch out for clichés. If you've heard it before and still use it, you're being either lazy or plagiaristic.

Do You Really Think Your Life Would Make a Great Movie? *The Art of Adaptation*

Someone once said that the true art of adaptation—adapting a true-life story, book, or play, into a movie—is *not* being true to the original.

So many students get screwed up trying to remain faithful to every aspect of the story, especially true stories. Let's face it, all you need are elements of truth.

Case in point: *A Beautiful Mind*. Based on the life and times of John Nash, game and chaos theory mathematician, Nobel Laureate, MIT professor, and schizophrenic, *A Beautiful Mind*, in perfect three-act structure, charts Nash's life: the build, the destruction, and the rebuild.

In Akiva Goldsman's script, under Ron Howard's direction, Nash becomes a modern tragic hero who survives through his own willpower and the love of a woman, who sticks by his side throughout.

The truth, according to Sylvia Nasar's biography on Nash, is this: Nash was mean-spirited, a master of the cruel put-down. Before he married Alicia Larde, he had married another woman with whom he had a child and abandoned them both to poverty.

He had many intense sexual relationships with men and was fired from the Rand Corporation for soliciting sex in a Santa Monica men's room. Alicia Larde did not stay with him. When his illness became intolerable, she divorced him, remarrying him in 2001.

The filmmakers left all this out because they felt these truths would tarnish the image of Nash they wanted to portray.

Was this ethical moviemaking? Moral? Was it smart filmmaking? Or were Ron Howard and Akiva Goldsman and the studio worried that including these facts would diminish box-office potential? Might these excluded facts have made a better movie, with a far more complex character?

The point here is that they did leave out these items. They slanted the stories to their own purposes. You can do that. You can keep or get rid of anything you want. You are not writing biography. You are making a movie. Even biographers leave critical stuff out.

Remember T. S. Eliot's words: "All history is a contrived corridor." Everybody becomes an editor to suit a point of view.

This behavior by the filmmakers reminds me of the whitewash job Mike Nichols did on Meryl Streep's character in *Silkwood*. The writers, and later Nichols, backed away from the booze-guzzling, sexually active Karen Silkwood because they felt that her behavior would diminish the force of her protests. What we got was a character (played magnificently by Streep) whose behavior was skewed. It was that very wildness that brought her to protest against the evil, but we never really see it. What a missed opportunity. Yes, it was up for and won Oscars, but instead of being just a good movie it could have been a great one.

I hate it when smart guys like Mike Nichols and Ron Howard back away from good controversy in the name of *possible* box office receipt loss. But Hollywood is first and foremost a business.

The point? Take what's available and use your art and craft to remain faithful to the essence of the story. Trim the fat. Add drama and strong visuals. Bring to high heat. And hope you succeed.

If I Haven't Lived It, Where Do I Find It?—*Tracking the Story Beast*

Let's say your life is boring beyond belief and the possibility of finding material for a story is as remote as finding your own old love interest. Let's say you're sitting around feeling sorry for yourself, wracking your brain for something to write about, when suddenly you wonder why you're so angry. Why *are* you angry? You're angry because your former love interest blew you off, and you want satisfaction—call it revenge! You like to take revenge on people who fuck with you, don't you? He or she got away with that shit! Who do they think they are?!

The truth is that the love interest is gone, but the thought, the feelings remain. As a writer in need of a story, this might be one. You're pissed. There's conflict. There could be revenge, getting the girl or guy back. Maybe some treachery, double-dealing, even death.

So how would you do it? How would you get back at the love interest who screwed you over and that evil creature who stole him or her away?

Maybe what you really want is revenge with a twist, getting the love interest again, making him or her realize what a stupid move it was to leave you in the first place, and then you become the one doing the dumping.

Start thinking, start writing.

Stories can start with pain, feelings of retribution, or longing.

That's what my Emerson College student, Duncan Birmingham, did with his story that became a screenplay and opened Hollywood doors.

He started thinking about a young guy who lost his father and took his place with his mother—in all ways but one.

Duncan, twenty-six, tall, lanky, with a bemused straight-arrow way about him (hiding a wicked wit), wrote the script, *Mama's Boy*, in class. After getting his MFA, he moved to Hollywood and in short order, with the script as his calling card, got an agent, a manager, and an attorney and created a stir.

In October 2002, after five months working on a script with producers, Universal hired Duncan to write a big-budget baseball comedy. His career was kick-started into high gear. He made a big chunk of dough up front; if the movie is made he stands to make in the high six-figures.

Here's Duncan talking about *Mama's Boy*, a small, dark, indie comedy that paved his way to a career as a Hollywood screenwriter:

"*Mama's Boy* is the story of Ed, a serious-minded young man who is overprotective of his beautiful but flighty mother. When his womanizing Shakespeare teacher begins a public romance with his mother, Ed sees this as a personal attack and declares a war on him that quickly snowballs out of control.

"For me, the sparking idea was the relationship between an eccentric young man who acts more like an adult than his young, party-girl, single mother. I really liked the idea of this strange family dynamic and thought a long time before I figured out what the actual plot would be.

"As a fiction writer, some ideas for screenplays come from stories I've written. Newspaper and magazine articles often spark ideas—the problem is those same articles often spark similar ideas to other writers or even Hollywood producers, too.

"Overall, for me everything spirals from the main character. Thinking up someone who would be interesting to watch for two hours inherently gets the ball rolling for your story. Once you establish a strong character, then you ask yourself what would really turn this character's life upside down.

"In Ed's case, he is a very lonely kid, always jealous of his mother's shady suitors. When he finally does make a friend (his teacher), he then experiences the double-bombshell of having his friend betray him to get to his mother. All this when he's fighting the uphill battle of starting at a new school."

Ed longed to be something. Important? A protector of his mother's virtue? What would a young guy like Ed do to carve out a place in his mother's heart? You start with a feeling, a need, and begin to play it out, to spin the yarn.

Don't Back Away Just Because It's Not Mainstream— *Indie Love*

A big question in the mind of every screenwriter is whether to take their screenplay mainstream or independent. High budget or low budget? High concept or low concept?

Mainstream means studio. I hear "It's not big enough to be a studio picture" all the time. This means that the agent or producer does not feel that the studio machine will be willing to pony up big bucks or big promotion for a movie too small, or too low-concept, to attract a big audience. In other words: Sorry, not enough potential profit. Won't attract a major star. Next.

I say to new screenwriters: Come up with a good story and write your heart out. If it's a well-written, strong story, you'll get noticed by agents and producers, who will guide your career. You might even get your screenplay made.

Maybe you want to write about incest (*Happiness*), pederasty (*L.I.E.*), or murder without morals (*Portrait of Henry: Serial Killer*).

The studios will touch some taboo subjects, but with a feather. How long will it take them to make a real-life movie about the gay world? Low dollar return doesn't encourage big production companies or studios to go out on a limb. Not those limbs.

If you have a story about a cross-dressing, hypochondriacal, Oedipal-driven homicidal maniac with a pet piranha, the indie route might be for you.

The catch here, of course, is that you have to write a great script. With a cross-dressing homicidal maniac as your main character, you had *better* write a great script.

But there is a dilemma. You've created an excellent cross-dressing, homicidal maniac. However, you know how tough it is to break into the business. An agent or manager wants to see a future in a client, one in which money is present. But you don't want to write ordinary drivel. What do you do?

You're caught in the crossfire between art and commerce, or between what producers think audiences want and what the audiences genuinely want—which sometimes is the same thing.

When William Goldman said that the only given in Hollywood is that nobody knows anything, he wasn't kidding.

When I teach I rarely try to talk anybody out of a story they want to tell. Something drives the writer toward a certain subject matter. To deny that urge, especially at the beginning stages, usually sends the writer, already frustrated, chasing after derivative trains, and ending up with formulaic crap we've all seen before.

So what do you do? Find out what the driving force is. What are you tapping into here?

Take a look at some of the 2002 Sundance entries' log lines and concepts.

Birthday Girl. *An English bank clerk sends for a Russian mail-order bride (Nicole Kidman) and gets more than he ever imagined.*

Short, sweet, with loads of implications. This log line kicked my imagination into gear. I want to find out what happens and why Nicole wanted to do it. She almost always makes good career decisions.

Coastlines. *Directed by Victor Nunez (Ruby in Paradise, Ulee's Gold). An ex-con (Josh Brolin) returns to his Florida hometown and gets involved with the wife of the local sheriff, his former best friend.*

Nasty triangle. Ex-con/sheriff/best friend's wife. Somebody's gonna suffer for this.

The Man from Elysian Fields. *A struggling novelist (Andy Garcia) gets a job at an escort service run by Mick Jagger and gets embroiled in the lives of a famous writer (James Coburn) and his hot young wife (Olivia Williams).*

A struggling novelist in jeopardy? What a concept. So what have we got here: a desperate need that leads to desperate measures, which will lead the writer to a legendary man in his own field, who has a young wife, who has hired the writer as an escort? Oh boy. But at what cost? And with Jagger in the mix? You *know* this could be good. The concept heats me up. Are you salivating?

One Hour Photo. *Photo lab technician Robin Williams is obsessed with a young suburban family.*

Again, tells little, suggests all. Can you see the slightly risqué photos coming into the shop, or something darker? Can you see Robin Williams developing and printing them? Can you see him leering at the family as they pick up the photos? Can you see him following the family home, checking them out? Is this a stalker movie? Is he obsessed with the wife, the daughter, the husband? All sorts of possibilities.

More intriguing log lines:

Lubov and Other Nightmares. *A computer nerd goes on a wild adventure with a lesbian assassin named Lubov.*

Miranda. *A librarian searches for his missing lover, Miranda (Christina Ricci), and discovers she has three identities: dancer, con woman, and dominatrix.*

What actor wouldn't want to play not one, not two, but three different roles in the same movie with all this good stuff going on?

In **Teknolust,** *a weird comedy, Tilda Swinton plays a biogeneticist who breeds three cyborg/automaton hookers (also played by Swinton).*

In **Britney Baby—One More Time,** *a down-and-out Wisconsin filmmaker expects to interview Britney Spears. The movie becomes a road trip where the filmmaker instead meets transvestite Britney look-alike, Robert Stephens.*

These stories have one thing in common: conflict. Character-driven, off-beat, and original, they promise to take us to worlds we have not visited before and dazzle us.

No matter how offbeat the stories are, if they're told and written well, they will get noticed.

CLASS FIVE
You're Writing in WHAT Genre?

A romantic comedy/Western/action thriller with fish-out-of-water, psychological, women-in-jeopardy, period-piece elements supported by sci-fi/horror/fantasy links with supernatural overtones?

Sure, send it over. My address? The moon.

In some of my film and book projects I committed a cardinal sin. I floated over borders and crisscrossed genres, making it impossible for sales departments in studios and publishing houses to sell the projects.

There's this screenplay I worked on for a year about a couple of airplane repo men who mistakenly kidnap a beautiful young woman from her very powerful father who will do anything to get her back. The kicker is that the woman is an extraordinary android, and the plane jockeys, who have had huge relationship problems with women to begin with, unwittingly fall in love with her.

The fliers will do anything to protect her, while her powerful father/creator will do anything to get her back. And the chase was on.

What did we have here? A buddy movie trying to cross-fertilize with a futuristic sci-fi thriller and a love story. This was the pitch and perception. When the agents and managers sent it around town, it was turned down everywhere. *Skyjax* never got off the ground.

More heartbreak in the city of heartbreaks. No one budged. It was an $80 million movie that nobody wanted to take a chance on. I learned a lesson—actually a couple of them.

One was that you don't write an $80 million movie that crosses genres because nobody in his right financial mind is going to risk that much dough on a hybrid that a studio sales department can't figure out how to sell. This was one that didn't make it. Then there was one that did make it.

In 1997, a book I wrote, *The Huntress,* was published. It is a true story about a mother-daughter bounty hunting team in Los Angeles. Dottie Thorson and her daughter Brandi lost their husband/father, Ralph Thorson, legendary bounty hunter, when one of the cons he put in prison got out and planted a bomb in his car. After his death, Dottie and Brandi discovered that Ralph had sold the house and had accumulated debt to the tune of $150,000. What were the women going to do? They knew one thing very well: the family bounty-hunting business. They grew up in it and worked it, so they became partners. USA Network made a movie and shot twenty-eight hour-long episodes. I wrote for the series, was a co-producer, made some money.

Why one and not the other? For one thing, there was no mistaking what the story was, who the characters were, and what genre it fit into. The studio could sell it. It had two women in jeopardy against a male-dominated world. Women as bounty hunters was different and plausible. They went after bail jumpers who ran big companies, others who ate rats under bridges, very bad guys, women who killed, old men, young women—in other words, they went after their prey everywhere.

The studio could *see* the story. They could sell it. And viewers watched it. It fit into a category.

The movie business, like most businesses, is category-driven. Sales departments sell categories and rarely will venture outside that tightly controlled atmosphere. Even though they might love everything about it, they will turn down a project because they don't know—or don't have time to figure out—how to pitch it to the public.

This practice, or lack of it, is to fiscal-minded people bottom-line, iron-clad wisdom. To the creative instinct, it stifles.

I'm of two minds about this. One mind says, *Yes, if you cross genres your script will be tougher to sell. But if you love what you are writing,* my other mind says, *don't stop yourself.* My practical side tells me to use my creative juices to saturate a genre with new and more wonderful characters, details, reversals, etc. My creative mind keeps moving toward the genre borderlines, trying to stretch as much as possible without getting cramped.

My advice is to understand the categories or genres and then, if you must, stretch their borders.

Everything about your story might work, except how to sell it—which is the kiss of death. If you confuse the sales staff, you lose.

Categories

1. THRILLERS

The very mention of "thriller" makes me sit up and pay attention. Thriller means suspense, not just action. It points to that most fabulous of all writing devices—dramatic irony—in which the audience knows more than the main character. "Don't go through that door!" we cry silently. "Don't get in that car!"

Look at all the sub-genres attached to the thriller: romantic-thriller; comedy-thriller; action-thriller; suspense-thriller (a redundancy if I ever heard one); psychological-thriller; political-thriller. I've heard X-thriller and noir thriller. And occult thrillers are currently hot. You name it, it's a thriller of some kind.

A thriller usually has one main character who stumbles in where he doesn't belong and screws up some major operation already in progress, usually run by the bad guy. This main character should be a major pain in the ass to the villain, who spends the whole movie trying to get rid of this pest.

Wouldn't you, if you had a plan you'd worked on for months, even years, and now some jamoke strolls in—the main character—and starts screwing things up? Somebody once said we should have more sympathy for the villains. These poor souls spend time, effort, and money planning this big deal (usually illegal and often lethal), then one afternoon the pest (stranger/hero) comes to town and starts ruining everything. So what if the villain is committing an illegal act? That's not the point.

Anyway, that's the thriller: Your main character bumbles in and spends the next two hours of movie time, isolated and in danger, trying to reestablish order from the chaos he has unwittingly created.

Take *Blue Velvet,* a noir thriller, the David Lynch sicko extravaganza that made more of an impact on me than any film I have ever seen. The kid/hero comes home to see his ailing father. One afternoon, in the middle of a vacant lot, he stumbles upon a severed ear, and the story kicks into gear.

The ear leads him to the discovery of love and sex and demented townie-creeps, led by Dennis Hopper, who are running the town from the shadows behind the town's external red rose–blue velvet exterior.

The hero/pest keeps finding clues, which lead to the downfall of the bad guys and an awakening of the pest from innocence to experience. It took my breath away.

David Lynch, an New York University art major, brought his visual world to the picture. I've seen *Blue Velvet* at least fifteen times. It changed forever my perception of what was possible in writing movies.

Lynch roars on. *Mulholland Drive,* which TV turned down as too odd, won Best Picture and Best Director in 2001 by the New York City and Los Angeles film critics respectively.

As a tyro scribe, stick to the tenets of this genre. Add dollops from other genres, but don't let them overtake the solid foundation of the genre you're working in.

Must for thrillers:

- Isolate your main character and put her in nail-biting jeopardy.

- Concentrate on suspense and tension over action.

- Make us identify with the main character's fears, needs, and courage.

- Give us a villain more driven and often smarter than the main character, and more dramatically terrifying—until the end when the hero usually digs deep and, by discovering the villain's Achilles' heel, prevails.

2. ACTION-ADVENTURE

Fifty-five percent of all pictures fall into the action-adventure category. The reason for this is just what the term action-adventure implies: lots of high-tech elements, blood, and adventure, and more visual than talky, which means foreign markets won't have to worry about language nuance. What dialogue there is is so simplistic that foreign audiences get it quickly. Action-adventure aims at the testosterone-driven teen market.

The hero can be an action-hero or a main character who sheds his identity to become the fantasy creature who does the bad guys in. Jean-Claude Van Damme, Arnold, Wesley Snipes, George Clooney's *Batman*—that crowd.

A main element of this genre: *reversals of fortune.* The hero hops into a high-tech truck to chase after the villain, *but* the truck has a ticking bomb under it that the hero doesn't know about. The hero is just about to rescue the girl *when* the girl turns into the villain, then morphs into a beautiful woman who looks just like the hero's dead girlfriend. The hero realizes what is going on and is about to nab the villain *when* the bomb explodes, sending the truck and the hero into a ditch. A dog comes up and guides the hero out, *but* the dog bites the hero, filling his body with a virus. And so on, until the hero figures out a way to get well and return to battle with the villain.

Action pictures have simple plots and simple characters, with one main objective that usually screws up the main character, who now has to take an alternative route to get his wish. Psychological insight muddies these shallow waters. Clever, ironic dialogue confuses the issues. Keep it simple.

Musts for action pictures:

- Concentrate on action and adventure over suspense.

- In the main characters what you see is what you get.

- Use many reversals of fortune for the main character in his or her quest.

3. ROMANTIC COMEDY

At least half the romantic comedies star Julia Roberts, and the other half, Renée Zellweger. Girl gets guy; girl loses guy, another girl gets guy, original girl fights for guy and gets him back. These date movies and "chick flicks" draw big audiences.

The key here is to find a territory that hasn't been exploited to death and then provide enough twists and turns to make the outcome unreachable—at least until the last moment, at which point the man and woman overcome ludicrous odds to show, once again, that love does win in the end.

The *Boston Globe* film critic Michael Blowen and I wrote a romantic comedy, *Best of Boston*, about a couple of reporters working for a *Globe*-like paper. They love one another but take each other for granted. She's a dogged crime reporter. He's the gossip columnist who once was a dogged crime reporter until he screwed up.

One day the local magazine names her Boston's Best Journalist and names him Boston's Worst. The story is what happens to their relationship as a result. With an upper-crust murder thrown in.

Not a bad concept. A production company optioned it. There was a lot of gab about the potential. Our problem was that we didn't make it tough enough on the main characters. They were too jokey and glib. None of that fierce sense of loss and betrayal showed up in them to make the audience respond as they should have. If we had gone for the turmoil of *The Wedding Planner* or *My Best Friend's Wedding* we might have fared better.

But we were too easy on them. In our version, that moment in their lives was not critical enough. The stakes were not high enough. Although the concept was strong, *Best of Boston* did not generate enough studio interest in the *plight of the characters*.

If you're going to work in this highly competitive genre, not only do you need a high concept but vivid, dynamic characters the stars want to play and audiences want to root for, characters in a life-or-death, high-stakes game.

What are your all-time favorite romantic comedies? One of the Katharine Hepburn–Spencer Tracy or Hepburn–Cary Grant films, or *Pretty Woman, Shakespeare in Love, The American President? Legally Blonde, Sweet Home Alabama*? What did you respond to in these pictures?

Musts for romantic comedies:

- There needs to be a fierce battle of the sexes.

- Your two main characters must be at the most critical moments of their emotional lives.

- Your characters have to overcome a barrage of unspeakable, often zany horrors in order to reach each other.

- Your characters must be strong and compelling, and in situations we can relate to.

4. STRAIGHT COMEDIES

I would give anything to be able to write a movie like *Big*. I would give not much to write an *American Pie* franchise flick (although I would like to have the box-office numbers). Straight comedies rely on timing, with foundations in tragedy, rising out of a dire situation, from which the humor emerges. If you strip away the jokes in these movies, you will find a pathetic, vulnerable human being in the midst of the worst crisis he or she has ever faced.

One of the tenets of great comedy is not to play for or write jokes. The characters have to play it straight; no mugging, please. Humor rises out of situation.

I have read scripts in which the writers tried to be too funny or clever, replete with old jokes, Marx Brothers routines, anything to get a laugh. I once saw a high school rendition of Neil Simon's *The Odd Couple*, in which every actor mugged, winked at the audience, you name it. It received not one laugh, not one, through the entire performance. *The Odd Couple!* Can you imagine how hard the cast had to *work* to accomplish that?!

They say that comedy is the most difficult to write. The Coen brothers come close to perfection in *O Brother, Where Art Thou?* and *Raising Arizona*. Billy Wilder worked comedic wonders with *Some Like It Hot*. *Tootsie* depends on a strong, driven, main character in jeopardy who is willing to do *anything*, including changing his gender, to get what he wants. *Best in Show,* an event comedy wrapped around a dog show, is one of the funniest movies of all time. Why? Against the characters' passions and obsessions to win, they play it straight.

Musts for straight comedies:

- Put the characters into utterly hopeless, tragic situations.

- Pull their obsessions from them, put them on display, and exaggerate them.

- Make sure the characters do not mug or play for comedy but treat their dilemmas as if they were Hamlet. What might seem slightly absurd to us is deadly serious to them.

5. HORROR

Horror flicks scare the hell out of me. I watched *Alien* through my fingers. I've listened to more horror films than I've watched. I remember seeing *Night of the Living Dead* with a clicker in my hand, cutting back to the ball game every couple seconds.

For days afterward, the *Scream* flicks made me sick. You might wonder why I keep watching these things that scare me to death. Aside from my own dark needs, the horror movies I've seen have been well made. In *The Shining*, for instance, Stanley Kubrick decided to eliminate all shadows, formerly a mainstay of this genre, and this turned out to be even creepier.

These successful horror movies did the job horror should do: give us an almost incomprehensibly evil villain, who for some indefinable (at least initially), demented reason wants to kill innocent, unsuspecting people.

The writers scare the hell out of the audience through many means, mainly by shock and surprise and hiding the creature until the last possible moment. (*Jaws* is an exception. We heard that music long before we saw Jaws, but talk about building suspense!)

In good horror flicks, the creature, no matter how awful, displays human fears, mainly the fear of being messed with. Usually the evil creature has been living a relatively quiet existence until man shows up and disturbs it. The shark and the alien were getting along quite well, thank you very much, until humans tramped all over their territories.

Sharp writers then play on *our* worst fears, making us love to hate how horror films make us feel.

If you write in this genre—which ebbs and flows in popularity—make your villain fiercely original, and at the same time so familiar in its emotional impact as to scare the shit out of the audience.

Musts for horror:

- The villain is a humanlike monster or monsterlike human. If your home comes under attack from the neighbors, might you become a monsterlike human? Take time to look at the story from the monster's point of view.

- As the movie progresses, the terror should escalate, the more horrific the dangers the main characters must face should become.

- In his fiction, Stephen King assails our greatest childhood fears. So should you—perhaps your own greatest childhood fears.

The key to mastering the genre you're writing in is to rent at least five movies in the category. Even more important, read five scripts of movies in the genre. Here are three websites that offer downloadable scripts or can steer you to sites that have them. Once you find what genre you want to write in you can find scripts that match the genre and read them.

Harvest Moon (www.harvestmoon.com) publishes award-winning shooting scripts in their professional format with the author's permission. This company is nonprofit and has the cooperation of the Writers Guild Foundation.

Simply Scripts (www.simplyscripts.com) offers free downloads of movie scripts for educational purposes. These scripts are not always properly formatted and might not necessarily be the shooting draft of the script.

Movie Script Database (www.iscriptdb.com) is a search directory for scripts online. Some scripts are free downloads, and others require a fee. Most of these scripts are properly formatted and the draft is identified.

Reading is essential. Seeing is not enough. You have to see how the pros do it on the page. Without this, you will remain hopelessly inadequate.

CLASS SIX
The Fourth Horseman: Plot

Plot is made up of the actions of a story. If the story is a series of events or situations strung together, plot puts the "how come?" or "why?" into the series of events—their cause and effect. Cause and effect examines the characters' patterns of behavior.

Story: Once there was a ring forged long ago in the depths of hell. This ring, over time, found its way into the hands of a young man and forever changed his life and those around him.

Plot: Once there was a ring forged long ago in the depths of hell. This ring, over time, found its way into the hands of a young man, whose destiny it was to try to return it to the depths of hell in order to destroy the ring and save mankind.

The **Story** of *Lord of the Rings* gives us the overall concept and situation: a chain of events about an ancient ring and a kid and what happens to them both along the way.

Plot brings the character's motivation and drive into play. The kid has to face great odds to get the ring back, *to save mankind*. The motivational "why?" creates a pattern of thought and action on the part of the characters. **Story** points to tidbits of action and event. **Plot** puts a beating heart, filled with need and want, on the story.

Let's look at it this way. In Tolkien's story, this innocent kid has been chosen to save mankind.

                    MANKIND
Hey, kid, got a minute?

                    KID
Sure, what up?
  (Mankind holds up a pretty RING)

                KID (CON'T)
Hey, nice . . .

                    MANKIND
Yeah, well, how'd you like to make
ten bucks?

                    KID
Sure.

                    MANKIND
I'm a little busy right now, so
could you drop this ring off for
me? It's just over that rise. Take
you no time at all.

                    KID
No prob.

                    MANKIND
The   sooner   the   better.   And,
kid . . .

                    KID
Yeah?

                    MANKIND
I been told that of all the kids
living in these parts, you're the
go-to guy for this kind of thing.
Am I wrong?

                    KID
No, no. I'll do it.
  (Mankind gives him a look . . .)

```
            KID (CON'T)
No, no. Believe me, I'll get it
done.


            MANKIND
No matter what?


            KID
No matter what.
```

So off the kid goes on his "no matter what" mission, with his best friend and a couple other tagalong buddies looking for something fun to do.

Along the way they meet some very bad people who also have an interest in this ring.

The farther they go, the stranger things get, and the more things are not even close to what they seem.

Even though the kid wonders what in the hell he's gotten himself into, he's more determined than ever to get the job done.

Welcome to plot.

If story is a chronicle of events, plot is a chronicle of events *pushed from behind by cause and effect*—the *why* of storytelling. Why the characters do what they do.

Plot = story + motivation.

Story is a misshapen though often exciting conglomeration of idea, concept, and notion. It's got some half-formed characters and some half-assed ideas floating around that give it some juice. But something about this *story idea* grabs your attention.

So you climb inside this story room and see what you've got. There are these ideas—things happen. You have characters who talk and act and interact. Add motivation and you have your plot. But what kind of plot?

You ask yourself: *Is this about a quest? Revenge? Coming of age? David and Goliath? What* is *this thing?*

As you build on it, you discover that it's fitting more and more into one of these categories. So off you go to look up what these categories are made of.

This is all about motivation. Is your plot character-driven, plot-driven, or both? Is this *The Graduate* or a Jean-Claude Van Damme flick? Is this *Rocky* or *Rabbit-Proof Fence*?

I don't think any writer ever starts out to write anything but a character-driven plot. But many scripts end up as pieces of action-junk because the writer has no idea who his characters are or what they want. Even if the writer knows what they want, he can't figure out how they can get it. "I'm stuck," the writer shouts, and promptly brings in a *plot device*: another ugly helicopter with its ugly pilot to try to mow the hero over.

If you get stuck, grab your character by the neck, hold her up, and shake her violently until she tells you what she wants in this plot. Revenge? Retribution? The Holy Grail? What?!

Once you get that information, you keep shaking, asking: *What would you do and be willing to give up to reach this objective?*

And then you listen to what the character has to say until you hear her shout the magic words, "Anything and everything!"—and you are convinced that she means it.

Now you've got the beginning of a plot.

Categories

From Aristotle on, writers have been trying to categorize plots.

When you're creating, building, writing, and finally pitching to the agents, producers, or studios, it helps to know where your movie sits.

Like most businesses, moviemaking is category-driven.

1. SAVE THE WORLD? NO PROBLEM—*THE QUEST PLOT*

In his excellent book, *20 Master Plots,* Ronald Tobias says, "Before plot there was story. Plot is story that has a pattern of action and reaction."

A strong character with flaws goes after something that will save the world, himself, his mother, somebody. The plot involves a series of episodes, each one more dangerous than the last, with heightened stakes, derring-do, and loads of reversals. We should be on the edge of our seats.

Hits: The *Indiana Jones* series. *Star Wars. The Matrix* series.

Flops: *Harry Potter.* A big, wonderful book turned into a flaccid flick. The characters, the story, and the plot are as flat as Churchill's ass.

The key to the quest category is the quest itself. Your character goes after something or someone and will not give up until she gets it.

If you're writing a quest plot, put a sign above your computer that says something like: "This is a story about so-and-so *who will do anything* to get such-and-such." Set your character in motion and, through a series of increasingly more life- and/or sanity-threatening episodes, your character will hopefully learn something while also saving the day.

It should be a simple story. The objective is always right in front of the character, but out of reach. Just when she's about to lay her hands on it, it slips away. Frustration and anger creep in, then a great desire to say, "Screw it. I'm not going another foot!" But by this time she's too invested and there is no turning back.

Your job as a writer is to come up with all sorts of external (visual) hurdles and internal (emotional) demons to prevent the main character from getting to her goal—thus making her work harder than she has ever worked before, which builds *character*.

In movies, character is as character does. Characters' wants and needs drive strong, savvy, compelling plots. Weak plots rely on external action to keep them going. These writers know so little about their characters, or care so little about them, that they seek objects to drive the plots forward.

T. E. Lawrence in the Robert Bolt–written *Lawrence of Arabia* drives the plot by his obsession to be an Anglo king of the desert and to right what is wrong. Lara Croft in *Lara Croft Tomb Raider* wants to solve a crime. The difference between these two characters is the degree to which the writers have looked inside their characters, pulled out their fears and wants and complexities, and translated those to the screen.

Fundamentally, you've got to have a goal for your character to chase after. Without a goal, you have no story or plot. This is the muddle that drove old Harry Potter down. What the hell was he after? I can't think of anything, or I can think of too many minor things.

Beware of getting caught in the Harry Potter trap. You probably won't have a series of bestselling books behind you to drive ticket sales.

Although most quest movies are big-budget jobs like *Gladiator* and *Spartacus,* some independent pictures share many of the same tenets on a smaller scale.

Musts for quest plots:

• The main character, perhaps a modern-day Don Quixote, is on a search for real meaning in a cynical world. Read the script to *Rushmore* or *Ferris Bueller's Day Off.*

- The character changes significantly as a result of the quest.

- The character starts after something he wants and instead ends up with something he needs. Read *Tadpole* and *Igby Goes Down*.

2. GO AHEAD, HONEY, I'LL GIVE YOU A TEN-MINUTE HEAD START—*THE HIDE AND SEEK PLOT*

Guys chasing each other. Women chased by guys. Tommy Lee Jones chasing Harrison Ford in *The Fugitive*. Tommy Lee Jones chasing Ashley Judd in *Double Jeopardy*. The innocents chased down by the uglies.

What I like to call "hide and seek" movies are typically episodic, big-budgeted, multi-locationed pictures fueled by low-tech characterization and lots of pyrotechnics. These movies usually waste big-name talent by hauling music video directors in to soup up the story with hot visuals and name bands. These flicks, like *The Cell* and *Vanilla Sky*, target eighteen-to twenty-four-year-old males.

On the smaller scale, you could write your own *Memento* about a guy chasing his own tail, if it *is* his own tail. He can't remember anything, so has written his recent past on his skin in order to try to discover what is real and what's not. It's brilliantly written as a puzzle that makes the audience work. It's tightly focused on the central character and his need to find the truth. It was shot on a low budget and won all sorts of awards.

The key to hide and seek is its constant movement and suspense. Take *Panic Room* with Jodie Foster. Mother and daughter move into a house in a large city. One of the rooms has a secret room. Bad guys break in. Mother and daughter hide in the panic room. The entire story revolves around the Jodie Foster character and her daughter—the innocents—trying to outwit the uglies, who will do anything to get at them.

Vulnerable characters. Enclosed area. Pressure, tension, and suspense. Mother and child innocents—in a box, versus a half-dozen black ops alpha males trying to pry the box open. Innocents become experienced as they elude the uglies, then turn on them.

In your hide-and-seek plot, how large is your field of play? An apartment? A city? A world filled with expensive locations? The TV series *Alias* travels the world. Each location is identified by music and a murky set, or a high-angled cityscape shot over rooftops.

When you write hide-and-seek, think compression. Compression of time and space and language are essential elements (see Class Four). The main characters are squeezed into tiny spaces with a clock ticking. Will the bad guys figure out how to get inside the panic room? Will the air give out before they do?

In hide-and-seek flicks, you want big suspense and tension, not just action. Simply put, action is two riders on horseback chasing another rider. Tension is the audience knowing that the rider being chased has a cobra crawling out of the saddlebag, up over the horn, toward his neck.

In other words, play up **dramatic irony**, which means that the audience knows just a little bit more than the hero. In this case, they know about that cobra. You want the audience to cringe, to want to rush up into the scene and shout: "Watch out for the cobra!" Tension and dramatic irony are key elements in this category.

Put your main characters in a vice, or lock them in a metaphorical closet (or a real one), and never let them out. If they do manage to get out, *let them do it by their own wits,* not your contrivances. Never bring in that Greek invention, the *deus ex machina,* the machine god, who suddenly appears and saves the day. In today's movies, there are no cavalries to bail out your characters.

When you're trying to figure out how your characters will get out of each jam, don't try so hard. Ask your characters. They have the answers, believe me.

The readers don't care how *you* will get your characters out, but how your characters will get themselves out.

Remember, in this kind of movie the chase is the thing. We're not in Westerns anymore where John Wayne chased down the bad guys. These days, the hero or heroine is the one being chased. For better or worse, John Wayne is dead and gone. Today's hero or heroine is in constant, nail-biting jeopardy.

These hide and seek plots have sub-genres—rescue, kidnap, etc.—all having to do with a simple straightforward plot: Somebody is chasing somebody else toward some bad end.

Your challenge is to make it original. Save the kid. Save the girl. Save the world. A race against time.

These plots all have **ticking clocks.** If you don't save the kid by midnight the ducks will be let through the trapdoor and peck him to death.

A ticking clock frames the time line. It puts pressure and tension on your characters to get the job done. Keeping your eye on the ticking clock also helps create what movies ought to be—tension-filled stories.

One of my favorite ticking-clock movies happens to be the movie that changed forever my way of looking at the movies: *Blue Velvet*. In it, the main character finds himself in the clutches of a corrupt town and its sadistic leader, played by Dennis Hopper. The hero sheds his innocence as he goes. Will he be able to solve the crime and stem the tide of corruption *before it's too late?* Will he be able to keep from becoming the next victim? Will he be able to save the dark woman (Isabella Rossellini) who took his virginity or the girl next door (Laura Dern) who stole his heart? I was on the edge of my seat, transfixed, scared to death, knowing what was waiting for him, and knowing also that he would never turn back.

Put a ticking clock into your story and watch the stakes rise.

Musts for hide-and-seek movies:

- All the characters revolve around one central event.

- The story unfolds in a series of rapidly accelerating events over a short period of time.

- The stakes are higher than they have ever been.

- Everything culminates in a riveting, slam-bang climax.

- Tell your characters, "You're on the clock!" Put pressure on them to get the job done. No characters should be hanging around the plot. If they are, write them out.

3. YOU DONE ME WRONG, YOU EVIL BASTARD, AND I'LL TRACK YOU TILL MY DYING DAY—*THE REVENGE PLOT*

Many moons ago, Charles Bronson starred in a movie about a guy whose wife was killed. Nobody had time to go after the killer, so Bronson's character decided to take matters into his own hands. *Death Wish* was so popular that it spurred three remakes.

Revenge is a popular motivation. The hero often lives a regular life. We get to know him and his friend or wife or dog. Some wretch comes in and knocks off the friend, wife, or dog, then the movie kicks into gear.

The hero or heroine goes to the cops, who aren't much help. Against everybody's advice, the hero, who knows next to nothing about tracking a killer, starts tracking the killer.

Along the way he battles the cops, his own ineptitude, and finally the killer himself. Straightforward stuff. Once again, we have a simple story, nothing too complicated.

If you want to write a compelling revenge plot, create complex characters and put them in a venue we haven't seen before. Maybe the crime is offbeat. Maybe the killer isn't who the hero thinks he or she is. Take *Reservoir Dogs,* a low-budget indie film about a handful of gangsters who screw up a jewelry store job. They rendezvous at a warehouse. In this confined place, suspicions mount and the men start killing each other off, thinking there's a cop/snitch among them. Space and time are compressed. The story is told in nonchronological order. The pressure mounts. The men, and the audience, feel as if they're in a cell. They can't breathe.

In many of these movies, the hero's moral justification keeps him going, and keeps us riveted to the screen. We want him to succeed. But it looks as if this hero, world-weary or off-kilter as he is, won't be able to fry an egg, much less catch a murderer.

The hero meets an army of reversals. Just when he thinks he's about to catch the culprit, bad stuff happens to him, throwing him off at every turn. Reversals are big items in revenge plots, which is another version of a chase movie, only in this case the good guy is the pursuer, not the pursued.

For instance, the plot to *In the Bedroom* is about a father avenging the murder of his son. *Hamlet* is about a son avenging the murder of his father.

The plot is the human engine driving the story forward. Remember that note above your computer: "This is a story about so-and-so *who will do anything* to get such-and-such"? When you get fuzzy about what you're supposed to be writing, stare at that note. It will get you back on track. This simple sentence illuminates the spine of your movie: Everything revolves around the spine. If you find yourself sailing off somewhere, away from the plot, tack back and get on course. Otherwise, you'll be carried away by seductive trade winds, never to be seen again. Why? Because, out of confusion, avoidance, and terror of being lost, *you will never finish the script!*

The reason I'm laying out these categories is to try to keep you in line with the kind of story you're telling. It's so easy to get swept away. God knows I've done it. It's the most awful feeling, being lost at sea, with no way home.

Musts for the revenge plot:

• Hero is usually an ordinary person who suffers a grave injustice, for which he seeks revenge.

• But first, he tries and fails to get official help.

• The better revenge plots show action *and* examine the motives for the revenge.

• The plot might be a revenge suspense, in which we know the villain's identity (*Hamlet*), or a revenge mystery, in which we don't (*Patriot Games*).

• However the hero punishes the villain, the punishment should never exceed the crime.

4. KICK SAND IN *MY* FACE, WILL YA?—*THE DAVID AND GOLIATH PLOT*

It's little guy vs. big guy. Take *The Insider,* the Russell Crowe movie about the tobacco company whistle-blower. He has to fight his company, the industry itself, his own conscience, the breakup of his family, and TV network news phonies. It looks impossible, out of the question, for him to go through this with so much at stake.

We think the guy is nuts, but his determination and need to right a wrong make us root for him against these insurmountable odds.

The key here is that it appears as if little David is no match for Goliath, but during the course of the story we find out that he is, and eventually so does he, he just hasn't realized it yet. He has reserves he hasn't tapped. That slingshot of his, if used properly, has loads of power.

Sometimes the enemy is not human. A disease, like alcoholism, becomes the Goliath. In *Leaving Las Vegas,* Nicolas Cage's character goes to Vegas to drink himself to death. There he finds new hope, in a woman, but even she proves no match for the insidious nature of the disease.

For me the best picture of 2000 was *Requiem for a Dream,* which in its message and even its execution, made *Traffic,* another very good film, look like a mere kissing cousin.

Do yourself a favor and rent *Requiem for a Dream.* Ellen Burstyn won an Oscar for Best Actress. Jennifer Connolly did a star turn that radically changed her career. The director, Darren Aronoski, already someone to watch, became one of the top directors in Hollywood overnight.

Here also is a movie with a nonhuman (but human-made) villain—drugs. Street and and prescription drugs and how they turned the characters into their own worst monsters.

In the Old Hollywood, in the standard texts on screenwriting, these Goliaths were almost all human, or even superhuman. In the New Hollywood, they are more sinister, more subtle, more devastating. They are human-created villains (like drugs) that become our Frankensteins.

Watch and read *Requiem for a Dream, Traffic,* and *Fight Club,* and you will not see old standard stuff. As a screenwriter, you cannot afford to play the old games or seem dated. The rules have changed. If you are not willing to challenge new territories you will get left behind. Look around. Read science journals. Read abnormal behavior tracts. Look at the behavior of your own family or friends in times of severe stress.

What comes out of them? Why did that woman down the street beat her son with a curtain rod, while he just stood there and took it? Because he would take anything she delivered, just so long as she paid attention to him. That's the kind of stuff that makes the readers of screenplays pay attention.

The screenwriter's mantra: Explore the human condition at great risk, in the modern day.

In my classes, some people complain that I'm a hard teacher because I don't agree with what other teachers have said in terms of the students' work. "My other teachers said I was great," they whine.

And my answer: "You have lots of potential, but your subject matter is too derivative. You're stuck twenty years ago, or ten years ago. That stuff's been done. You're worrying too much about formula and not enough about what you see in the world around you—why people do this or that, even in your own neighborhood."

The old Goliaths are fuzzy, dead men. They haven't got a shot against the modern hero.

Remember Duncan Birmingham and Rachel Grissom, former students now working in Hollywood? Duncan's spec script is about a sixteen-year-old kid who literally climbs into his dead father's shoes and becomes him in his relationship with his mother (in all ways but sexually, and that might be next). Rachel's heroine hooks up with a weird and fascinating gang-of-three cemetery thieves who lure her into their dark world. Original stuff.

If you're not original and you decide to follow conventional means, you will fail. If your capacity to work creatively is there, take chances. Use standard means of laying out the screenplay, but get down inside and find the rare juice of creativity that you possess and free it.

After you get the necessary stuff from screenwriting books, throw them away. Don't read all the retread junk they lay on you. Most of it is old, standard, and lazy.

Read new scripts and some old scripts. Language changes. Ideas move forward and take on new colors. If anyone tells you, as someone recently told me, to not read anything made after 2000, tell them to take a hike.

Some screenwriting gurus travel throughout the land, espousing the early movies as models for the modern sensibility. How about breaking down *American Beauty* instead? Something relevant to today.

As much as we try to turn the old-time classics into models for today, they're not. Movies reflect the age in which they were written. The language is different, character sensibility has changed, and the issues are not the same. That's not to say that those movies aren't wonderful or important. They are. But they should not be the models on which today's writers should be basing their work.

If you want to succeed in today's world, read today's successes—and failures.

The old villains, the ancient Goliaths of movies past, wear frayed, ordinary armor and see-through masks. They are not sophisticated or complex enough for today's modern hero, not when we have characters like the ones played by Brad Pitt in *Fight Club*, Guy Pierce in *Memento*, and Billy Bob Thornton in *Sling Blade*.

Villains drive movies forward. The more fascinating, deeply rooted, and dangerous the modern villain is, the better off your script will be. Make your Goliath the best, most daring, potentially devastating creature you can.

Who's the Goliath in *American Beauty*? Kevin Spacey's inner modern man at war with society and himself? Yes. The world at large? Yes. The family he is tied to but can't let go of? Yes. Is this the story of a modern man who is not buying the bullshit family ideal story/pabulum fed to us from the conservative right—keep your family together, protect family values, even if they kill you—and decides to do something about it? Yes.

This ain't George Bailey's neighborhood in *It's a Wonderful Life*. In *American Beauty*'s neighborhood, they brutalize each other, they come apart at the seams, a father lusts after his daughter's friend, and a wife screws her competitor. The next-door neighbor is gay *and* homophobic, beats his son, and, in the end, murders the hero. Now *this,* ladies and gentlemen, is a modern American neighborhood. Face it. Love it. It's what goes on behind the modern façade that matters these days. You, the writer, have to take this undercurrent and bring it to the surface.

George Bailey probably thought about screwing the next-door neighbor's daughter and maybe he even did. But that was then, when things like that were not put up for all to see. This is now.

What I'm also talking about here is man against self, the most severe villain of all. John Nash, Russell Crowe's character in *A Beautiful Mind*, battles imaginary enemies created by his own fear, by his schizophrenic twin self.

Ed Norton's character in *Fight Club* battles Brad Pitt's character, his own creation, his other self brought out from behind his own human wall. The main character in *Memento* fights for control of his own memory. Man against self. In *In the Bedroom* the couple fights their own grief that comes from the loss of their son.

Our Goliaths are the fears we possess within and how we manifest them into the villains without. It's your job to take these internal demon-monsters and create from them visible and visual monsters we can see on the screen, in whatever form they take.

Musts in David-and-Goliath movies:

- Goliath must far outmatch David in his or her power.

- The David character uses wits to overcome the power of Goliath, and there is never a secure moment for him.

- The plot builds in a series of plans made, plans enacted, and plans thwarted, until reaching the climax where David, through his cunning, usually prevails.

5. I MEAN IT, IGNORANCE WAS A MUCH EASIER GIG—*THE COMING-OF-AGE PLOT*

Change—young change—is at the center of this category. This is the favorite category of young writers because they haven't lived long and this is what they know.

Most coming-of-age scripts I've read lack conflict and drama. This is because the writers haven't been willing or able to take chances with their stories or characters or to stack the deck against the young hero. The writer might not have met great adversity so has little experience to draw from.

Let's take a look at *Tadpole*, an indie film that came out in 2002. Like *Rushmore, The Graduate*, and *Spanking the Monkey, Tadpole* is a coming-of-age tour de force. Fifteen-year-old Oscar Grubman, son of a wealthy Manhattan family, arrives home from prep school. Oscar is in torment; he's madly in love with his stepmother (Sigourney Weaver). Oscar quotes Voltaire and is determined to make love to his stepmother. Instead, he gets seduced by her pal, Diane (Bebe Neuwirth), and hit on by all their friends. He learns a big lesson in the end.

Learning big lessons, as well as small ones, is a capstone for coming-of-age flicks.

Musts for coming-of-age movies:

- Your character ought to be sliding, screaming, or erupting into adulthood.

- Establish your character so we know him well enough. When the bomb explodes, we want to see a big change from what he was before.

- Show how your character handles this bomb. Does he try to run, confront it, etc.? How he reacts will say a lot about him.

- Show how little moments become, for him, big moments. How does he handle each one in this process of maturation?

- Your character must pay an emotional or psychological price as he makes the transition from innocence to experience.

- Make sure your character *learns* small, important lessons about growing up; don't rush the transition. You've got one hundred minutes of screen time to tell the story.

In the Final Analysis

In my classes, rather than steering a student away from an original concept, we play around with plot and characters, looking for the best way to tell the story—always keeping in mind that there is something about that concept, that *urge,* to which the writer continually needs to pay attention.

That is what I try to get them to respond to. Sometimes it's impossible to reach right away, but eventually, as the story unfolds, the writer understands the urge to stay with and pursue that original gust of creative wind that carried the story in the first place. This is the writer's *need* to tell the story.

Some stories, for instance, arise out of the need for the main character to make a choice at the end. Maybe a woman must choose between two men. It might be that the writer feels that she needs to make this choice herself. As the creator, she has to understand why she possesses this need and why she would give it to her main character. Maybe the character will choose neither of the men. She would instead tell the guys goodbye and choose to be alone for now. It should be your character's choice, not yours.

In some cases, the writer can't decide what to do, throws up her hands, and decides to go on to another story. But she will invariably come back to the same concept from a slightly different angle. It's funny that way, and telling, and it happens all the time.

As a writer, recognize your need to tell a particular story and then allow the character to live it. Ironically, the character might show you the way out of a dilemma you've been facing for a long time.

As I mentioned earlier, I always seem to write the David and Goliaths. The main character is a victim of his own weaknesses, who, in order to overcome the odds, must reach way down and pull out a handful of slingshots to slay the dragons of his fears.

I try, in all my work, to slay my own insecurities, over and over, in different forms. I respond to my gut fears and try to write my way out of them. It's a lifetime preoccupation that's become an occupation. A lifetime obsession turned into a profession.

In my attempt to overcome these odds, my character moves from innocence to experience. He comes of age.

My advice: If you are writing a coming-of-age story, read *Rushmore* and *Igby Goes Down,* then make a list of all the things you didn't know about how to create stories and characters like this.

DRILL: *Each week in my classes I ask the students to read at least one, usually two, scripts of produced movies that have something to do with the script they're writing, whether in theme, genre, or plot.*

I ask them to turn in at least one sheet on each script, listing all the things they didn't know about how to put a screenplay on a page.

By jotting these down as you read along, and typing them afterward, you'll get an education that money can't buy.

CLASS SEVEN
The Fifth Horseman: Structure

A few weeks after the Spielberg war movie *Saving Private Ryan* came out, *Newsweek* invited a few top-notch screenwriters for a symposium, among them Robert Rodat, who wrote the picture, Tom Stoppard and Marc Norman (*Shakespeare in Love*), and Don Roos (*The Opposite of Sex*). In the symposium, Rodat railed against three-act structure as the bane of young screenwriters' existence.

Newsweek's question: *In film school, screenwriters are taught formulas. Screenplays have to have three acts: thirty pages, sixty pages, thirty pages.*

Rodat: "It's hideous! And they get you when you're *so* young and *so* malleable that you believe this stuff. It's been a real challenge to for me to take that stuff and try to blast it out of my brain. Otherwise, you're going to end up with real formulaic films."

Hmm. Can you imagine that? Ironically, I cannot think of a major film in recent memory that follows a more rigid three-act structure than *Saving Private Ryan*. Could this be a case of do as the screenwriter does, not as he says?

So should you write your screenplay in the three-act structure or not? "If it was good enough for Aristotle," a student once said to me, "it's good enough for me." Fair enough. Can you write a screenplay not in the three-act structure? Yes. Can you write a screenplay without structure? Yes. Will it turn out any good? Possibly. But probably not. Then why take the chance?

Like any other paradigm, you should know the rules before you can break them. Rodat and other naysayers can call how they structure anything they like. The truth is that they use the principles of three-act structure in their work. I can only guess what makes them suggest otherwise.

Every writer I know, or have read, who works in Hollywood, writes with a beginning, a middle, and an end, which is three-act structure. Studios and producers think in three-act structure; their notes address three-act paradigms.

Ah, structure. You need to know a few things up front.

People mix up plot and structure. Structure is the bones, the architecture, the plans on how to hold up plot. Plot has no bones, no skeleton. It's an organic process.

Plot is the sweet- or sour-smelling people who drive through and around a story and make it a living force. Structure is the LEGO network of shapes and forms that hold up your story. Structure is static; plot is kinesthetic.

Structure is the fifth horseman of the screenplay; it holds up everything. Why didn't we start with structure in the first place? Without the substance of story and plot, there's nothing for structure to support.

Structural musts:

- Make the first ten pages so startlingly magnificent that only someone who perishes mid-read will be prevented from going on.

- Read the first ten pages of twenty scripts from the same genre in which you're writing. See how those writers did it. Study how they introduce characters, story, tone, place, etc. Take notes.

- After you write your own dramatically magnificent ten pages, promise yourself that none of the pages that follow will fall below their excellence.

In every script there's what's known as **the Bomb,** or the **Inciting Incident.** You'll find the explosion at around page ten.

This bomb starts the story. This bomb blows up in the main character's face, throwing the hero and most of the other characters into utter chaos. The rest of story is about your main character trying to pull his or her life back together—and not doing a very good job of it.

In *A Beautiful Mind*, John Nash meets a secret government agent who hires him to decode Communist infiltration through magazines and newspapers.

In actuality, as we later discover, this is the moment that Nash's paranoid schizophrenia kicks in big time. The agent is a figment of his wild mind, and so is a lot else about his life, including, as he later discovers, his roommate.

Much more often than not, the villain of the piece throws the bomb. The villain comes hard and fast and hurls the bomb on your character's life.

The story setup is this: In the first ten pages, we see life as it is lived by the characters. When the bomb hits, that life is forever changed. The bomb could be schizophrenia kicking in, a car accident, a murder, a plague, or a young genius janitor being discovered solving an impossible equation on a blackboard at MIT.

The bomb stops one life, starts another, and begins the movie.

Whatever problem erupts at the bomb will have to be resolved by the end of the movie.

Draw a line from the bomb to your climax, and you have the spine of your movie. Nothing should waver from that spine. Hamlet learns from the ghost that Claudius and Gertrude killed his father. For the rest of the story, everything Hamlet does has to do with proving if what the ghost said was true or not. Period.

If you wander from the spine, you'll lose the story thread, give up, and the story will never get told. This is the chief reason why you fail without structure.

ACT I	ACT II	ACT III
Problem/setup	Characters in conflict	Problem resolved
pages ten to fifteen bomb explodes, establishing problem	leading to:	climax, where problem is resolved

Act I: The Setup and Overview

The first ten minutes of any movie establishes the world as your main character knows it. It might be a world at war or in a meadow (but there had better be something interesting going on in the meadow).

At around pages ten to fourteen, the bomb explodes, hurling your character out of whatever comfort she has in that world. The character finds herself in a new hell where nothing will ever be the same and the past cannot be recaptured. Confusion, uncertainty, and fear grab her. She reaches out to find nothing but more misery or danger. She desperately searches for some way out of the chaos and, finding little, has to start reaching down inside herself for some answers, and so the journey begins. Villains rise up and inner demons stalk her.

Throughout the rest of Act I and into Act II, the character tries to restore order to her shattered universe.

At the end of Act I, another bomb hits—the first big turning point that gives her a notion of what she's really up against. She faces more danger, but at least she can now identify the danger. This really means nothing, but she has to keep fighting. What else can she do? The doors to the past have closed, and at present she can't stand still without being devoured by the villains, who want to prevent her from solving the problem, or the internal demons, who have always acted against her own best interest. She has to keep moving toward something—a solution—that she can only vaguely see or understand.

Act II: The Confrontation

General wisdom says that most movies fail in Act II. As the longest of the acts (half the movie at fifty to sixty minutes long), Act II is the stretch where the main character meets all sorts of obstacles from the visual and visible world of people, places, and things, and from the internal world where she faces and overcomes her own demons.

Act II is where the writer and her character often wander off together into the desert and get lost. They perish and the script dies, and another fifty-page story gets buried in the drawer. Why does this happen? The writer does not get to know her character well enough and gets led by this inadequate creature into oblivion. She didn't do enough prep work.

She forgot to refer to her character bios. She doesn't have a clue to her character's fears or wants. She was impatient to get started on the story, thinking she would work it all out in the actual writing. She forgot to do a mini-treatment or a scene breakdown (see class nine).

She forgot to explore the backstory, the chief mental and physical problems the main characters had before coming into this story: the insecurities, fears, phobias, bad attitudes, the characters' own personal saboteurs.

In *In the Bedroom,* for example, a middle-age couple (played by Sissy Spacek and Tom Wilkinson) have a college student son who's dating an older woman (Marisa Tomei) with two kids and an estranged husband, the scion of a local powerful family.

One day the estranged husband, in a jealous rage, murders the college kid, and the rest of the story focuses on his parents trying to pull their own lives back together by grieving and then avenging their son's death.

When I read the story idea I could not wait to see this movie. It had all the elements of great storytelling:

- Small elegant Maine coastal town, Camden.

- Younger man/older woman affair torn apart by murder.

- Class struggle. Middle-class family versus town big-wigs.

- A couple forced to face the death of their son, and each other, against great odds, on a small, personal scale.

- A low-budget movie that attracted top acting talent.

So with all this wonderful material, what could go wrong?

After a saw the movie I went home and wrote a review. I often do this when a movie affects me. I vent. I toss out ideas that often make me sound like a sour, irritated ass. Call it mental masturbation. Here it is:

In the Bedroom is like a film school effort, with a tension-absent Act II and self-conscious directing.

While Act I starts with an original world, Act II is glum and tedious. How many ways can two characters show grief—dozens, in this rendition. The actors work overtime to bring the material to life, but they can't overcome the weight and quicksand storytelling. As the lights came up, I heard a woman behind me in the theater say, "Insufferable." That about sums it up. The characters were not delineated enough, even for fine actors to capture.

Under less self-conscious and precious directing—with its lingering shots and "meaningful" pauses—the movie could have been the jewel some critics have called it.

I feel that some of these critics wrote more about what they would have liked to see than what was in front of them. Or maybe they felt that *In the Bedroom* was one of the best in a generally mediocre lot of 2001 movies.

In Act II, the pacing plodded, stumbling along on spindly legs. The director held his shots for so long he must have been brought up on Eastern European cinema. Where was the editor on this? Or better yet: Why did they (whoever *they* is) allow this director, and editor, to take this self-indulgent route?

Once the son is murdered, even the dialogue takes on a halting, artsy-fartsy "meaningful" first-year film school feel to it. The pace slows to inertia, as if grief is supposed to stultify the world.

After a well-paced Act I, the filmmakers had nowhere to go, the movie went to sleep for sixty minutes, then picked up again when the father decides to take revenge and kill his son's murderer.

And so on.

The point is that *In the Bedroom* has lots of good things going for it—the concept, the twists, the actors, the *potential*. Let's go back to the origins, the script and story.

After the murder, the story had nowhere to go but inside the parents' grief. Of course they were devastated by their son's murder, who wouldn't be? But did we have to spend sixty screen minutes watching people pine over a lost one in such deadening repetition?

Penny Marshall had the same problem in *The Awakening,* in which a troubled Robert DeNiro spent Act I in craziness, Act II in recovery, and Act III in craziness again. In Act II, Marshall and her filmmakers had nowhere to go. They found nothing to replace the tension of Act I.

What did the filmmakers do? They bloated, or floated, the story with other characters and events that didn't matter. We were forced to watch other mentally challenged people make it through the day—all the while waiting for the chaos of Act III to give the story energy again.

So it is with *In the Bedroom*: Act III, when the father decides to take revenge, is when things pick up.

In Act II, characters are supposed to be reacting and in constant escalating turmoil, to the bomb of Act I. The movie shouldn't go flat.

Maybe the writer-director saw Act II as a way in which he could show human beings reacting to devastation. We are bombed and we retreat, we fall back, we head for cover to recuperate. Only when the coast looks clear do we come out again.

Not in movies. Movies are not real life. They are acts of compression—real life compressed into a few terrifying, damning, exalted, wild and wonderful moments, filled with sound and fury, signifying everything.

Movie characters should not be allowed to retreat for more than a few moments, and screenwriters shouldn't encourage their characters to retreat for long before challenging them to move ahead. Your job is to force the characters out of their retreats and into the heat of frenetic life. The characters will resist. Who wouldn't want to go back to bed and pull the covers over their head?

But that's not allowed in movies. Your job as a screenwriter, especially in Act II, is to:

- *Force* your characters out of their comfort.

- *Close* all escape routes.

- *Identify* and then attack their fear centers so they won't be able to sit still for one moment.

- *Make sure* the villains know where they are, forcing your heroes out, if the heroes can't bring themselves to do it.

- *Create* an unrelenting vise pressing against the characters. Once the characters are out in the open again, *don't let up*. These characters are abruptly forced to change habits, outlook, list of priorities—in preparation for radical change, at this the most critical moment of their lives.

- *Compress* time, space, and language in an all-out effort to force the characters to face the brutalities of the outside world and the terrifying demons of their inner selves.

Act II is all about confrontation. It's about breaking behavioral chains that your character has dragged along behind her all her life, and is now compelled to break—at this most critical moment in her life.

Don't be afraid to put your character through the wringer. That's your job. Act II is the place to do it, with physical and emotional violence. Rain down on your character torment, doubt, and living on the edge of madness.

And never let up on her. If you do, the story turns soggy. Never give her a break.

Throughout Act II, your character tries to restore order—failing, succeeding, only to fail again. This is a journey. She is *forced through circumstance* to go on. As the main character, she is the one most challenged, who will make the biggest change by the end. She is on a mission to resolve the problem and restore order. With good luck and her own canniness, she will slay her demons and beat back the adversaries and prevail. But this is, after all, the most critical moment of her life, so she will not have it easy. In fact, one of the tenets of screenwriting is that you will *never make it too easy on your main character*.

Fear motivates the character and drives her on. She will pick her way through hell and find wisdom, self and otherwise, along the way.

She will screw up, fall back, get whacked by major reversals, but through hit and miss, trial and error, hopefully she will gain understanding and clear away the debris of her life.

In this wake-up call of a story we will root for her. She becomes a heroine to us. We want more than anything, considering what we see her go through, for her to succeed.

Act III: The Resolution

By the end of Act II and beginning of Act III, your character is more conflicted than ever, but sees a dim light way out on the emotional and physical horizon. A mirage? Who knows?

But she wants out of this misery and will do anything to fight or think her way to freedom.

Out of this need, and from what she has learned along the way, she sees that dim light as a solution. She stands alone at the edge of the swamp between her and the jungle thicket and wonders if she has the stamina or juice to go on.

She would turn and run if it were not for two things. One, she can't turn and run because there is nowhere to go. Two, she knows in her heart of hearts that if there is a solution, it is on the other side of the jungle.

She buckles up, gets the lay of the land, makes a plan based on what she has already discovered, and moves ahead.

In Act III, the resolution act, she fights her greatest battle. If she thought she had already been through hell, the last leg of this journey will make the earlier stuff pale by comparison.

She knows the problem will not go away by itself. She commits herself to go through this last door, and does.

The rest of Act III is the working out of the decision she made at the beginning of Act III to move forward. She fights the chieftains, her own inner demons, and the mightiest of her adversaries.

In Act III, the main character *acts* by vigorously pursuing the objective that will make or break her—the problem's resolution. At the climax she'll meet her greatest challenge face to face.

In the climax, the biggest scene in the movie, everything gets tied up. She wins or loses, or partially wins, leaving a modicum of hope.

Make sure the climax is the payoff to what began back at the bomb.

Your job is to make the journey fascinating, original, exciting—through your fascinating, original, and exciting main characters. Not an easy thing, as many of you already know, but possible, if you have the tools and the story, a story that is not clichéd or derivative. Something original.

This is the overview, begun in Act I: the problem's setup.

Read screenplays in the genre you're writing. Watch for the act breaks. Take each screenplay and divide it into the three acts. Taking each act, make a list of the central actions.

You will see how the three acts break down. This exercise will take some time, but when you're through you will know better than ever how the pros do it. I cannot stress enough how valuable this exercise is.

We have not been brought up to read screenplays. We don't know the form unless we study it. And we certainly won't be able to write strong screenplays without knowing the form.

Do yourself a favor and buy or download five of your favorite screenplays, read them, and break them down into acts. They will become templates for all future scripts you write.

CLASS EIGHT
The Nature of Character

Heroes

A schizophrenic bisexual Nobel Laureate (*A Beautiful Mind*). A maybe-murderer who has lost all ability to remember and has to write everything down on his body (*Memento*). An absent sixty-year-old philandering head of household who, after many years, loses everything and returns home to his whacked-out family of misfits (*The Royal Tennenbaums*). A spoiled rich kid whose mind has been stolen by a cryogenics firm (*Vanilla Sky*).

In the past, characters lost their dignity, honor, self-esteem, homes, and jobs—now they lose their minds.

Consider a handful of critically acclaimed indies: A rather likable pedophile (*L.I.E.*) A frantic website designer who loses his wife to suicide and confronts "sympathetic" nutcases who have their own agenda (*Love Liza*). A precocious fifteen-year-old who has an obsession for Voltaire and is sexually obsessed with his stepmother (*Tadpole*).

Or a woman who fails at dating takes a nymphomaniacal veterinary clinic secretary as her lover and becomes a sadistic serial killer (the spoof *May*). In Chicago, sordid *Blue Velvet*–type lives intersect for perverse, sadistic fun and games (*Design*). An anal-retentive photo developer (Robin Williams) stalks a local "perfect" family (*One Hour Photo*).

There are no George Baileys anymore, folks. No more Rockys. Forget about Superman. Gone, all of them. As much as we might have loved being brought up with some of these heroes, they reflect an age that has passed into memory.

Today's heroes are far cries from the muscle-bound guys like Sylvester Stallone or the cybermen like Arnold. Today's heroes are more closely aligned with that golden age of moviemaking, the 1970s, in which the antiheroes played by Dustin Hoffman and Jack Nicholson made their bones. But even they are not that mentally challenged.

Today's heroes are complex amalgams of tortured, idiosyncratic, demon-pursued, vulnerable, often neurotic, even psychotic characters, men and women, whose inner lives crawl out on the surface for all to see.

As the language and knowledge of psychology came to the front, an entire new generation of characters with dark pasts, incomprehensible presents, and uncertain futures emerged. More mysterious, more angst-ridden, they face ghosts, mental disorders, and fears their predecessors may have suffered from but couldn't comprehend or even name.

Let's revisit the Andy Garcia movie *The Man from Elysian Fields,* in which an unsuccessful writer gets a job at an escort service. One of his first jobs is to escort the beautiful, young wife (Olivia Williams) of an older, world-class writer (James Coburn).

A struggling writer, you say? What's the big deal there? Struggling writers are like locusts. But this writer is willing to do anything to support his family and what's left of his writing career. And look at what he must do to chase the illusive muse, not to mention the almighty buck.

The question behind almost all characters is this: What is the character willing, or forced, to do to get what he or she wants? The answer should be: anything. The field is open. What is your character willing to do? Not you—your character.

As the writer, you have to place your character at that proverbial critical moment and then squeeze. For your character, the further into the story he travels, the more he realizes there is no retreating. You, the writer, have slammed those doors shut.

The character, of course, wants to go back, but in that direction is nothing, less than nothing. Ahead is the way to resolve the problem. Back there is death or, worse, *ennui.* There isn't anything worse than a character saddled with ennui for turning a picture into a dishrag.

Look what happened to Will Hunting. In the beginning, Will is a prisoner of his own fears, hiding in Southie, among his pals, working at a nondescript job as a janitor. He's a mess. He can't go much lower. He's also a genius tormented by his own insecurities. He is his own worst enemy, the evil villain in his own life.

Okay, so the writers have many choices. The one they choose is to bring Will, yelling and pounding, out of the darkness of his prison into the light of the world. How to do it?

Gradually, slowly, piece by piece, they set up a series of incidents designed to tug and yank and pull Will out of his cave.

They first assailed his genius by tempting his ego. They encouraged him to solve a complex math problem on the MIT blackboard. They didn't turn their character into a janitor at MIT, the top math genius school in the world, for nothing.

So now Will is exposed for the genius he is. He tries to retreat. Too late, Will, you've been found out.

But the writers can't let it go at only his genius; they need their character to experience a full frontal attack on all his fears and insecurities.

To get at his heart they created the Minnie Driver character—a lovely, smart, exotic Harvard student, to whom he begins to open up. Will resists her, too, but not for long. He tries to retreat from her but, alas, she is too compelling and his heart says, "Give it a shot, stupid."

Item number three creates the deepest problems. Will's psyche. His emotional past. The part of himself he has shrouded in a cloak of darkness.

Enter the Robin Williams character, a shrink, who probes the depths of Will's self-protection mechanism. This mechanism has been in place forever and nobody gets past that sentry. Will resists mightily and, as a result, now tries harder than ever to retreat.

In all scripts, it's essential to study how the writers work with their main characters—truly the most important relationship in writing a script. Writers and characters. Creators and creations. If this connection is not solidly linked, all else fails.

You might say, "What about Robert Altman? What about *Gosford Park*? What about *Nashville*? What about all those ensemble casts that worked so magnificently?"

My questions to you: Who among you is Robert Altman? At this point in your careers, who among you possesses the genius for making that kind of movie? Who can, with a look or a word, bring a character to life just like that, like magic?

For the time being, early on in your career, concentrate on bringing one central character to life. It's difficult enough to create one strong central character per script, much less five.

Will Hunting's heart, genius, and psyche are being simultaneously assailed by secondary characters who represent the paths by which he can escape from his prison.

But like all of us, Will falters, he doesn't want to make the effort, a mighty one to be sure. He wants to go back to Southie and the confines of his little apartment.

But there, in the personages of his pals, his last refuge, is an answer he doesn't want to hear. Ben Affleck's character tells him that he is no longer welcome there, for his own good. "You," Ben's character tells him, "can offer the world a great deal more than you can give from down here in Southie." Out of love, he tells Will to go.

Will Hunting has had the doors to the past sealed by a squadron of people who help him enter the present, providing help for the future. By an act of will, he makes the final decision to move forward. At story's end, when his genius and his psyche have been laid out before him, and his past is not the dark secret that it was in the beginning, he will chase his heart and love will hopefully prevail. He will find the girl and begin a life.

Once you've forced your character to move forward, what compels him?

Here's where a little character legwork will do wonders.

In her excellent book on character archetypes from mythology, *45 Master Characters,* Mia Schmidt breaks the archetypes into simple categories: male heroes and villains, female heroes and villains. As Linda Seger in *Creating Great Characters* did before her, Schmidt provides the tools for thinking about character needs—what you need to think about when you're coming up with your own characters.

Like creating a story, there's no easy plan. Nobody's going to hand you the total meal. You've got to cook it up yourself. But these writers offer you ingredients. They steer you in the right direction. There's enough here to offer you options so that you can cross-fertilize character aspects, borrow from this one and that, and come up with something original.

No matter how many treatments or scripts I read, I always find myself asking the question: What does the character want? To get out of a jam? To save the day? To get the guy? To get rid of the girl? To kill the bastard who murdered her son and ruined her life?

Yesterday afternoon I read a treatment about a guy who wins the lottery. It was fuzzy, soft in the middle, discombobulated. Like a drunk on the street, the story kept veering off, stumbling around, loosing its footing, careening toward who knows where.

Why? The main character didn't know what he wanted; neither did he have the tools for discovering it. He kept looking for something to do. Meanwhile, all this *stuff* was going on around him. The other characters seemed to know what they wanted, but he—the main character—didn't have a clue.

Your main character doesn't need to have all the answers, but at least she has to be going after something that will ease her pain. Maybe she'll fail and try something else, but at least there's movement.

Your main character, at the most critical moment of her life, is looking for a way to resolve a problem. She's tried this, she's tried that. She's hit a wall, she's veered off and tried another route toward what she believes is the solution.

Take a good, hard look at the crisis she meets at the moment of the bomb. That moment establishes the problem for her. Somehow, by the end of the story, she will have to resolve that problem and restore order to chaos.

Villains

A few years ago I started a novel based on a guy who terrorized me. In truth, I terrorized myself out of fear for this guy. He was in charge of the English department where I taught. When he came into the department the halls cleared out.

The former chairman ran a smooth ship on which everyone worked as a team, but the new guy had his own way of steering the ship: through intimidation. Whereas the former guy said, "Let's all sail together and as a team we'll do great things," the new guy divided everyone so he could conquer.

The new guy, who had a lot of insecurity issues of his own, played Iago. He whispered in the ears of this one and that one, denigrating one faculty member to another. Bitterness and fear roamed the halls. The department became a ghost town.

It was ugly. I loathed him and feared him. I was afraid of losing my job; in fact, he threatened me with the possibility.

In my novel he was the same egomaniac with an inferiority complex that he was in real life. He was well educated but frustrated by his inability to get published in any significant way. His insecurity stemmed from a life of unrealized expectations.

The heroine of the book is a woman teacher who came into the department and discovered the chairman's last desperate attempt at publication. If he couldn't get his own work published, he would steal a sharp grad student's work and make it his own. The heroine, who has her own issues with male authority figures, discovers this. The chairman is willing to do anything to protect himself; the heroine is determined to uncover the crime. The wrinkle here is that the two of them had begun an affair before all this comes out.

In the real story, after a faculty uprising, the dean removed the chairman and he went back to intimidating his students in the classroom. In my version, I made the hell more personal.

The chairman is a manipulative, insecure, but powerful villain who, by story's end, would fall prey to his own vulnerability and a strong woman's determination.

I love villains. I love to hate them. The hate feeds into my own insecurities and desire for revenge, all of which I try to hand over to my main character without making the main character the almighty me. Tricky. I take the essence of my fear and dump it on my character, who has to live a life of his own.

Without a strong villain, the hero or heroine has little to fight against. Conflict wanes and the story goes limp. Without his great villains, James Bond would have been just another fey British government worker who liked his martinis shaken, not stirred. Without Hannibal Lecter, we have no story. Without Glenn Close's character in *Fatal Attraction,* are we willing to watch the Michael Douglas character's family life?

WHAT A VILLAIN DOES

1. *He drives the story toward catastrophe.* By the time the hero comes on the scene, the villain usually has something already in place. By the time James Bond got the news from his superior, all those great villains had been planning (for months, sometimes years) to take over the world. I used to get irked that all Bond had to do was sashay in, spend a couple days ruining all that work, *and* get the girl, then sashay out.

   The villain has the plan that the hero is going to screw up.

2. *Has all the real fun.* The villain sets the agenda, defines the story itself, ruins lives, usually acts without strong moral or ethical restraint, has a big plan to do big things, believes that he is destined, in his own way, for greatness—and is loaded with complexity (let's hope).

3. *The villain acts.* This character is driven by God only knows what: obsession, revenge, rage, a sense of his own importance, or the absolute belief that what he or she is doing is noble or right, or to which he is entitled.

   Ask yourself: What are my villain's motives? Why does she do these things? Out of what emotional, psychological, or sociopathic/psychopathic well does this character drink?

   Usually the villain thinks he's the hero. At some point this character believes, through self-justification or self-delusion, that he's on the right course.

   One of the things a writer should always do is to establish the villain's logic for what he or she does. The reader should be able to see clearly that the villain has a plan and a way to carry it out. In fact, it might be, on certain levels, a good plan. If the writer makes it clear from the beginning that the villain is pure evil, wrong-headed, and stupid, the story does not do what it's supposed to—give the main characters complexity, intelligence, and logic, and not forecast the end.

   The more fun (by which I mean creative fun) you have with the villain, the better the movie will be. The villain is not reactive, he's proactive.

   The hero is reactive until he refuses to be the punching bag anymore and becomes proactive.

   The villain always acts. He kills, manipulates, drives himself and others crazy, protects what he has worked hard for, and obsessively wants and needs whatever that thing is that he's chasing after, whether it's world domination, to screw with Clarice Starling's head (*Hannibal*), or to seduce young boys (*L.I.E.*).

   In the New Hollywood, more than ever before in the history of film, the villain wrestles with his own character; he is his own worst enemy. Often, the villian is another part of the hero.

If you look at the best of the independent and studio films, you'll see this Janus-faced complexity. In a very good British film, *Croupier,* the main character (powerfully played by Clive Owen) recognizes the "two" of him—Jack, the real day-to-day person, and Jake, the wilder character in the novel he's writing.

In *A Beautiful Mind,* Russell Crowe's character battles his schizophrenia. He is his own worst enemy, or rather his disease is.

In another powerful import, *Lantana,* the Anthony LaPaglia character is an Australian police detective who is beset by his own crumbling marriage, self-doubt, a murder mystery, and an affair he's having. In these movies, and dozens of others, we are fascinated by the complexity of the main character, who battles against self.

4. *Is a slave to the appetite.* Somewhere way back in the quagmire of his dark childhood soul, Kevin Spacey's character in *Seven* got all tangled up in the deadly sins. He has been preparing forever to carry out his mission: to display to the world the most grotesque examples of what these seven deadly sins are all about. In his twisted mind, he seems to believe that he is doing the world a favor by showing how truly awful a human mind can be.

He is on a mission of mercy. He has an appetite for providing absolution through death. He sees himself as a modern God, who must give up himself, as God gave up his only son to crucifixion in order to save mankind.

By using God and his son, Christ, as his team of mentors, he carries their message and mantle and issues their dictums. He whets his appetite for being the modern Christ as he absolves and forgives through the taking of lives, reenacting the seven deadly sins, and their punishments.

The Kevin Spacey character believes he is a hero of some rank and, if you turn it up a bit, he is. He will, by vivid example, show to mankind what one of its own is capable of, with a warning: Tread not in my footsteps.

In this villain you've got a real sicko with a inky past, a mission with Judeo-Christian roots, and a mind that is thorough, determined, and prepared. Look at what he does to the Morgan Freeman character and especially to poor Brad Pitt's character.

The Kevin Spacey character drives this movie. He is the fun one to write, unencumbered as he is by the patina of civilized behavior that governs the others.

5. *Is smart and vulnerable*. Watch out for the tendency to write your villain as a pure bad guy. Make her smart and vulnerable and give her something to do other than going around slaughtering people.

Here's a tip that might solve a bunch of your problems. Ask yourself the question: What is my villain afraid of? Or, if this guy is so smart, maybe he's too smart for his own good. What's he hiding behind his surface brilliance? Or, what is he most afraid of having revealed? What is he hiding? What is his greatest vulnerability, and how can the hero find it, attack it, and bring the villain down?

We all try to hide our insecurities and vulnerabilities from the public, right? We slide those smarmy things behind our strengths so others won't know we're, in critical ways, just a sack of quivering flesh.

Your villain became a villain for good reasons. What are those reasons? Why does this character act like such an awful human being?

Once the hero discovers the villain's vulnerability, he will attack it.

And of course the villain, once he discovers what the hero is trying to do, will try to stop him at all costs—providing more conflict and drama.

Take a movie you like. Read it or watch it. In one page, write down the central conflict between the hero and the villain and how it plays out. For instance, place the adversaries in Act I and define the nature of their conflict. In Act II, watch how it escalates, and in Act III, discover how the conflict becomes a fight to the emotional (and sometimes physical) death.

You will be astonished by how much this exercise will help you in the creation of your own story.

This axis or spine, which begins at the bomb and culminates at the climax, drives the story. It holds the entire story together. Everything that happens in the story revolves around this spine and defines the chief adversaries. The villain and the hero battle on the spine.

Remember that the villain drives the story toward some awful end. For the villain, the hero is at first a pest, then a deterrent, then a force to be reckoned with. Their conflict becomes a battle of wills, with the end result leaving only one of them standing.

If you pay attention to the idea that this is the most critical moment in *both* the hero's and villain's life, your story will bubble with conflict and tension and grow into a very hot property.

CLASS NINE
The Dreaded Mini-Treatment and the Tedious Scene Breakdown

The mini-treatment takes up just four pages but will be the most difficult four pages you will ever write, and encapsulates the entire story you will write in the screenplay. It's almost as onerous as the terrifying scene breakdown, which you'll learn about later in this chapter. If there were ever twins from Hades, here they are.

To get to the mini-treatment you should follow a simple regime. The first thing to do when you start to formulate the movie idea is to write down anything that comes into your head that looks as if it belongs to your idea. Shotgun the idea. Let it rip. Soon, your mental editor will come on the scene and start to dismiss certain extraneous ideas as soon as they come up (although some of them you'll retain for later when you write the actual script).

By the time you've shotgunned a number of pages, you will start to whittle down and condense, whittle and condense, until you can fit the major plot and story elements into a workable six or seven pages.

At this point you go through it again, eliminating anything that is not absolutely necessary to the plot or story. By the time you finish this process you will have that four-page, double-spaced, 12-point Courier font, mini-treatment.

Basically, the mini-treatment is a four-page summary of the

highlights of the story, broken down into acts. Page one includes the action of Act I; pages two and three carry the action of Act II, and page four carries the action of Act III to the climax.

I assign my students the mini-treatment, in this form, so they can focus on the main story points. Without a rigid, four-page, double-spaced, 12-point Courier font, they would tend to run the story out to seven or more pages, put it in single-space format, and make it 8 or 10 point. The reason they give for doing this: not enough space to tell the whole story.

That's the point. You don't want the whole story. You want to focus only the major elements and turning points so that we can *see* the story unfold. It's all about spotlighting the story, not how many details you can cram into a half-dozen pages.

I warn them that if I get anything other than four pages of double-spaced 12-point Courier prose I will turn it back to them unread. During my teaching life, I have been met by a number of shocked and disappointed faces belonging to students who didn't believe me.

Write it as if you're telling a story to a five-year-old with a short attention span. Use generalities to keep the flow and specifics to nail the big turning points.

I'm including three mini-treatments and scene breakdowns from three of my students, you'll notice that the styles in each are slightly different. Pick the one you're most comfortable with. Like scripts themselves, treatment styles also vary slightly. Here's the mini-treatment from Katherine Follett, a quiet, determined grad student from Vermont.

UNTITLED MINI-TREATMENT
by Katherine Follett

Act I: Upstate New York in the present day. Four friends await news from NYU film school concerning their ambitions to be stars in the movie industry. Rachel, a smart, funny, college-age girl, bides her time working in a bookstore. Her closest friend, Riley, unassuming but razor-minded, runs his own shady Internet business. Kind, reliable Mike is hoping to escape a life of apprenticeship for his father's electrician's practice. They spend their afternoons at the shabby diner where Dale, classically tall, dark, and handsome, waits tables for minimum wage. They meet there one afternoon, letters from NYU in hand. When they open them, they each find a rejection. Their egos are crushed; the working-class surroundings of the tacky diner seem to spell their fate. But back at Rachel's apartment is an old screenplay she and Riley have co-written; it's a caper film about a bank robbery. Convinced that they're bound for stardom, they decide to film their movie on their own terms. Problem: They have no money for sets, actors, costumes, etc., only a super-8 camera, some sound recording equipment, and a couple lights.

Plot Point 1: While mulling over how to film a blockbuster on a shoe-string, Rachel jokingly says, "Hey, why don't we just rob the bank and film it that way?" The foursome exchange looks; they've been dis-secting this screenplay for years—it seems air-tight. It just might work.

ACT II: The bank in the next town over is unglamorous, but it has money. Super-8 in hand, they begin scoping out the place. Dale opens an account and shamelessly flirts with the dippy blonde teller. Mike waits in the lobby, studying the security cameras. Rachel observes the parking garage, orchestrating their getaway. Nights, they meet at the diner to lay out plans, thought out mostly by Rachel and Riley. Guns or no guns? Dale and Mike don't want this to get too real, but as co-directors, Riley and Rachel win out. Dale ineptly learns how to aim and shoot a gun.

The plans are set, a timed rehearsal run gone through. On Tues-day morning, Dale, Mike, and Riley walk into the bank. Mike sets up lights, and Dale, all charm, explains the situation while Riley films. They're going to be filming a bank robbery for a "school project," and they need to "borrow" the bank, so act scared, duck when I point the gun at you, give us the money in this conveniently large duffel bag. Mike, masked, shoves an enormous wrench through the front doors and cuts the power to the security cameras. Meanwhile, in the parking garage, Rachel hops into an unmarked white van they have seen parked there every weekday, unlocked. Reading from a manual, she hot-wires the van.

In the bank, they shoot. The tellers are far too nonchalant—Dale did his job too well. Riley yells at them. The blonde teller can't help smiling at Dale, even when Riley insists he point the rifle in her face. Each time they must re-shoot, Riley cleverly insists that they leave the money in the bag and add new cash. But as they continue to pile money in their bag, the bank staff starts to get antsy. Something's up.

The manager demands to see some proof that they're doing this for "a project." Meanwhile, Rachel carefully drives the van to a pre-determined spot, a handicapped parking space on the second deck. She hangs a stolen handicapped card on the rearview mirror.

Dale and the manager argue while Mike and Riley become very nervous. Finally, Riley insists that this bank robbery is going to go down how a bank robbery should—he forces Dale to point the gun at the manager and insists that everybody get down or they'll be killed. When the manager questions the legitimacy of the gun, Riley insists that Dale fire it. It is, in fact, real and loaded. They insist that the bank staff get on the ground, not to touch the alarm. They finish the job with almost everyone involved (Dale, Mike, the manager, the teller) quite shaken. Riley, by contrast, seems jazzed by his sense of power. On their way out, Riley tosses Dale the camera. Mike arrives at the parking spot first and hops in the back. Riley follows next. Sirens. The cops see Dale and chase after him, but with Dale's athleticism and small-town cop ineptitude, he manages to lose them on the first floor of the parking garage, all while filming the chase, until he lands safely in the van. Slowly and casually, Rachel drives out of the parking garage. They return to the apartment, jubilant.

Plot Point 2: Later that night, while the foursome party, the cops knock at Riley's door. It might be just because of the noise, but they're spooked, and Riley insists that they run.

ACT III: In the van. Arguments ensue about whose fault it was that the cops came. The alarm must have been pulled. Riley is furious at Dale, Rachel at all three of them. She is driving north, toward Canada. By dawn, they're at a laughable border crossing—one old man in a brick shack. Despite coy Rachel, the man insists on seeing the back of the van. When he does, Riley, gun in hand, forces him inside, filming while he ties him up. It's clear that Riley is over the line, but finally Rachel concedes and they drive on. They see lights, imagine sirens. In the back Riley taunts the guard, aiming the rifle at him. Mike gets up front and insists Rachel pull over. In a cornfield, there's a showdown. Riley wants to keep running and take Dale with him; this is the best scene yet. Trying to win back Dale, Rachel reveals her feelings for him. Riley is furious; they had been a team, he thought. Mad with jealousy, he takes Dale and the guard off in the van. Rachel and Mike walk back to the road, and Mike reveals that he had been accepted into NYU. Realizing what their crimes have cost them, Rachel tips off the police on Riley's possible whereabouts. In the police car, finding the van, Mike and Rachel are horrified to discover that Riley has insisted on filming the guard's death scene by Dale's hand. Riley is arrested; the film will prove that Dale, now an emotional mess, was coerced. As Riley is taken to jail, Rachel insists that Mike take the film they have made and create a masterpiece at film school.

Strengths and Weaknesses

Act I (page 1) sets the story nicely. We meet the four main characters and their variety of personalities. They all have hopes of getting into NYU film school. Hopes are dashed. At the bomb, depression sets in. Then they discover an old screenplay about a bank heist. Act I ends with Rachel suggesting actually robbing the bank while shooting the movie. Solid setup act. We get to know the characters and their mood swings as they deal with disaster and hope. A small indie feature, not expensive, a movie within movie.

Act II (pages 2 and 3) puts the confrontation into play. They stake out the bank. Dale and Mike, the conservative ones, argue with the more liberal "co-directors" Riley and Rachel. They hit the bank, a clever rendition of movie/robbery/chaos/humor, and by the end of Act II they escape. But later that night a cop comes to the door and they freak, making their escape once again.

There's potential for all sorts of trouble and reversals of fortune. Anything can and does go wrong both inside and outside the bank. This all depends on the execution, but at this point the story remains strong. The escape can be dramatic, and even the knock on the door and flight set up well.

Thus far, the pieces of the puzzle fit well. I don't see any fat on the body, no dangling subplots to carry the story off somewhere. The locations are simple, the budget moderate. I want to find out what happens to the characters, who are showing pressure from the heist itself. The action and tension are changing them in interesting ways. We have an ego loose-canon case in Riley.

Everything will depend on the details and execution, but so far so good.

In **Act III** (page 4) the characters are trapped in a moving vehicle, arguing, blaming, tense. Good. Tension rises. Crisis looms. Their intention is to get away clean, but will they?

Now they split up and the movie takes a dip. With Riley, Dale, and the guard going off in the van, and Mike and Rachel walking down the road and with Mike's admission that in actuality he had been accepted to NYU, the stakes flag. Rachel calls the cops, they discover that the guard died, and so on. To me, the end is not as satisfying as it could be.

When you split up the characters, a movie automatically spreads out and loses steam. The end needs work to make what comes earlier achieve its optimum effect.

Katherine did a very good job though. She carried me through the tough setup and the very difficult Act II confrontations, only needing work on the resolution.

You've noticed that a mini-treatment contains no dialogue, only narrative. It should sweep along from one point to another as if carried by a big wind.

The mini-treatment establishes the foundation for your story, which will change as you write the screenplay. I write at least a half dozen mini-treatments along the way. I need to; otherwise I'll lose focus.

As the story changes, even during the writing, I need to refocus on what I have. The mini-treatment is the way to do it.

Scene Breakdown

After the mini-treatment comes the scene breakdown, which is a scene-by-scene delineation of the story. By using the location and the central action of each scene (the reason why the scene exists in the first place), you can see the story from yet another perspective. If the mini-treatment is an overall rendition of the story, the scene breakdown nails it down point by point.

We've all written scenes cluttered with off-focus material. This exercise makes you concentrate. Each scene is about one central thing. Each scene has a beginning, middle, and end, like a mini-screenplay. Focus and structure are the keys. Each character in the scene has a personal agenda that flies in the face of the others' agendas—creating conflict, the juice that drives story forward.

On my advice, Katherine rewrote the ending to her screenplay. Here's the scene breakdown for her revised script:

SCENE BREAKDOWN

ACT I

1. Bookstore where Rachel works: Riley films Rachel's intro.

2. Outside Mike's dad's electrician's shop: Riley films Mike's intro.

3. Daisy's Diner: Riley films Dale, the foursome discusses NYU; their hopes for stardom become apparent.

4. Rachel's apt.: They watch their awful student films.

5. Rachel's front porch: She finds a letter from NYU in her mailbox—rushes to . . .

6. Daisy's Diner: The foursome collect and open their rejection letters. They are devastated.

7. On the job with Mike: Rachel films Mike's bleak future.

8. Daisy's Diner: Rachel secretly films Dale sucking up to fat, stupid customers.

9. Riley's cavernous bedroom: Rachel films Riley working; they decide they can't live this way. The contents of Riley's room hint at a darker side.

10. Rachel's apt.: They collect equipment and try to adapt their screenplay; each person has about twelve roles.

11. Bleak early spring, railroad tracks in industrial park: They scope out locations, potential "banks." Looks grim.

12. Daisy's Diner: Decide it's impossible. Rachel jokingly suggests they rob the bank.

ACT II

1. Next town over: The foursome scope out the bank, notice the parking garage next door.

2. Inside Circle Bank: Dale opens account, flirts with cashier. Mike scopes security system. Cross-cut to—

3. Parking garage: Rachel and Riley rolling through the run-down parking garage, formulating a getaway.

4. Rachel's apt.: Specs laid out—who gets masks? Do we need guns? Mike agrees to steal his dad's hunting rifle and teach Dale to shoot.

5. Residential street: Rachel sees handicapped tag in car, gets idea, steals the tag.

6. Sandpit behind town: Dale incompetently learns to shoot, Riley watching, fascinated by firepower.

7. Circle Bank: Practice-run/scope-out. Riley, Mike, and Dale subtly choreograph their robbery. Cross-cut to . . .

8. Parking garage: Rachel drives around, checking the getaway plan.

9. Circle Bank, next morning: The day of the robbery: Lugging equipment, Riley, Dale, and Mike enter and assure bank tellers/customers it's "Only a movie." Cross-cut to . . .

10. Parking garage: Rachel driving through garage, excessively nervous.

11. Circle Bank: First take. Dale flirts and teller giggles. All other employees circle around and ogle the shot.

12. Parking garage: Rachel ditches her car, is able to open the van. She is the only one conscious of the severity of their actions.

13. C.B.: Other tellers want turns being the one "held up." Mike has dismantled both the camera and the alarm system while the filming provides a diversion.

14. P.G.: Rachel unloads the van and hot-wires it from a manual.

15. C.B.: Riley gets nervous, yells at the employees. The cash starts to pile up and the manager becomes testy.

16. P.G.: All set, Rachel begins to sweat. Where are they?

17. C.B.: Manager demands to see credentials, Riley starts to lose it. He insists it start to look like a real robbery. People are scared, a shot is fired. Mike's turn to take off to . . .

18. P.G.: Mike makes it to the spot, into the van. Informs Rachel of the breakdown of their plan.

19. C.B.: Bank robbery ensues. Riley exits, followed by Dale. They make it to . . .

20. P.G.: Riley makes it to the van, while Dale runs in afterward, terrified. Sirens. They force themselves to be calm while pulling out of the garage.

21. Rachel's apt.: Celebratory party. Bought tons of shit. A late knock on the door turns Riley paranoid, sets them running.

ACT III

1. The van, near dawn: Friendship breakdown. Argue over who is to blame for bungled robbery and how they are going to get out of it. Riley wants to run; Rachel wants to stop and plan.

2. Somewhere in farm country: They pull over, and Riley takes the gun and threatens to take Dale (the star) to finish the movie by any means necessary.

3. Cornfield: Trying to pull Dale to her side, Rachel reveals her feelings for him. Furiously jealous, Riley takes Dale and the cash and runs off.

4. Cornfield: Rachel and Mike chase after Riley. Mike reveals he got into NYU.

5. Cornfield: Standoff; Riley's madness enables Rachel and Mike to seize the gun, camera, and cash. Leaving Riley there, they get into . . .

6. The van: Swing back to town to drop Mike off, with the tapes, to head off to NYU. Rachel and Dale head toward Canada.

7. Train station: Mike films himself getting on the train.

Now we can see the characters begin to emerge. In Act I, Riley is darker (even his cavernous bedroom suggests it) and the frustration at having been rejected at NYU is more poignant. The environment in which they live takes on character. Mike's "bleak future" with his father comes up. "Bleak early spring" sets a mood. We get a better sense of smart, driven young people with some hope in a murky place, only to have the hope dashed—until the suggestion to rob the bank arises.

In Act II, with the plan, we get the sense of new hope. The cross-cutting sequences among the characters and between inside the bank and those outside give us the sense of space, danger, and anticipation. A key here is the juxtaposition of the their bleak world and their young hopes, and that the only way out of this world is by taking the biggest chance ever. The stakes are high.

They pull it off and celebrate, after which the cops knock and they are on the run again, in more trouble than ever. They might now have to pay for their crime. The mood swings and changing fortunes make this compelling. Katherine is building a story through her characters.

In Act III the friendships break down and there's a gun and a corn-field standoff. Rachel and Dale head for the border to an uncertain future. Mike will carry the banner for them all.

Bittersweet ending brings complexity to the story.

Mike Demer's last script was about a shrink who holds his sessions while driving a cab through Manhattan. Mike is tall and thin and works like a dog, and he's funny.

His bio: "I was the youngest of three brothers, meaning those two connected and then there was me. I was ignored a lot growing up. But I had things to say, stories to tell, and after spending a half-dozen years in the 'real world,' I applied to grad school and found my way at Emerson College. Writing screenplays. It's hard as hell, inventing worlds, but it's rewarding like nothing else. And my brothers can't tell me to shut up."

```
                "HELL INC." MINI-TREATMENT
                      by Mike Demers
```

Mini-Treatment: *For a good time, go to Hell . . . Exit 6 off the Mass. Turnpike*

ACT I: Nobody's heard of Hellick, Massachusetts. With Lenox next door, a plush green example of wealth and pride, Hellick is the oppo-site, riddled with potholes, dead brown grass, and dilapidation. Lenox has wanted to buy Hellick for years, to store their trash there and make it the muddy doormat to lovely Lenox. This naturally offends Hellick. But with bankruptcy looming, and the likelihood of losing Hellick to the state, which will sell it to Lenox, the selectmen scramble to turn things around. While Buck Barnum lobbies to sell the town to a celebrity, like Chevy Chase or Kim Basinger, the selectmen call Granger Todd after they see him on the cover of an old *Ad Week* magazine.

Meet Granger Todd, a brilliant ad man whose inability to keep "it" in his pants destroyed his career. He can't buy a job until he's asked to change Hellick's image from the decaying zero that it is to a wealthy tourist destination. His pay is a storefront downtown, and if he succeeds in Hellick, his property value skyrockets, and he's back on top. Hoping to score a couple bucks—and a couple babes—Granger heads for Hellick.

Shacking up in the guesthouse of the virtuous chairman of selectmen and high school principal Dawnie Collins, the comedy begins. The men love him and the women "love" him. At the town meeting, Granger dazzles, proposing dropping the "ick" from Hellick because a town called Hell commands attention.

Plot Point 1: Despite the virtuous Dawnie's resistance, they drop the "ick" and the transformation from Hellick to Hell begins, a deal with the devil that proves to be ruinous as well as rousing.

ACT II: Reverend Baker, a quiet black family man resigned to empty pews and a church in decay, just wants to save somebody, anybody, and is convinced by Granger that if he jazzes up his sermons and renames his church, the pews will fill and the church will get the paint job it's desperate for. Told he'll save more souls in a populous Hell than a dilapidated Hellick, the reverend agrees to become a public access TV evangelist at the First Church of Hell, which irks his wife, who wears the pants in the family. PJ McKay, the town cop who once promised his wife a baby "the day Hell freezes over," and whose job is to chase out the riff-raff from Lenox, is persuaded to be nicer, to make Hell a friendly place so visitors come back and spend money. Lola, a high school senior/Martin Scorsese wannabe who needs an original film short to get into film school, gets her chance at something original, and damning, when Hellick becomes Hell. Clyde Lyman, another selectman and owner of the hard-up Hellick Watering Hole, is engaged to Dawnie Collins, but when he gets a whiff of money, Dawnie becomes second fiddle. Clyde renames his bar "Hell Hole" to attract business and becomes driven by greed, to Dawnie's dismay. As tension mounts between them, Granger moves in. Meanwhile . . .

Merchants get into it, replacing old awnings with new ones reading *Hell of a Diner, Drugs from Hell* (pharmacy), etc. The school symbol changes from the Hellick Ducks to the Hell Devil Ducks, which are ducks with horns and pitchforks. Tourists begin appearing, and Hellick's profitable transformation to Hell parallels Granger's own return to success. But when Dawnie tires of Granger's lechery and goes to kick him out, he tells her his wife and child are dead, appealing to her sympathy. It works. He gets to stay.

Granger creates publicity stunts to put Hell on the map.

Stunt #1: In the search for a famous fugitive, Granger instructs Clyde Lyman, owner of the Hell Hole bar, to claim to have seen him, promising media attention for the town and a full cash register, to boot. It works. Media and police converge on Hell, seeking quotes and information, and Clyde's bar is packed. Hell makes the local news.

Residents are overjoyed, but Dawnie expresses the usual concerns at the next meeting, wanting a virtuous town, but Clyde, her fiancé, says Hell will make them rich! Dawnie is disgusted with Clyde, love on the rocks, and she soon leaves Clyde for Granger. But just as Granger's reeling her in, psyched to be finally getting the girl, his wife and child show up. They're not dead, as he'd said. Dawnie's pissed and blows him off. But the show goes on.

Stunt #2: When winter arrives, and the town freezes over, Granger has Lady McKay, once promised a baby by PJ "the day Hell freezes over," take her husband to court. It's all a sham, and the judge rules PJ must have the baby or do jail time. It makes national news and a Jay Leno monologue. Hell, Massachusetts, makes the *New York Times*.

Lola sends out her video, and Hell is exposed as a sham, a publicity stunt, and tourists begin arriving in droves to have a burger in Hell, to buy T-shirts reading: "I've been to Hell and back," to send postcards from Hell to family and friends. Hell has become the Vegas of Western Massachusetts, famous, rich, and saved from Lenox. But where there is Hell, there is evil. The reverend's children, once meek and giving, are now fighting over the Gameboy. Clyde is stealing from the town treasury. Debauchery is widespread.

At a "Taste of Hell," an extravaganza with costumes, bonfires, and tourists, everything erupts. PJ is a celebrity cop, and the reverend is defrocked by the diocese for escorting sin into God's house.

Plot Point 2: As Granger tries convincing Dawnie that advertising is harmless, still trying to get her in the sack, his own son catches fire.

Act III: He tries rescuing his boy, but tourists block him, cheering the burning boy on, snapping photos. They've seen Hell on *Hard Copy*. They think it's a show, a stunt. The reverend finally appears and saves the boy's life. He finally saves somebody, which is all he ever wanted. Granger, in tears, tries confessing his advertising sins to the media, but they're more concerned with the priest that just saved a burning boy in Hell. Granger gets knocked unconscious by a snowball. When he wakes, he learns that Hell has burned down. The town is ashes, broke again, and doomed. All seems lost.

For Sale signs pop up everywhere as residents sell their Hell property to relocate to obscurity. To hell with Hell. Hell votes two to one to put the "ick" back, though the reverend moves his family to Lenox. Clyde, caught stealing from the town, is impeached, and Granger quits advertising, opening a candy store instead. But the town is broke, foreclosed on by the state, about to be sold to Lenox, until:

Famous celebrity director brothers show up and buy the town for a cool couple million, pleasing Buck to no end, who wanted a celebrity from day one. They're going to make a movie about Hell going to hell, calling it *Drop the Ick*. The town is saved from bankruptcy. Lola is on set for the shoot, working as a production assistant, her path toward directing having begun. Dawnie, Granger, and Granger's boy are there, too, as they film a dripping brush painting over the "ick."

Strengths and Weaknesses

Handled properly, probably as a satire, this could be a fun movie. It takes aim at small-town mores, community anger and envy, and desperation. A former star ad man on the skids, with a sex addiction, coming to bail this town out is a riot. The story is strong, but execution is all.

In Act I we have a strong setup, a dying town on the verge of bankruptcy. The town next door, Lenox, wants to annex this dump, but the people of Hellick will fight back. The stakes are high: survival. Enter the formerly successful Granger Todd, who we know is a rake and slightly crooked. On his last legs, with one final gasp, Granger is the human embodiment of the town. He will take the job, mainly for the bucks and Dawnie, to whom he takes a liking. So far, so good.

A lot of characters parade by us in Act I. I worry when this happens because usually it means that the central characters lose their thrust and identities amidst a thundering herd. But Mike seems to have this under control.

In Act II, the merchants smell dough and go for the makeover. Meanwhile, Dawnie leaves her ugly, capitalist boyfriend for Granger, whose wife and child suddenly show up. The writer knows how to play comedy by using a series of quick reversals that put the reader in the position of knowing just a little bit more than the characters do. This dramatic irony works wonders on a story like this. Granger works his magic with publicity stunts, along with the "when Hell freezes over" promise. Hell itself becomes a self-fulfilling prophecy.

I am not wild about the coincidental nature of the fire that destroys the town and the snowball that knocks Granger out, although these events do pull everything together in Act III so that the town can come back from its ashes and bankruptcy. These events also allow Granger to get the girl and retrieve his boy.

The mini-treatment provides an overall view of the story, and the scene breakdown particularizes that view. In the breakdown you'll notice that Mike has added and subtracted elements to make a better story. So if you see items in the mini-treatment that are absent in the breakdown, or vice versa, you'll know what happened. The breakdown is essentially a way for the writer to find, on a scene-by-scene basis, a logic and pacing to the story.

Scene Breakdown [In this one you'll notice the absence of numbers beside each scene—another accepted way to do this]:

Act I: Various images of Hellick's decay: swamps, sign for water ban, and town meeting *tonight!*

Three selectmen (Dawnie, Clyde, and Buck) phone Granger Todd, best advertising guy in the biz, to offer job of jazzing up town's image, to attract tourists. He readily accepts.

Granger, in crappy New York apartment, hangs up phone, resumes shameless womanizing.

At town meeting, selectmen explain Hellick is bankrupt, but Granger Todd, a New York City image expert, is coming to save them!

Residents talk hopefully about Granger Todd.

On school bus, selectmen pick up slovenly Granger, have second thoughts, but he's smooth and wins them over perfectly. Granger instantly has eyes for Dawnie, Clyde's girl.

Bus passes Hellick sign, inc. 1705, pop. 665.

Granger tours Hellick with selectmen, gets the scoop.

School bus drops off Clyde Lyman at his bar, then Dawnie at her high school, after she offers her guesthouse. Dawnie's shocked when Granger kisses her.

Granger's dropped off at guesthouse.

Dawnie tells Clyde that Granger kissed her and gets angry when he doesn't believe her. Lola, a high school senior, says she needs an original film short to get into film school.

Granger locks up guesthouse, starts walking.

Granger harassed by town cop, PJ McKay, then wins him over.

PJ tells Granger his wife wants a baby, and that he'll have one when hell freezes over. Ha ha ha.

Granger visits his storefront, hooks up with random girl #1.

Reverend Baker tells his wife about Granger, says town meeting is tonight.

Plot Point 1: At town meeting, Granger's smooth, wins residents over perfectly, persuades them to drop the "ick" despite Dawnie's reservations, wanting to be virtuous for the children.

Dripping brush paints over the "ick," rewrites pop. 665 as 666.

Dawnie, on phone with Clyde discussing Granger's immorality, sees random woman #2 leave guesthouse, says she's kicking him out.

Granger tells Dawnie his wife and son died, gains Dawnie's sympathy.

Granger tells PJ about Taste of Hell, the extravaganza that'll save the town from bankruptcy.

Various shots of new awnings being hung, school bus and cruisers being repainted, etc. Town's taking on decidedly red hue, and residents have skip in step.

Granger comes up with plan to save the church, which is being closed by the diocese for low attendance. Reverend says he'll try the idea, but must ask his wife about renaming church.

Wife says no damn way.

New "First Church of Hell" sign being hung anyway, the reverend shaking head, in big trouble with wife.

Granger hanging sign of his new candy store, "Sweet as Hell," as PJ pulls up.

Dawnie begins to have feelings for Granger, but fights them.

At Clyde's bar, Granger talks Clyde into first stunt (publicity stunt #1).

Police and media converge on town to interview Clyde Lyman, who claims to have spotted the famous fugitive, the Animal Cannibal. Hell makes the news.

Lark! Police find actual fugitive by swamp!

Residents celebrate. Various shots of growing debauchery: drunks, littering, fights.

Clyde and Dawnie fight. Love on the rocks. She wants Granger.

First sermon at First Church of Hell is a huge hit, moneymaker.

News gets hold of damning video footage, Hell is humiliated, Granger's plan in jeopardy.

Granger spins the bad publicity into good publicity.

Knock on Granger's door. Dawnie? Nope. It's his wife (Ivy) and son (Evan, age eight), *alive*. Ivy says she's fed up with motherhood.

Dawnie sees Granger's wife and son, is hurt by being lied to by Granger, who said they were dead.

Town meeting, Granger says Taste of Hell is seven days away, has devil costumes for residents.

Granger apologizes to Dawnie, says he loves her. Dawnie says Clyde's a crook, but Granger's a liar, no better. Ouch.

Various shots of town preparing for Taste of Hell. It's Halloween meets Vegas: costumes, games, rides, bonfire supplies.

Weatherman says freezing temps overnight, an early winter. Granger asks PJ if he's ready for his stunt.

At McKay house, Granger sends PJ off in one car, accompanies Lady McKay in another.

Granger and Lady arrive at town courthouse. Media frenzy awaits, in the center of which is PJ.

Reverend's wife says the town's become the devil's playground as kids fight over Gameboy.

Dawnie visits Ivy and Evan, Granger's wife and son.

Ivy says Granger's an advertising liar, a chameleon, whose sperm made son retarded. (Kid has weird fascination with fires and firemen.) Dawnie's flabbergasted at this woman.

Judge rules in favor of Lady; PJ has to have the baby. Outside, reporter says history has changed. Hell's frozen over. Anything can happen now.

Dawnie says Granger's not saving the town, he's destroying it. The devil! To think that she trusted him! Granger's hurt.

The reverend, in a devil costume, winds up a dazzling sermon for parishioners who throw money at him, entertained, but are not saved. The reverend looks tortured.

Man approaches the reverend, pulls down his stretchy devil neck, yanks out white collar. Defrocked by the diocese for escorting sin into God's house.

The reverend wanders outside to bonfire, costumes, games, media, a marching band of devils playing the devil's music. It's Taste of Hell, a smash hit. And it's snowing.

PJ, now a celebrity cop with horns, signs autographs while Clyde Lyman prods women into bar with pitchfork.

Granger, dressed as shepherd, tries to convince Dawnie advertising is harmless.

Plot Point 2: Screaming erupts. Granger's boy, Evan, is on fire.

Granger tries to reach him, but tourists have surrounded the boy, taking pictures. They think it's a show. Granger flips out, tries to save him, but the music is too loud. Finally, the reverend appears and saves the boy's life.

Granger's in tears, tries to confess ad campaign to media, but media won't give him the time because a priest, dressed as a devil, just saved a burning boy in Hell.

Snowball cracks Granger in the head. He's knocked out cold.

Granger wakes in hospital, learns Hell burnt down, and media blames the candy store owner who ran around throwing snowballs saying, "I made them drop the ick!" It caused a riot.

Town meeting is in the school auditorium, until they find money to rebuild town hall. Selectmen approve adding the "ick" and impeach Clyde Lyman, crook.

Granger tells the reverend his boy is okay, with only minimal burns because he wore fireman's flame-retardants. The reverend says he's moving to Lenox, the spiritual capital of western Massachusetts.

Famous director brothers offer to buy the town for two million dollars, so they can make a movie about Hell going to hell called, *Drop the Ick*. Now they can rebuild Hellick.

Granger says he's quitting advertising and going into candy full-time.

Outside, For Sale signs everywhere sticking through thick snow that blankets street. Mass exodus from town.

Close-up on "Hellick" town sign, population six hundred and sixty-five. Pull back to reveal production company and famous director brothers filming a dripping brush painting over the "ick," crossing out six hundred and sixty-five and rewriting 666.

Strengths and Weaknesses

It's your turn. In a few sentences write what you feel the strengths and weaknesses of this scene breakdown are. Are there fundamental problems with the story or structure? Be hard on it. Don't mince words. The very toughness with which you go after this should reflect the toughness and thoroughness you would use on your own.

Rob is mild-mannered, a poet, with a fierce sense of place and a dedication. Here's what he says about himself: "I grew up in the Midwest with five sisters and a brother. Out of that turmoil emerged a strong sense of the world around me and a sensitivity to its stories. I was educated in writing at the University of Washington in Seattle and at Emerson College in Boston."

```
       "MANIFEST DESTINY" MINI-TREATMENT
                by Rob Arnold
```

"In a Midwestern wasteland, a young man's newfound daughter forces him to reconcile a criminal past."

Act I: JIMMY HICKS, twenty-three, comes from a nothing background in central Nebraska. His father is an alcoholic trucker prone to fits of violence. His mother died when he was fifteen. Jimmy has been in jail on and off since he was seventeen and is now doing time for attempted armed robbery and drug offenses. He hates his father, who beat him regularly, and resents his brother, who took responsibility for him when their mother died. At the prison, Jimmy works on a road crew, cleaning litter and roadkill off the highways. He is up for parole soon. Jimmy's older brother, DAVID HICKS, twenty-eight, a recovering alcoholic, writes obituaries for a local newspaper, and attends church and tries to lead a decent life with his wife, away from his family's history of failure. One day David visits with news: Their estranged father, BILL, is dying of cancer. Jimmy receives the news with self-interest: perhaps it will help in his parole hearing in a month. He asks David to attend the hearing because it looks better if family is present. David leaves without promising anything. When Jimmy's parole hearing date arrives, David doesn't show.

Jimmy makes parole and travels to his hometown to stay with David but receives a cold welcome, especially from David's wife, PAM. He gets a job at a local slaughterhouse to convince David he's changed. At a tavern after work, he runs into TAD, an old friend and bad influence. Tad tells Jimmy he saw Jimmy's old girlfriend, ANGIE, twenty-two, with a child.

Plot Point 1: Jimmy looks Angie up and finds her a gaunt waste. She reveals that she spent Jimmy's abortion money on drugs. Jimmy is furious, but suddenly her jealous boyfriend pulls up and Angie panics, making Jimmy leave out the back door. Outside, Jimmy sees a SIX-YEAR-OLD GIRL playing alone. She sees him and waves. He runs off.

Act II: Jimmy is convinced that the girl he saw is his daughter, but Tad tries to make him forget about it. They go on a drinking binge and get in a fight with some guys at the bar. They run away and decide to visit Jimmy's brother to harass him. David is asleep when they arrive and is not pleased to see them. He knows Tad is a bad influence on Jimmy. He yells at Jimmy for his irresponsibility and tries to make Tad leave so he and Jimmy can talk. Instead, Jimmy leaves with Tad. David yells after him to remember they have a sick father. Jimmy shrugs and gets in the car.

The next day at work, Jimmy talks to a co-worker about family. The co-worker talks about his children and how he wants them to have a better life than he's had. Jimmy nods.

Tad is waiting for Jimmy after work. At Tad's house, Tad and a friend share some crank. Tad and his friend plan to build a meth lab but need money for supplies. They offer Jimmy some crank. Jimmy declines, but Tad insists. Stalling, Jimmy borrows Tad's car to go to the store and get some beer. Instead, he drives to Angie's house and parks outside. He hears raised voices and sees Angie and her boyfriend arguing in the window. The boyfriend hits Angie and she falls to the floor. He continues yelling. In another window, the little girl is looking out at Jimmy in the car. They make eye contact and Jimmy drives off.

Back at Tad's house, they pressure him once more to join the team. Unnerved by his experience, he agrees. They decide to rob a liquor store, using Jimmy's meatpacking smocks as disguises, and

Tad's BB guns as decoy weapons. The next night, they do the last of Tad's crank and drive to the liquor store. As they're psyching up for the robbery, a police car pulls up. An off-duty police officer, KIM, twenty-eight, goes in. On her way out, she sees Jimmy and recognizes him as David's younger brother and comes over to talk. She asks how parole is going, wishes him luck, and leaves. Spooked, they decide to hit a convenience store by the highway instead.

At the convenience store, they rush in, weapons drawn. The clerk ducks beneath the counter and comes back up with a shotgun. He fires at them several times, injuring Tad. They barely escape. In a parking lot, Jimmy assesses Tad's wounds, decides he'll need medical attention, and drops him off at the hospital, taking his car. Tad is not happy. The next day, Jimmy goes to David and tells him what happened. David wants him to get help. Jimmy agrees, but he wants to see his daughter again. In the morning, David awakes to find Jimmy gone.

Nobody seems to be home at Angie's house, so Jimmy breaks in. As he's looking at some photographs, he realizes he's being watched. The little girl has come out from a back bedroom. He sees she has bruises on her arm and asks if she wants to leave. She nods and they go. In the car, he tries to talk to her but she doesn't talk back. He explains he's her daddy, but she doesn't respond. He realizes she'll need clothes.

Plot Point 2: Jimmy returns to get clothes, but Angie and her boyfriend, BEN, return. They're arguing and Ben is getting violent. Jimmy grabs the girl and hides in a closet. Angie opens the closet door and sees Jimmy. The boyfriend is furious and pushes Angie out of the way. Jimmy tries to run but is caught. The boyfriend draws a gun and beats Jimmy with it. They scuffle. Somehow Jimmy manages to get the gun and shoots the boyfriend several times, killing him.

Act III: Angie, in shock from the events, hits Jimmy. Jimmy, also in shock, pushes her away and grabs the girl. Angie tries to call the police, but he rips the phone out of the wall and throws it out a window. He runs to the car and drives off.

On the road, Jimmy tries to talk to the child. She remains silent. He begins to think something is wrong with her. Jimmy calls David from a pay phone on the road. The girl still hasn't spoken. David's wife tells Jimmy that their father has been hospitalized and that David is with him. Jimmy gets directions.

Jimmy and his daughter find David outside Bill's room. Jimmy confesses the shooting and cries on David's shoulder. His daughter wanders off into Bill's room. Realizing she's missing, Jimmy looks for her. David takes the opportunity to call the police. Jimmy finds his daughter on Bill's lap and explodes in anger, physically intimidating the weakened man and blaming him for all his problems and difficulties. He tells Bill to stay away from his daughter. Bill apologizes, but Jimmy is relentless, wishing him a painful death. David enters and calms Jimmy. He has news: The police are after Jimmy but David gave them misinformation, buying some time. Jimmy grabs his daughter and they rush down the hospital corridor.

At his car, Jimmy thanks David and says farewell. David wishes him a good life. Then, Jimmy and his daughter drive away, into the west.

Strengths and Weaknesses

In Act I, Jimmy Hicks, the protagonist, is in jail for armed robbery and drugs with a history of violent fits. He has an alcoholic brother and a violent alcoholic father, who is dying of cancer, and a dead mother. The Nebraska landscape is as desolate as his life. Jimmy has nowhere to go except up, we think. We also know that Jimmy can be violent and will take advantage of any situation—including his father's cancer to get him out on parole, which works. At home he finds coldness, an old pal, a former girlfriend with a kid, and her angry boyfriend. In order to keep our interest we have to hope that Jimmy has a sense of humor or at least a cynical take on the world.

In Act II, Jimmy's convinced that the six-year-old girl he saw while escaping from his ex-girlfriend's house is his own daughter. It's been six years that he's been in jail and the girl even looks like him. Now he's got a mission and reason to live.

Jimmy's brother, David, wants Jimmy to stay away from his friend Tad, a bad influence. Jimmy defies him. At Tad's, where a meth lab is about to be built, they decided to knock off a store for dough. Jimmy also goes over to see the girl he thinks is his daughter and finds bruises on her arms. They meet a female cop. They rob the store. There's no end to the pressure and action. The key here is to make Jimmy sympathetic, which the writer does. He's a victim of his father's violence and drinking. He wants to save his daughter. And the writer has made everyone around Jimmy seem worse than he is. It's almost as if Jimmy is the only one we *can* like. The writer wants the audience (in this case, the reader) to pray for Jimmy's recovery. But let's face it: This could be a hard guy to like and a tough story to get involved in. It's so damned desolate. But so, on the surface, was *Sling Blade*.

At the end of Act II, Jimmy kills the boyfriend. Now he's really in deep shit. There is no way out, it seems, and this is just where you want your character to be at the end of Act II—in a place from which it seems he will never escape, because in Act III you will send him on the most harrowing journey he will ever face, with no guarantees.

In Act III, Jimmy is on the run. He senses something is wrong with his daughter, as a result of the beatings and bruises and probably fetal alcohol syndrome. He kidnaps the girl and goes to his brother's, where he finds out that Dad is on his last legs. At the hospital we have the family showdown. Father, two sons, source of all pain. When Jimmy sees his daughter with his father he flips out, taking her away, as if the mere presence of his father will infect her, as it did Jimmy.

Family still prevails though, when brother David waylays the cops, allowing Jimmy and his daughter to get in the car and head west, to perhaps a better life together.

Once again, the proof will come out in the execution, but Rob Arnold's story resonates. I care for what happens to Jimmy and his daughter, and even though he commits murder and robs a store, he battled his way through and earns the love of his daughter and the promise of a better life.

Do you think so, too?

SCENE BREAKDOWN—MANIFEST DESTINY

ACT I

1. A prison road crew cleans litter along a highway. JIMMY HICKS, twenty-three, is among them.

2. Jimmy in his cell at night. It's decorated only with a photo of his mother. He reads a bad Western novel.

3. Jimmy talks with a parole review board. Jimmy is approved for a parole hearing.

4. The road crew cleans along the highway during an autumn rainstorm.

5. Sunday. In the prison, a minister speaks with prisoners about redemption. A guard enters: Jimmy has a visitor.

6. In the visitation room, Jimmy's brother, DAVID, twenty-eight, tells him their father is dying. Jimmy, unsympathetic, hopes it'll help his parole case. He asks David to attend the hearing.

7. Jimmy's parole hearing. His parole is granted. David never shows.

8. Jimmy rides the bus into town. He calls David.

9. David takes Jimmy home. David's wife, PAM, is not happy. Jimmy says he'll work at the slaughterhouse to make money.

10. At a slaughterhouse on the outskirts of town, Jimmy speaks with the foreman and is given a job killing horses.

11. Jimmy comes home to hear Pam and David arguing about him. Angered, he goes to his room.

12. At the slaughterhouse, Jimmy is shown how to kill a horse.

13. At a tavern, Jimmy runs into TAD, twenty-three, an old friend and bad influence. Tad tells him about his ex-girlfriend, ANGIE, twenty-two.

14. Jimmy visits Angie and insists they talk. She reveals she spent his abortion money on drugs. A truck pulls up. Angie panics and makes Jimmy leave out the back door.

15. Out back, Jimmy sees a SIX-YEAR-OLD GIRL playing alone in the dirt. She sees him and waves. He pauses, then runs off.

ACT II

16. Jimmy finds Tad at the tavern. Tad gets Jimmy drunk off his concern. They get in a fight with some guys and leave.

17. Tad and Jimmy drive around looking for trouble.

18. On a highway overpass, Tad and Jimmy drink and throw their bottles to the concrete below. They decide to visit David.

19. David is asleep when they arrive and explodes in anger. Jimmy laughs at him. David reminds Jimmy they have a dying father. Jimmy shrugs and leaves.

20. In the bedroom, David's wife asks about Jimmy. David tells her that their father used to beat Jimmy.

21. The next day at the slaughterhouse, ERNIE, who is in his thirties, and Jimmy talk about family. Ernie is saving money for his kids.

22. Tad is waiting for Jimmy after work. Tad explains he can score some good crank to make money.

23. Jimmy meets with a drug counselor. Tad picks him up afterward.

24. Tad and Jimmy visit GREG, Tad's connection. Greg needs money to start a meth lab. Jimmy stalls, going to get beer.

25. Instead, he drives to Angie's and sees her boyfriend strike her. In another window, the girl makes eye contact with him.

26. At the liquor store, Jimmy buys some beer and drives back to Greg's.

27. At Greg's, Jimmy is pressured to try a sample of crank. They agree to rob a liquor store for the cash using BB guns.

28. Outside the store, they do more meth. A police car drives up. The officer recognizes Jimmy and talks to them. Spooked, they decide to rob a convenience store instead.

29. They rush into the store, BB guns drawn. The clerk gets a shotgun and shoots several times. Tad is hurt. They flee.

30. In a parking lot, they inspect Tad's wounds. He took some shots in the side and arm and needs medical attention.

31. Jimmy drives Tad to a hospital and leaves him on the curb. Tad is not happy: Jimmy has taken Tad's car.

32. At David's house, Jimmy confesses and claims he wants to go straight and not back to jail. David says he'll help.

33. In the morning, David wakes to find Jimmy gone. A police car arrives, looking for Jimmy.

34. Outside Angie's house, Jimmy makes sure nobody is home and then breaks in through a back window.

35. Inside, he looks at some photographs. The girl comes out of her room, with bruises on her arms. He takes her.

36. At a park, he asks her name. She doesn't reply. They play together on the playground. Jimmy shows real tenderness.

37. At a diner, Jimmy tries to talk with her. She is quiet and unresponsive but smiles a bit when he offers ice cream.

38. Jimmy and the girl go shopping for food. She still won't talk. It's clear something is wrong with her.

39. They sleep that night in the car by the highway. Jimmy realizes she'll need some clothes.

40. In the morning, they drive back to Angie's house. Nobody seems home. David tries the door: It's open.

41. In the kitchen, he finds a grade report. Her name is Emily. The report shows that she needs special education.

42. In the girl's room, David roots around for clothes, throwing some in a bag.

43. As they're about to leave, he hears a car door close and voices approach the front door. He panics and hides in a closet.

44. From in the closet, he hears Angie and her boyfriend, BEN, argue about Emily's whereabouts. Ben is getting violent.

45. Angie opens the closet door and finds Jimmy and Emily. She screams. Ben draws a gun and beats Jimmy with it. They wrestle. Jimmy grabs the gun and kills Ben.

ACT III

46. Jimmy finds Emily hiding in a corner, scared. Angie hits Jimmy and tries to call the police. Jimmy breaks the phone.

47. Jimmy puts Emily in the car and stops. He has forgotten the clothes.

48. Inside, Angie is screaming. Jimmy grabs the bag of clothes, wiping blood off it.

49. Jimmy finds Emily terrified and hiding in the backseat when he returns. He tries to calm her but hears sirens.

50. Jimmy drives fast down the road, trying to coax Emily from out of her hiding place. She doesn't respond.

51. Jimmy calls David from a pay phone. David's wife tells him that David is at the hospital, visiting their father, BILL.

52. In a gas station bathroom, Jimmy washes his face. His eye is swollen shut, and his lip is cut open.

53. Jimmy buys an ice-cream treat from the gas station. He offers it to Emily. She takes it.

54. Jimmy and Emily drive in silence to the hospital.

55. At the front desk, they get directions to his father's room. The nurse wonders if Jimmy needs some patching up.

56. They find David in the hallway. David is concerned about Jimmy. Emily wanders into their father's room.

57. Jimmy tells David what happened and starts to cry. David grimly holds him.

58. Jimmy enters the room and finds Emily in Bill's lap. He becomes furious and fights with his father, slapping him.

59. Out in the hallway, David phones the police.

60. In the room, Bill apologizes but Jimmy is relentless, blaming Bill for all his problems. David enters and calms Jimmy, saying he called the police but he bought him some time to escape.

61. Jimmy, Emily, and David rush through the hallways of the hospital.

62. David wishes Jimmy a good life.

63. Jimmy and Emily drive west.

Once again, the scene breakdown particularizes the generality of the mini-treatment. In this case, Jimmy's journey is the focus, and we follow him through jail, parole, home, discovering his daughter, drugs, armed robbery, homicide, family woes, and finally hope.

The scene breakdown gives the writer a chance to focus on the beats of a story, how the story unfolds through character and turning points.

Once you complete the scene breakdown and feel that you have the story in hand, begin to write. Start with the opening scene and build through the structure. Remember, the bomb appears around page ten, then Plot Point 1, on page twenty-five to thirty, that takes the character in a completely new direction (either emotionally or physically or both). Act II will find you and your character in the vast desert of conflict in which he or she battles external villains, environment, etc., and internal demons. At the beginning of Act III (three-quarters through the script), the character finds him- or herself in position to make a final assault on the villains and the demons—as Jimmy does here against his father, his brother (who in the end turns out to be his ally), and his own fears. In the end he deserves another chance.

It's the most frightening journey, this last leg, because once into it, there is literally no turning back. The character is usually alone and running scared. The committee in the character's head is screaming at him. He keeps losing focus and getting it back. Up ahead he sees the climax, the biggest battle of the story. Is he prepared? Can he face this and win? This is, let's face it, do or die.

Never forget that this is the most critical moment of your character's life. Life as he or she knows it will change forever; it already has. This kind of crunch moment is why we go to movies and can sit back watching events unfold that we, thank God, don't have to face in our own lives. Yet we can identify; we can root for; we can weep and scream out.

Structure is the bowl into which you pour your story and plot. The mini-treatment and scene breakdown are the intermediary steps between the concept or idea and the actual writing of the script. They are the bridges to give you form and substance and a path to follow.

Now you're ready to take the final plunge yourself. But before you do, I have some bad news for you. Bad news and good news. The news is this: Before you start to write the script itself, do what the pros do—expand the scene breakdown into a twenty- to thirty-five-page single-spaced document. This becomes the entire story—every beat, every nuance, and all the major actions of every scene—in single-spaced prose.

By doing this you will have solved the story riddles that can plague you later on. My students hate this part; they hate the idea of it. But after they begin the arduous process of building their story before they actually write the script itself, they gradually begin to realize that this is perhaps the most critical step of all.

Once they finish this story treatment they see that writing the script itself is a cinch; it's fun. They won't be shocked to find out that they screwed up and missed an entire part that should have been included, or have included a large section that shouldn't have made it into the script in the first place.

After this step, the heavy lifting has been done, the beats have been placed, the characters have been established, and their wants and needs and fears have been brought to life. The relationships are solid, the motivations and logic are intact. In other words, this detailed short story or novella establishes the story line in a comprehensive way that removes the terrors or omission later on.

When you start to actually write the script you don't have to worry about those things and can concentrate on the characters and their nuances, the way they speak, their wit and anger, their complexities and secrets.

Here the writing becomes what it should—a joyous romp.

To do this, take each scene of the breakdown and expand it, starting with the beginning of each scene and carrying it through to the end. Some scenes can be handled in a short paragraph, others will take up a half-page or more. They should be single-spaced and thorough. You should be comprehensive in the use of salient details and bits of dialogue, interior feelings of the characters, etc. You are telling a prose story.

You will be astonished at the thoroughness, and then the confidence, you gain in your story as you build it through the process.

And then you can take the final plunge.

CLASS TEN
How to Break into Hollywood

You Need a Crowbar, Otherwise Known As a Great Script

Breaking into Hollywood as a writer means having a knockout script as your calling card. This masterpiece should have "talent" written all over it, money-making talent. As you gaze west across America, with the masterpiece tucked into your laptop case, you know you've taken the screenplay as far as you can. You've rewritten it at least a half dozen times, you've given it to anyone who's agreed to read it and offered take-no-prisoners analysis. You've pored over the notes they've given you, taken what you truly believed to be good ones and made the changes. You've spent months crafting it, and now you're ready to take it to the marketplace.

One of my favorite Hollywood stories concerns writer/director Colin Higgins, who has made a number of big pictures. While Colin was at UCLA Film School, he worked part-time as Robert Evans's pool boy. While cleaning the pool one day, Colin asked Evans if he would read a script he was going to submit for his thesis project. Evans said, "Sure kid," and tossed it into a pile.

A few days later, Evans picked it up and started to read. By the time he finished *Harold and Maude*, he knew he had found a masterpiece. A movie was made, a career started, and one of the great independent pictures of all time went off into the world.

Let's say you have finished, rewritten, and polished your own masterpiece to a point where you are satisfied. What do you do now?

The possibilities:

- Move to LA

- Don't move to LA

- Make the movie yourself

1. Move to LA and get a real job. Do it! What's the problem? You're young. You want to write movies for a living or get into the film business in some capacity. How many movie jobs are in Sadsack, Tennessee? How many producers or agents have you run into in downtown Sadsack?

Take the plunge. Drive that rickety old car out there and find a place to live. Get a shit job at Bobo's Eatery in the Valley. You hate it, but you have this script, this masterpiece, and it keeps you going when you're down.

In your non–Bobo's Eatery hours you hound everyone for names and contacts and generally make a sweet pest of yourself.

You meet tons of people doing what you're doing—trying to get their script read. And with persistence you will get it read. I know someone who send an agent a dozen white roses every day, for two weeks, begging her to read his script. Finally she did. She didn't like it, but she read it. It's called access. Gaining access.

You might even land a job as a production assistant at a production company, placing you closer to the flame. You might get hired in the mailroom at CAA, William Morris, Warner Brothers, Paramount, or an independent production company.

Your only aim is to get your masterpiece read by somebody significant who can get it to somebody *more* significant, pushing your script up New Hollywood's ladder. If the masterpiece is good, it will get attention. *You* will get attention. Everybody wants good material, and they don't care from whom.

Once you get close to the flame, you start to talk about the script, maybe casually spark an industry person's interest. Maybe they ask you what it's about. This is what you've been waiting for: to pitch your idea. If they like it, they'll hopefully ask for the script. Are you ready to pitch your heart out? You had better be.

What exactly is a pitch?

A pitch is a brief, compelling, verbal rendition of your movie. You want to pitch agents, producers, studio heads, anybody who can move the script forward. You practice your pitch on strangers at cocktail parties, to mirrors, in the shower—all the time. Try it out on your friends. You need to be ready with the pitch because you never know when you'll have the opportunity to use it.

In pitching to producers, agents, etc., you have at most five minutes. Some of the great story pitchers give Oscar-caliber performances. They get down on their knees or fly around the room, playing all the parts. If you're not a thespian or drama queen, make sure the pitch is straightforward, original, and dramatic. It should unfold logically and stun the audience with its visual and storytelling brilliance.

Start with a short, pithy attention-getter, a *log line,* which is a dramatic one- or two-sentence rendition of the movie. Example: What would you do if a very rich man offered you $1 million to spend a night with your wife? *Indecent Proposal.*

If you need a jump-start in developing the log line, check newspaper listings for movies showing on TV that night, or *TV Guide* or Done Deal at Scriptsales.com, a top screenwriting site, which also supplies most recently bought or optioned screenplays and their log lines. These are industry-grade log lines to movies *that the money people are buying.*

After the brilliantly sharp log line, begin the story in a casual but visual way with the opening scene and the main character. Draw us into the world. "It's a hot, humid night in Phoenix. Gisele, twenty-two, a breathtakingly beautiful Italian diamond merchant, stumbles her way out of a bar. She's a little drunk and a lot unhappy. She wants to go home tonight and climb into bed, alone. But that's not going to happen . . ."

Move rapidly through the rest of the story, introducing the other characters as they appear. You hit the big moments—the bomb, the turning point at the end of Act I, the turning point at the end of Act II, *but no climax*. Never give them that—unless they ask.

And then stop talking.

If the person you're pitching is asleep, get up and tiptoe out of the room. If the person starts asking questions, you've got interest.

There are other pitching venues: organized pitch fests where studio execs, directors, and producers listen to your pitch and comment on it, suggesting changes. If they like the pitch they'll tell you to finish the script and even send it to them. Instant contact.

If you live in LA you will have access; it's where the business is and where the people who run the business live. It is as simple and clear as that. Everybody struggles in the business, even the top dogs, *and they all live in LA.* They moved to LA because that's where the action is.

But the action is not for everyone. It might not be for you, but you'll never know unless you take a shot at it. From Kansas City you can *say* you don't like the action, but you won't know unless you live in it. There is no substitute for living close to the flame. I say go, take the chance. You're not going out there cold; you've got your best friend with you—the masterpiece.

2. Okay, so you can't move to LA just yet. You've got family, a job, responsibilities. You might be better off staying put for the time being. You might be buying time to work on your masterpiece, sculpting the script into the fine piece of art that it deserves to be. You might not be like the others—the impatient ones—who wrote their screenplays in a hurry and left in a hurry.

You're more cautious, more deliberate. You plan. You're not into spontaneous combustion, but logic. Call it good sense.

From your home far away from LA you can seek out, via phone, mail, and the Internet, agents and managers and production companies. You can write and call them. You can build a log line and hone your mini-treatment. You can develop your pitch. You don't want to pitch anyone, however, until you have a completed script. What if someone says, "I like what you've told me, send it to me." And you say, "Well, it's not quite ready."

The agent or producer on the other end is hot to see your work, and you don't have it to show? There goes your chance. Almost as bad as sending your sort-of-okay masterpiece before its time. There's no better way to kill interest than with a bad script, or a great pitch and no script to back it up.

When you finish your screenplay you can send it to screenwriting competitions (on search engines, search for screenplay contests), where producers and agents look for new talent—new talent that wins or comes close to winning.

If you need help, send your script to online websites that promise to read your script for free in exchange for you reading submissions by others. You can send it to script doctors who charge anywhere from $200 to $3,000. I feel that with basic research you can find someone qualified to read and evaluate your script.

Some people say, "Never pay anything to anyone!" They seem to have control issues that you shouldn't have to get involved in. I've used online services for a fresh set of eyes, and invariably, I've come away with some good advice. Isn't that what I was looking for? The best method is having someone in the industry, or close to it, read with your best interests in mind and give you excellent feedback.

You can give the script to your friends and family, but doesn't your mother love everything you do, or hate everything you do? Does your sister the fashion designer know how to read scripts and give cogent criticism? If you're giving it to her, let's hope so.

To reach agents, the best method is through contacts. Some say it is the only method because agents do not have time to read query letters. Do you know someone in the industry? A friend, relative, someone you met at a party or conference or seminar? Get them to read your script. If they like it, they will pass it on.

I agree that agents don't have time, but I also know people who have sent query letters to agents who have read them and asked for the scripts and the writers got representation. Write a one-page cover letter, explaining to them that you have written a script—a romantic comedy or a psychological thriller—about such and such (this is where you insert your powerful log line), followed by a brilliant two- or three-line pitch about the rest of the movie—without the ending.

If you have some expertise in the subject matter of the screenplay—you worked for the very same government agency your main character works for in the story—include that. Or include anything that might get the agent's attention: awards, expertise. Agents read scripts for two reasons: they like the idea, or they think some other agent might like the idea and beat them to it.

Go to the Hollywood Directory (HollywoodDirectory.com) or to various websites that list theatrical agents and send them the letter only (not the script), along with a stamped, self-addressed postcard, with two little boxes marked "Send the script" or "Don't send the script." In other words, make it easy for them to either accept or reject your idea.

In the letter you might also mention that you saw a movie you loved written by one of their clients. Next time you see a movie you love, write down the name of the writer, call the Writers Guild of America, West or East, and ask for "Representation." When the person comes on, ask who represents the writer. They'll tell you.

Production companies normally will not read scripts at all or unless you sign a release form indemnifying them from stealing your idea. Production companies have many projects in development. Your script might have elements they are already using in another project. Worry not. If something unsavory happens, you will have recourse, with proof, later on. The odds are they will steal nothing from you or anyone else. It's not worth it.

Still, people worry about their work being stolen. To protect against that, go to the Writers Guild of America website (www.writersguild-ofamerica.com) where you will learn how to register your screenplay.

3. Make your own movie. You've heard the stories about maxing out credit cards, begging relatives, borrowing from anybody, defraying all costs. Will you beg, borrow, or steal to make your own movie?

Why would anybody want to? Lots of reasons. There is nothing like the on-the-job training of making your own picture, from script to shooting to postproduction to editing, to marketing—always with the idea that you might strike it rich. What a rush! What a headache! It might be one of the most emotionally draining, spirit-destroying, ego-gratifying, neurosis-inducing exercises of all time.

Valerie Weiss was on the last leg of getting a Harvard Ph.D. in biochemistry while at the same time writing, shooting, and directing her first feature, *Dance by Design*. I met Valerie when she asked me to speak at the Harvard Film and Drama Program, of which she was the head.

Here's the story of:

THE MAKING OF *DANCE BY DESIGN*
by Valerie Weiss, Ph.D.
Filmmaker in Residence
Dudley Film and Drama Program
Harvard University

I always wanted to make movies. Growing up, the closest, most accessible thing to it was theater. I honed my acting and directing skills by doing plays. Then everything changed. Digital video technology became a consumer's medium and, like a painter or a poet, a filmmaker could afford to practice her craft.

I was in my third year of graduate school at Harvard University working toward my Ph.D. in biochemistry. I had been studying theater and biology in parallel since high school. I had been directing plays in Boston and at Harvard University's graduate student center, Dudley House (go.to/dudleyfilm).

Because Harvard does not have a graduate program in film, our students earn their doctorates in a wide range of disciplines, including math, archaeology, Spanish literature, computer science, history, and biology. Half our participants are scientists.

We decided to write and produce our own collaborative feature film. We would start in September 2001, completing it by the following May. A feature film in nine months, written, produced, edited. No problem.

Our highest priority was that it be a fun film. Growing up in the eighties, I was influenced by dance films like *Footloose, Flashdance,* and *Fame.* That must explain why I always hear a soundtrack in my head and live to go dancing. We decided that the feature would be an eighties dance movie.

I had learned about treatments from Chris Keane's lecture. I was impressed with the way he organized ideas and provided guidance for avoiding pitfalls of the first screenplay. I watched all the movies he recommended.

I had always been involved in the performances of the actors in films; it was difficult to switch gears and observe story structure. I began to understand the level the story worked on and to separate the screenplay from the production.

We needed to work quickly, but we were all full-time students. I recruited a team for the project: Ph.D. candidates from the divinity school, computer science, architecture, romance languages, Spanish literature, English, and graphic design departments, and an M.D./Ph.D. student. It was an international crew from Spain, Mexico, Holland, Puerto Rico, and the United States.

We agreed on the basic story. We identified plot points. Plot Point 1 would be when Angela's best friend Andre's night club got closed down. Angela needed a final project for her thesis in order to graduate; she offers to design him a new dance club.

This rekindled her passion for architecture, which sets up the conflict: to pursue dance or design. We focused on character development. What they did in the story, who they were.

We found the theme: a real-life story about how one decides whether or not to go for one's dreams and the effects of the decision. This was the most important moment in the whole project—the moment when *Dance by Design* became *our* movie. We had moved past the model that had inspired us and began to put our real beliefs and impressions into the film.

Then came homework. I assigned people sections of the screen-play. By the next meeting we had a first draft—very rough.

This method almost backfired. We were close to a final draft. I went away for Thanksgiving. While I was gone, the architecture student put some final touches on the script and checked for authenticity. When I returned, we met to read the draft. It was a mess! He had expanded all the dialogue and inserted foreign phrases everywhere to capture the pretentious culture of the design school. He gave Angela a lesbian relationship. We were outraged, even though some of the language changes did add flair.

In December, we cast the film with local professionals. We found a lead who could act and dance. We found a director of photography. Because the writing team had bonded so well, each of them took a role.

We began shooting February 3, 2001, shot on weekends, and wrapped April 1. While we kept to our schedule, we did not complete the editing by May. As we learned, postproduction is the longest phase.

We got feedback from professional editors and directors. Our most common mistake was writing scenes that were too long. We learned to dip in and out of a scene without needing to start at the beginning each time. You want to start right at the action.

Luckily, rewriting dialogue is possible in editing, but there would have been so much time and money saved on the set and in the cutting room if the story were pared down to its essence on paper.

We had the premier in Boston, after which we sent it to festivals. We're now awaiting word about that. I am eager to begin writing my next film using the lessons I learned from this one. My advice is that when you are developing your craft as a writer or filmmaker, keep working on it. Take Chris's advice for applying structure, and force yourself to put in the time every day.

Even when your project does not have the shape you want, you need to keep working on it until it does. It is easy to give up a project that is frustrating for a promise of a new one, but you will make the same mistakes on that second project. Don't move on until you have learned all you can from the first.

Good luck!

Val

The Rejection Pitfall

One the things you will encounter is rejection, from everyone. Writers get rejected almost as often as actors, about whom I've heard get rejected on the average of thirty-four times before they get a callback.

People in Hollywood don't like to say no. Instead they say, "It's not right for us," or "We're not making this kind of picture right now," or "Thanks, but we have something similar in development." What they're saying is no. The writer doesn't get solid feedback. Call it silent rejection.

Michael Schiffer (*Colors, Crimson Tide*) tells the story about early in his career when he really needed a job. He had pitched an idea to a woman studio executive who loved the idea. In fact, she was on the verge of making an offer.

The phone rang, and she took the call in the other room. When she came back a few moments later, she was not nearly as receptive. In fact, she did an about-face, thanked Michael for his time, and passed on the idea.

Michael called his agent, saying he thought for sure he had it. The studio executive as much as said she would buy it for development. What happened?

His agent said he knew why. That phone call she had gotten was most likely from her boss, who fired her. "You were pitching to a person who no longer worked for the studio."

Rejection is a way of life. Don't take it personally; it's not about you but about so many other things. The best thing for you to do is nod and move on.

Titles

A title can be a real turnoff. It can sour the pitch. If a title is boring, tasteless, derivative, or forgettable, call it untitled. The title is a reflection of your general ability to write.

Would you see a movie called *Next Door* or *A Black Veil for Lisa* or *Drifting Souls*?

Don't let anyone tell you otherwise: Titles mean *a lot!* If you can snag a great one right away, go for it. If not, get as close as you can.

Don't drive yourself crazy trying to find it. It will show up—like a great relationship—when you're least expecting it. It might come out of something a character says or from that thesaurus you've been scouring for days, or you might reshape it from an already existing title.

I found the title for one of my books, *Dirty Words,* in a conversation with my niece at dinner one night at an Outback restaurant in Orlando. The story was about plagiarism, and she said, "You mean, dirty words. There's your title." Just like that.

How about *Bad Day at Black Rock*? Says it all, doesn't it? How bad can a bad day be at a place called Black Rock? Exactly. How unforgettable is *The Good, the Bad, and the Ugly*?

Will the title fit on a movie marquee? Or does it have so many words that they will trail down the building and onto the sidewalk?

Pearl Harbor. Is there any doubt what this movie's about? Here's how *New York Times* critic A. O. Scott began his review: "The Japanese sneak attack on Pearl Harbor that brought the United States into World War II has inspired a splendid movie, full of vivid performances and unforgettable scenes, a movie that uses the coming of war as a backdrop for individual stories of love, ambition, heroism and betrayal. The name of that movie is *From Here to Eternity*." *Pearl Harbor* is a New Hollywood title. It says what it is; there's no mistaking the time and place and significance. Like the movie itself, its title bangs you over the head. *From Here to Eternity* came from James Jones's hugely popular novel. The producers weren't about to change it, but don't think they wouldn't have if they could.

A boring movie title means, to me at least, that the creators put about as much effort into it as they did into the rest of the movie. *Enormous Changes,* a 1983 flick about New York City women starring Ellen Barkin and Kevin Bacon, was written by the inimitable John Sayles. It could be the worst title ever. "Hey, Bob, have you seen *Enormous Changes*?"

A title should titillate: *Whatever Happened to Baby Jane?* It should perhaps create mystery: *The Haunting.* It should allude to something about the picture itself, with irony or a double or triple entendre: *Dead Wringer.* Or how about a title that overstates what it is: *Atom Man vs. Superman,* or *Triumph for the Son of Hercules.* Pass the sledgehammer.

A title should suggest some kind of action and intrigue. It should startle. *Fight Club.* In the dark city, in an underground fight club, a deviant soap salesman entices a overeager insurance adjuster to rule the world.

In *Psycho* we get exactly that in the person of the Anthony Perkins's character. Hitchcock loved one-word titles. *Vertigo, Frenzy, Notorious, Spellbound.* They fit on the marquee, they grab you, and notice how each one conjures up a feeling or sense of emotional or psychological danger.

A good title grabs you, points you in a direction, and guides you toward the center of the movie.

Last Writes

Before you do anything, get that masterpiece written, edited, and pored over until there is not one more thing you can do. The script has become a living thing, deep within you now, deeper than any creative effort you have ever made. It is now part of you. And now you have to let it go, send it off into the world for others to embrace and rip apart and reject and maybe option or buy, then give it to complete strangers to change and rip apart and do unspeakable things to.

Meanwhile, you, the fickle lover, are on to a new passion, a new script, a new lover. The muse has introduced you to a new toy—an idea. And something strange happens. That old passion gets put into perspective, that wonderful place where art can rest in the world outside yourself, while you have already entered a new world with your new work.

I get out the note cards, call up Final Draft on my Mac, and start plugging in ideas. I write and rewrite myself into another world, with new, barely formed creatures roaming around. I'm as lost as they are, but we will find one another and start relationships. And who knows, we might find another way to chart the story of our lives.

There are no vacations in this racket, only exits and entrances.

CLASS ELEVEN

DON'T KISS ME THERE: An Original Screenplay

by Christopher Keane

I've included a full-length screenplay-in-progress, an annotated version of *Don't Kiss Me There*. It's what they call in the business a dramedy—a comedy drama—about three tormented teens who battle an evil divorce lawyer in order to keep their families intact.

Here I try to show you what my thought process was in writing the script. Along the way I have inserted notes, using the screenwriting principles from the preceding chapters.

It's been a process in itself. I hope you get something out of it.

Don't Kiss Me There: Where the Idea Came From

When I was fifteen and living in Florida, one balmy evening I impulsively kissed the wrong girl, and there was hell to pay. I kissed her and she told her boyfriend, Danny D., the high school football team fullback, a big, ugly, bruiser of the guy.

Not only did Danny get pissed at me, he got the rest of the team to join him, and for six months they stalked and brutalized me. The second mistake I made, after the kiss, was to fight back. I strapped on ego-gear and loaded up with self-justification and struck back. With my mouth.

At one point during this brain cramp of mine I agreed to a boxing match with the team's left halfback, Karl T., during which he pummeled me to the canvas.

The following Friday, at a dance, wearing my wounds on my face and my heart on my sleeve, I got pumped up with self-righteousness and agreed to meet the right halfback, Bill A., in Junez, an out-of-the-way, dead-end part of the landscape, for a confrontation.

A dozen so cars drove out to Junez. The cars pulled up in a circle, leaving the lights on, Italian style. As soon I got out of my car, Bill A. kneed me in the groin. When the pain bent me forward, he hit me with an uppercut and I went down in a heap.

They left me for dead. The cars drove off, and I remained there in Junez (did I mention it was raining and my head ended up in a mud puddle?), with my lights on, the engine going, and some insipid love song playing on the radio.

That was not the end of it. A week or so later, I actually went to the wrong girl, Carol S., and told her that I had meant the kiss and that I wasn't sorry. Why I did that I can only guess. Death wish? An extension of my life-long romance with masochism? A need to explain to the girl that I really did care for her, as if that mattered?!

One night later that week, at a local joint, Danny D., her fullback boyfriend, beat the shit out of me. I went to the hospital and pressed charges.

Nothing came out of it. The charges were dropped. My best friend's father, a lawyer, handled the case. Danny D. was told not to come near me again. I was told not to go near him, or his girlfriend, again.

That incident has always haunted me. What had possessed me? What made this fifteen-year-old guy, me, the dunderhead, walk into that mess? And then spit at it, daring it to show its face?

The girl was in love with someone else. She was beautiful and sexy. Did I, an overweight, smart-ass, mouthy kid from a middle-class family, think I was entitled to her? Did she even care?

In the midst of the chaos, I bought weights and stopped eating cake for breakfast. I lost fifty pounds in a very short period of time, got mono, and have watched my weight ever since. Was this a variation of that infamous brutality diet: You *will* lose weight—if you live.

In the ensuing years, I have written short pieces, sketches, all manner of look-sees into the heart of this incident.

When I decided to write the script I had a situation, not a story. Kiss the wrong girl and you will get beat up. *If you knew you'd get beat up,* I asked myself, *why'd you do it? Even if you didn't know for sure, what possessed you? What was the motivation, the fear, or obsession that drove you toward this madness?*

Another David vs. Goliath replay? I had to open it up, find a villain and a character who, through the experiences, would change.

Danny D. and the football team were villains I had seen before and I didn't want to write a kid-gets-sand-kicked-in-his-face-by-high-school-football-players story.

I remembered my friend and his father, the lawyer. I remembered the way the lawyer looked at my mother, how he had looked at my mother in the past. *Hmmmm,* I thought.

My parents often had big fights, and half the time seemed to be on the verge of splitting up. Somewhere in the midst of trying to turn situation into story, I remembered the interest the lawyer had shown in my mother, real or not. What about a *divorce* lawyer brought in to mediate?

Brought in by whom? The wife, of course. Aha! Things started falling into place. The fat-kid hero who kisses the girl. The football player is gone, replaced by the lawyer and his shitty son, a younger version of himself. *Keep it tight,* I kept telling myself.

The wrong girl is dating the lawyer's son, but not for the obvious reasons. The divorce lawyer is a serial seducer of vulnerable clients. He uses his divorce-lawyer profession to "help" women get away from their awful husbands, while at the same time comforting them, and *sleeping* with them.

I thought to myself, *What if the girl's parents have already split, helped along by the lawyer? Our hero, seeing that this human virus-lawyer might soon be infecting his family, decides to do something about it. With the girl's help, they go up against the lawyer in order to what? Save their families!*

A log line is born: Two witty but tormented teens battle an evil divorce lawyer to keep their families intact. Aha!

The truth is, I didn't get what this story was all about until I had written four drafts. This happens. My instincts told me I had something here, but what?

I thought initially that this was about a kiss gone bad. It was precisely that, and more. But I didn't have the *more* until I got the drafts written.

I also decided to make it today rather than back then. The story is not about the past. I could think of no good reason to put it there.

DON'T KISS ME THERE

by Chris Keane

FADE IN:

DAWN—with the sun at our backs, climbing over the horizon, painting the world a deep amber glow.

We're MOVING west, skimming over a blue choppy surface. Below us is water. Ocean water. Specifically, the Atlantic Ocean.

A wide BEACH comes into view, with hotels lining it—we TRACK UP AND OVER the hotels and head inland.

We hear a young man's voice:

> ROGER (V.O.)
> My sister, Bang, says it all had
> to do with dark impulses. A whole
> slew of dark impulses. Way down
> inside of everybody, ready to
> explode. Which they did. All at
> once.

I've always liked this device of a narrator starting the story, especially a personal story about a moment in the main character's life. Its use tells us who the main character is, that there's a reason for telling the story, and that there's a kind of confessional behind the telling. I feel it draws the reader in. This device is obviously not ideal for most movies.

The landscape looks suspiciously like Florida—flat, dull patches of suburbs, golf courses in bright pastels, sleepy commerce coming awake, retired people in shirtsleeves taking early morning walks in relative darkness.

A SOUND begins—of a golf ball being struck, then another, solidly.

> I know Florida and all its quirky, romantic, weird manifestations. It helps to be able to see, and feel, the place you write about. I often ask the question of my students: Where does this take place? Many of them shrug, as if it doesn't matter. It does matter. It should matter to you for all the sensations about the sense of place you're trying to covey. Later, the studio might want to take it out of Florida and put it in Burbank for cost reasons. That's not your job.

And now we're crossing over a major interstate, and TRACK-ING lower—into a upscale neighborhood, where we see:

—A BIG HANDSOME RICH GUY in his mid-forties pounding golf balls off his back patio toward a dew-heavy fairway.

—A *FORT LAUDERDALE SUN* newspaper truck rolling out of an upscale mall's parking lot and down an empty highway.

—A medicine cabinet opening on: dozens of bottles of prescription anti-anxiety/depression pills, reading: PAXIL, XANEX, NEURONTIN, etc. A WOMAN'S hand reaches for the bottles, unscrews them, and pops pills into her mouth.

                                                        CUT TO:

> I like the arrival beginning category of how to start a picture. Here we spiral down into a neighborhood. In *American Beauty* we spiralled down into a neighborhood. It gives the reader the feeling that even though lives have gone on here, our spying on these lives is just beginning.

EXT. STREET—EARLY MORNING
We're moving through a nice middle-class neighborhood.

And up a driveway toward a well-kept home, landscaped—with the spinge-chik-spinge-chik sound of a sprinkler system.

> ROGER (V.O.)
> We live here. Mom and Dad. My sis-
> ter, Bang. And me. We had a dog,
> Rex, who ran away from home last
> October. He must have known some-
> thing.

ON: a five-year-old, dinked-up red Plymouth convertible.

> ROGER (V.O.) (cont'd)
> That piece of heaven is my
> car . . .

ON: a beige SUV.

> ROGER (V.O.) (cont'd)
> . . . that's the family tank.
> Actually, I'm the family tank. The
> family tub . . .

MOVING through the front door (with "ROYCE" on a wood plac-
ard), and into:

INT. LIVING ROOM—TRACKING THROUGH

> ROGER (V.O.)
> My mom decorated all this; that's
> what she does . . .

A quite nice interior with modern art and low-slung furni-
ture on Belzerian rugs, a screened porch, and a pool out
back.

TRACKING along a hallway and into:

A DISASTER OF A BEDROOM
The room is piled high with male teenage crap. On the walls:
giant POSTERS of determined golfers on raw, rugged land-
scapes that look vaguely Scottish.

> ROGER (V.O.)
> I have this gift, they say. Golf.
> Fat kids can't play many sports,

            except golf. I put my weight into
            it and hit 300-yard drives.

On the bed, tangled up in the sheets, is a sleeping ROGER
ROYCE, 17, overweight, a decent-looking kid, if you like the
sloe-eyed, I-don't-give-a-shit type. He always wears over-
sized clothes, including his perpetual cardigan sweater,
fluffing them away from his body to cover his fat stomach,
which is horribly embarrassing to him.

                    ROGER (V.O.) (cont'd)
            My great grandfather was the Scot-
            tish national champion. I inher-
            ited his genes. To make money,
            which the Scottish are also fond
            of, I teach fat, middle-age rich
            guys to play golf. They're awful
            but they get better. My father,
            who teaches school, says I have
            the teaching gift, just like him.

On the night stand is an ALARM CLOCK—of a golfer addressing
his ball: It's 5:30 A.M., and now:

We are TIGHT on Roger's baby face, when we hear:

The BASH of the golf club hitting the ball, followed by a
BASH! BASH! BASH!

**Okay, so here's the main character. Like any movie character you meet
for the first time, the impression should last. Example: A few years ago a
half-dozen friends kept saying to me, you've got to meet Antonia; she's
extraordinary. For months I heard about Antonia—her brains, her beauty,
her charm. I mean, wow! The night arrived. A party at a pal's. I was nervous. Who wouldn't be, having been prepped by friends—not to mention
what I had done, in my head, to the image of this woman I had never met?**

　　　**It was a raucous party, loads of fun. As I moved among the crowd I
kept hearing a woman's voice shouting. "Hey, motherfucker, kiss my ass.
You heard me. I am not getting on a plane in one hour and flying to
Chicago to spend one shitty night with you. Come here. Fuck you!"**

　　　**I rounded the corner and entered the kitchen, where I saw, sitting on
the floor in a puddle of spilled beer, legs splayed, drunk as shit, dirty—you
guessed it: Antonia.**

That first impression has never left me. How do you want to present your main character—all the characters, for that matter—to the world? Big question.

I don't know if this is the best way to intro Roger. I do know that he's going to change during the course of this story, so I had better set myself up for that.

                    BANG (O.S.)
                (cranky)
       Roger! Get up . . . now!

Roger struggles out of bed and into a pair of shorts, T-shirt, unlaced tennis shoes, and stumbles out.

IN BATHROOM
Roger looking in the mirror, dry-brushing his teeth, once around the gums, water on the face, hands through curly hair, and out the door.

IN LIVING ROOM
Roger stumbling through.

IN KITCHEN
At the fridge, Roger stuffs a plate of last night's left-overs into his face, washing them down with milk from the carton.

                    ROGER
              (shouting)
       Bang!

A 15-year-old GIRL, sassy, dark, thin, and sullen, cranky with sleep, stands in the door.

Although sleepy you know she's takes no shit and tells you what she thinks. This is BANG, Roger's sister.

                    BANG
       You know, if I didn't want that
       subwoofer so much I would not put
       up with this! Are you ready?

IN BREEZEWAY—IN MURKY LIGHT
Roger and Bang peek through a window. Their POV of:

MASTER BEDROOM
In this large suite, a WOMAN—slender, elegant, wearing a
sleep mask—lies alone on a huge bed. This is DARLENE ROYCE
(38), their mother.

On the nearby couch, a MAN sleeps, tangled in sheets, almost
exactly as we found Roger. This is LLOYD ROYCE (42), their
father, an older version of Roger.

Their separateness and coldness to one another is obvious.

IN BREEZEWAY/THROUGH BEDROOM WINDOW
Roger and Bang staring at them, frowning.

> **So now we've meet the family. We get a pretty good idea of them: Bang,
> Roger, the parents who sleep apart in their bedroom. Something awkward
> and painful is going on.**

IN DRIVEWAY—EARLY MORNING
They hop in the Plymouth, top down, and drive off.

                    BANG
          They had another fight last night.
          A real bad one.

                    ROGER
          I heard.

                                        CUT TO:

EXT. NEIGHBORHOOD STREET/5:50 A.M.—DRIVING
Roger and Bang listening to a MOOD TAPE of: surf crashing
against rocks.

                                        CUT TO:

EXT. CORRUGATED WAREHOUSE PARKING LOT—6:05 A.M.
Pulling into the lot filled with early and late-model cars,
with haggard-looking parent-types behind the wheels.

The sign reads: NEWS STATION. B. ZELLER, PROP.

IN THE WAREHOUSE
Packed with people folding and bagging daily newspapers—*THE FORT LAUDERDALE SUN*—at wooden stations lining the walls.

Roger and Bang approach a stall with "ROGER ROYCE" magic-markered into the green wood—with stacks of unfolded and bagged papers . . .

> ROGER
> Where's our folder?!

ON: MR. ZELLER, an ugly scraggly faced guy with zits, checking out Bang.

> ZELLER
> (to Roger)
> What's your problem, Royce?

> ROGER
> Your nephew. Our folder.

> ZELLER
> He wants a 20 percent increase.

> ROGER
> This is extortion. We'll tell your
> boss.

> ZELLER
> Who will give a shit.

> BANG
> Oh, that's nice, Mr. Zeller.

> ROGER
> Twenty percent it is.

> BANG
> Roger!

> ROGER
> (to Zeller)
> I should have been more sensitive
> to your nephew's needs.

With Bang, moving off:

> ROGER (cont'd)
> He's not worth the aggravation.

> BANG
> For you, nothing is.

Roger is hurt by this, though he doesn't want to show it.

> CUT TO:

EXT. NEIGHBORHOOD/6:30 A.M.—DRIVING
Roger's at the wheel, with Bang high up on the backseat,
uncomfortable, flinging papers.

The surf-crashing-against-rocks tape crescendos.

> TIME CUT TO:

NEIGHBORHOOD
A BULLDOG runs into the street, yapping. Roger aims the Plymouth at it, chasing the dog back to its yard.

From the carport: The dog's owner races out, yelling.

> ROGER
> (to Bang)
> I'll do the Murphy's.

Grabbing a paper:

> ROGER (cont'd)
> Observe.

Holding up the paper with a thumb and two fingers, Roger
slings it.

FOLLOWING the paper's flight through the air and across the
lawn, it CATCHES the dog smack on the forehead, sending it
into Mr. Murphy, as they both go sprawling.

BACK IN THE CAR

                         ROGER (cont'd)
It's all in the wrist.

                         BANG
All in your behavior.

EXT. HOME/DRIVEWAY—7:05 A.M.
Roger and Bang pulling in. They climb out and head toward
the house. SOUND of a couple arguing.

Roger and Bang, heads down, skulk up the path.

                    DARLENE ROYCE (O.S.)
         . . . what has happened to us? I
         can't do this anymore, Lloyd. I
         can't breathe!

                    LLOYD ROYCE (O.S.)
         So you want a divorce? That's it,
         right?

                    DARLENE (O.S.)
         Isn't that where we're headed? We
         don't have a kind word. We don't
         touch . . .

                    LLOYD (O.S.)
         You don't think this is as painful
         to me?

                    DARLENE (O.S.)
         Am I so repulsive that you can't
         stand to be in the same room with
         me?

                    LLOYD (O.S.)
         You asked *me* to leave our bed.

                    DARLENE (O.S.)
         You couldn't get any farther away
         from me if you tried.

> LLOYD (O.S.)
> What do you want? I don't know
> what you want!

> DARLENE (O.S.)
> What do *you* want? Why is it always
> *me?*!

IN HOUSE
When Bang slams the door shut, Roger glares at her. The conversation stops. Roger and Bang move across the living room carpet.

> DARLENE (cont'd)
> Roger. Bang.

They halt, to see: their mother: elegant, a professional woman, looking younger than her age (38) but haggard.

> DARLENE (cont'd)
> Breakfast.

> ROGER
> Not hungry, Mom.

> DARLENE
> Get in here, please.

> TIME CUT TO:

KITCHEN—BREAKFAST TABLE
As Roger wolfs down his food:

> BANG (O.S.)
> Did you know that by watching how
> a man eats you can tell what kind
> of lover he is?

Roger stops.

Darlene, despite a cool exterior, is frantic beneath and very unhappy. She tries to put on a good face, but it's not working.

> DARLENE
> (to Bang)
> Is that what they teach you in school?

> ROGER
> And astrology. And minor Canadian poets.

> BANG
> And golf grips!

> DARLENE
> I wasn't speaking to you, Roger.

Rummaging through her handbag, she fishes out a cigarette. Prescription bottles (the same ones we saw in the medicine cabinet in the opening sequence) fall out and scatter.

Roger and Bang look at each other. Embarrassed, Darlene scoops the bottles back into the bag.

LLOYD ROYCE, their father (42) enters. Professorial. Wears glasses. In a jacket and tie.

> LLOYD
> (to Darlene)
> Honey, please don't smoke in here.

With a look at the kids, Darlene returns the cigarettes to her handbag. She hands a stack of envelopes to Roger:

> DARLENE
> Would you mind?

Roger takes the envelopes and begins to lick them shut.

> LLOYD
> (to Bang)
> I hear you've been taking a lot of bathroom breaks at school.

> BANG
> Who told you that?

                              LLOYD
                    What's up, Bang-o?

All staring at her, waiting:

                              BANG
                    I've been . . . my stomach has
                    been . . . Isn't that invasion of
                    privacy?

                              ROGER
                    Exactly.

                              DARLENE
                    What's wrong, honey?

                              BANG
                    I don't know.

                              LLOYD
                    Go to the infirmary, okay?

                              DARLENE
                    Female problems?

                              BANG
                    Mom!

                              ROGER
                    Family problems?

All eyes rivet on Roger. Bang gets up and hurries off, as
Roger shovels the last of his food into his mouth and follows her.

On his way out, turning back:

                              ROGER (cont'd)
                    What's going on with you two?!

                              LLOYD/DARLENE
                    Nothing.

                                                    CUT TO:

The opening pages establish the world of the story. Here we have a troubled family, living in Florida, a bond between brother and sister. We have a handle on the main character—half-asleep but a worker, kind of dazed by it all but not wanting to show vulnerability. We don't have to like him, but we do want to be curious enough about him to find out what happens next.

   We also should have a pretty good idea of what this world is like, because pretty soon it's not going to be like this anymore.

EXT. NEIGHBORHOOD STREET—7:30 A.M.
Roger and Bang drive through an upscale neighborhood, toward:

A DRIVEWAY—LEADING TO A SPRAWLING, ELEGANT HOME
Roger pulls behind a shiny black Lincoln and gets out.

                         ROGER
            Come on.

She doesn't move.

                         ROGER (cont'd)
            What's with you?

                         BANG
            I hate it in there.

                         ROGER
            It's not polite.

He raps on the front door.

The door opens on an overly made up, cheerless, middle-age woman—MRS. VICTOR FERRIS (45), a seething mountain of DAR/Junior League resentment.

                         MRS. FERRIS
            Roger.

                         ROGER
            Good morning, Mrs. Ferris.

                              MRS. FERRIS
            You know where he is.

Passing by her, into the house:

                              ROGER
            Yes, ma'am.

                              MRS. FERRIS
            Hello, Bang.

Slipping by them and into the house:

                              BANG
            Mrs. Ferris. Your oleander needs
            watering.

                              MRS. FERRIS
            Thank you, dear.

BACK PATIO
Roger and Bang approach—to the SOUND of a golf ball being
struck.

The ball striker, VICTOR FERRIS, Esq., mid-40s, an extraordinary presence—handsome, charismatic, a big-time divorce
lawyer and local force of nature.

This is the same guy we saw hitting balls in the opening
sequence. He has his own backyard tee box. Victor sends a
big banana slice toward the GOLF COURSE that adjoins his
property.

                              VICTOR
            Goddammit!

                              ROGER
            You're dropping your left shoul-
            der, sir. Stick your thumb down
            the shaft. Follow through.

                              VICTOR
          Hello, Roger.
                         (darkly)
          Bang.

Not a big fan:

                              BANG
          Mr. Ferris.

                              VICTOR
                         (to Roger)
          Show me.

Roger takes the driver, tees one up, and hits a perfect
looping draw way out there.

                         VICTOR (cont'd)
          See that, Dickie.

ANGLE ON: DICKIE FERRIS, 17, a slicker, younger, leaner version of his father, with dark, teen-idol good looks, standing in the doorway.

                              DICKIE
              You've got your games, Poppo, and
              I've got mine.

He looks lasciviously at Bang, who turns away but still
likes the attention from the most popular boy in school.

Victor takes the club, tees one up, squares his shoulders,
and hits a wonderful one, long and straight.

                              VICTOR
                         (to Roger)
          With your help, son . . .

Dickie's irritated at "son."

                         VICTOR (cont'd)
              . . . I'm going to win the tour-
              nament this year. Take note.

TIME CUT TO:

IN BREAKFAST NOOK—LATER
Dickie and Bang sit opposite Mrs. Ferris—dark circles under
her eyes, sullen, drinking coffee.

Dickie pushes his food around.

> MRS. FERRIS
> Perhaps you should eat at Jerry's
> Drive-In, Dickie, if you're so
> dissatisfied.

Dickie slides his eyes toward Bang, who pulls her dress down
over her knees.

Enter Victor, with his arm around Roger's shoulder, leading
him past the table, toward the front door.

> VICTOR
> (to his wife)
> Get my briefcase.

> MRS. FERRIS
> (with a withering look)
> Of course, darling. How remiss of
> me.

Dickie watches Victor and Roger leave together.

> DICKIE
> There goes your oversize brother.

> BANG
> Who will one day give you a over-
> size lip.

She rises and follows them out.

AT FRONT DOOR—MOVING TOWARD DRIVEWAY
Slipping Roger two twenties:

                    VICTOR
        Knowing you're here each morning
        means a lot to me.

                    ROGER
        I have other clients, Mr. Ferris.

                    VICTOR
        Fire them.

                    ROGER
        What?

He pulls another two twenties out and hands them to Roger.

                    VICTOR
        You heard me.

Off Roger's hesitation:

                    VICTOR (cont'd)
        Tell them you're busy.

Bang tags along behind, with Dickie following.

                    VICTOR (cont'd)
        You may be on tour one day. Do you
        want me in your corner? It's a
        quid pro quo world, son.

                    BANG
        Roger wants to be a divorce
        lawyer, Mr. Ferris, just like you.

Detecting something insincere in her voice:

                    VICTOR
        Is that so? It's not easy trying
        to encourage profoundly unhappy
        couples to act with reason. "Call
        me a human bridge my clients can
        traverse, in order to pass from a
        world of night into the sunlight

of freedom . . ." Oliver Wendell
Holmes. Another lawyer who did
alright for himself.

                              TIME CUT TO:

MOVING TOWARD THE SHINY BLACK LINCOLN—
Where Mrs. Ferris waits with his briefcase.

                    VICTOR (cont'd)
          Hit 'em long and straight, guys.

Victor climbs into the car and drives off.

As Roger moves on ahead, Dickie, carrying his gym bag,
sidles up to Bang.

                    DICKIE
          How about if we go swimming later?

                    BANG
          What about boxing practice?

                    DICKIE
          I'll blow it off.

                    BANG
          What about your thirty or forty
          girlfriends?

                    DICKIE
          I wouldn't need them if I had you.

                    BANG
          That would mean everything to me,
          Dickie . . . so that I could pass
          from a world of night into the
          sunlight of freedom . . .

                    DICKIE
          I hope it won't be long.

                    BANG
          Before you gag on your own ego?

                              DICKIE
                    You know, your mouth . . .

                              BANG
                    Keeps flies like you off the food.

Bang joins Roger at the Plymouth. Dickie loads his gym bag
in the trunk of his own car (a Lexus), which is filled with
sports equipment, including golf clubs.

IN THE PLYMOUTH
                              ROGER
                    Stay away from him.

                              BANG
                    Oh yeah like, right, I want to
                    join a harem.

                              ROGER
                    I mean it.

                              BANG
                    Why would I want to hang around
                    with the best-looking, richest guy
                    in school?

Off Roger's look:
                            BANG (cont'd)
                       (loud, sarcastically)
                    Oh, Roger. Isn't Dickie so cool!

Dickie, making a face, watches them drive off.
                                                    CUT TO:

EXT. WINN/DIXIE FOOD STORE
Roger pulls into the parking lot with Bang riding shotgun.

                              BANG
                    Get me some supers.

Getting out, heading for the market:

                              ROGER
                    Get your own supers.

                          BANG
            When you pay me!

Bang starts to get out.

                          ROGER
            I don't want company, thank you!

Staying where she is:

                          BANG
            Who said anything about it?!
            Supers!!!

                          ROGER
            All right!!!

                                                    CUT TO:

INT. MARKET
Roger carries a Danish and cup of coffee. He takes a box of
Supers off the shelf and heads for the checkout. Turning the
corner, he sees *his mother with Victor Ferris!*

Shocked, Roger ducks back and peeks around the corner, to
see: Victor pulling Darlene close and nuzzling her neck.
Darlene pushes him away, but not forcibly. As if this has
happened before?

Roger recoils. He has SUDDEN FLASHES OF Victor replacing his
father in various situations:

—in the MASTER BEDROOM with his mother and Victor in bed
together.

—at the BREAKFAST TABLE, with Victor instead of his dad.

BACK TO SCENE
In the market aisle, Roger sees Victor playfully walking
beside Darlene, heading in his direction. He turns and runs
for the checkout, taking the Supers, coffee, and Danish with
him, ducking through the line, slapping down some cash.

Okay, so we're about sixteen pages in. We've met the important characters, including the ugly villains, Victor and Dickie Ferris: rich, arrogant, entitled.

Roger's bomb has just exploded: The big-time lawyer he coaches
and his own mother doing something shocking in the market!

Up to this point, there might have been something upsetting going on.
Now "might" has been removed from the equation. Roger freaks.

Go back to the log line: witty, tormented teens battle an evil divorce
lawyer to keep their families intact. The story has now begun, which
means that the spine of the story has been established. By the end of this
journey, that problem will have been resolved. This spine will keep you
online. This is the plot. Everything else, the feeder material, the emotional
relationships with other characters, are the subplots.

Remember: Plot carries action. Subplot carries emotion. Plot the kids
having to save their families. These teens will do anything to save their
families.

IN PARKING LOT
Roger, dazed, hurries across the lot, throwing the bag on
the front seat. He climbs behind the wheel.

                    BANG
          What's up, Rog?

                    ROGER
          Jesus Christ! Jesus Christ!

                    BANG
          You got my . . . ?

                    ROGER
          Jesus CHRIST!!!

He GUNS the car, throwing Bang against the seat, and tears
away, nearly clipping a couple on his way out.

                    BANG
          What's UP???!!!

Roger looks into her innocent 15-year-old eyes: He can't
tell her.

                                        CUT TO:

EXT. SCHOOL PARKING LOT—8:28 A.M.
Roger, very edgy, walks along, with Bang trailing behind.
They head toward a modern, low-slung single-story school
building—passing students.

Nobody pays attention to Roger, while everybody greets the
wildly popular Bang.

Roger, stuffing a candy bar into his face, tugs at the red
cardigan sweater around his large middle.

> BANG
> Roger . . .

> ROGER
> Just . . . just . . . you
> know . . . just . . . don't
> even . . .

> BANG
> Okay, well, sure, whatever!

Up ahead Roger sees a dark-haired BEAUTY with black spiked
hair, knee-high black leather boots, and a very short mini-
skirt. Very hot. She's Jessica Rabbit, Catwoman; a rocker
girl extraordinaire, enigmatic. A sex-bomb.

This is MANDY SILVERA, 17. Roger stares at her. He can't
help it. She's a vision. Bang notices Roger's reaction and
doesn't like it.

Beside Mandy is Dickie Ferris, class lothario, with his arm
around her. Bang doesn't like this, either.

Look out. We just met the love interest. Catwoman. Rocker girl. As if our hero hasn't got enough on his hands—here comes Jessica Rabbit. Are we putting this guy in a vice or what? You've got to befog your main character. This is the big moment of his life. He's got to be primed for change.

IN SCHOOL HALLWAY
Roger moves along, agitated and confused by what he saw in
the market, Dickie with the girl, everything!

MALE VOICE
Roger.

Roger stops and turns, to see Lloyd Royce, his dad.

LLOYD
We'll be working in the sand trap
today, son.

ROGER
Dad?

LLOYD
Yes, son?

Roger can't get the words—any words—out.

BANG (O.S.)
Hi, Dad.

Lloyd turns to the approaching Bang:

LLOYD
Hi, Pumpkin.
                    (changing gears)
About this morning, kids. Your
mother and I have been under a lot
of stress lately. So . . .

ROGER
Stress. Uh huh.

LLOYD
What's with you, Rog?

ROGER
What's with me? What's with *you?!*
What's with *Mom?!*

Roger tears off, leaving Lloyd and Bang perplexed.

CUT TO:

INT. CLASS ROOM
A characterless beige box. On Roger, distracted.

> ROGER
> (by rote)
> . . . Jack Kerouac, a rebellious
> young writer, said, and I quote:
> "Screw story . . . grab your char-
> acters by the balls and run . . ."

Lloyd Royce, also the English teacher, gives his son a look.

> LLOYD
> There you are, class, one of Ker-
> ouac's more gritty profundities.

Mandy Silvera stands in the doorway, the same slender, spike-haired beauty we saw earlier. She's the baddest, sexiest, punk chick you've ever seen. Hot hot hot.

She hands a sheet of paper to Lloyd and takes a seat next to Roger, who can't keep his eyes off her. She, on the other hand, can't care less.

> MANDY
> Kerouac also said, "I don't give a
> shit what a character says. It's
> what he *does* that matters."

Lloyd looks at the sheet she's handed him.

> LLOYD
> That's exactly right, uh . . .
> (looking at the sheet)
> Mandy. Silvera. A transfer stu-
> dent, people. Welcome.

> ROGER
> "There are only thirty-two sto-
> ries, and I've written all of
> them, but there is only one plot:
> Things are not what they seem."
> Jim Thompson.

                    MANDY
Another good one.

                    LLOYD
Remember that, class: Things are
never what they seem. Here's
another one: "If you want to bring
a man down, discover what matters
to him most, and take it from
him."

                    MANDY
Kerouac?

                    LLOYD
                (quietly)
Lloyd Royce.

The bell rings and they all parade out.

                    LLOYD (cont'd)
Roger . . . ?

But Roger's already out the door and down the hall.

                                        CUT TO:

EXT. PARKING LOT
Roger, stuffing a candy bar into his mouth, climbs into his
car, when:

                    MALE VOICE (O.S.)
Rolls . . . !

Dickie Ferris walks up, with Mandy Silvera.

                    DICKIE
Rolls.

                    ROGER
What?

                    DICKIE
What's with the attitude?

                          ROGER
          What do you want?

                          DICKIE
          You know Mandy here?

                          ROGER
          Jack Kerouac introduced us.
                    (to Mandy)
          How you doing?

                          MANDY
          Just fine, and you?

                          ROGER
          Better now that the sun is behind
          a cloud and I can see you.

She smirks at this.
                          DICKIE
                    (to Roger)
          Still pounding down those carbs.

                          MANDY
          I'd like a ride home.

                          DICKIE
          Mandy needs a ride home. That
          means you, Rolls. I'm busy.

                          ROGER
          Yeah, sure, come on.

They get in. Dickie gives Mandy a kiss. She gives him a hot
one back. Roger starts the car and drives off.

                                              CUT TO:

INT. MOVING PLYMOUTH/TOP DOWN—DAY
Roger peeks at Mandy, whose skirt is hiked up over her fish-
net thighs. She's carrying a bunch of schoolbooks and a cell
phone.

The crashing-waves tape thunders over the speakers.

Roger rips open a candy bar and pops it into his mouth, chewing angrily.

                    MANDY
          You're in a good mood.

                    ROGER
          When did you move here?

                    MANDY
          Last week.

                    ROGER
          Where from?

                    MANDY
          West Palm Beach. Is that the deal?
          I gotta answer questions to get
          this ride?

                    ROGER
          No, sorry.

                    MANDY
          Wanna know my bra size? I don't
          wear one.

                    ROGER
          What's up your butt?

                    MANDY
          You, babe. I'm having a family
          tragedy. Do you mind?

This catches his interest.

                    ROGER
          Yeah, like what?

                    MANDY
          Got a month?

                    ROGER
          That bad, huh? Me, too.

                         MANDY
          Mi family tragedy is worse than *su*
          family tragedy.

Roger stuffs the last of the candy bar into his face.

                         MANDY (cont'd)
          Do you always eat so . . . loud?

                         ROGER
          When I'm nervous.

                         MANDY
          I won't bite you.

                         ROGER
          Too bad. I could use a good bite
          right about now.

She leans over and digs her teeth into his shoulder. He
howls in pain.

                         MANDY
          How's that?

She is so hot. He doesn't know what to do with this.

                         MANDY (cont'd)
          Why does Dickie call you Rolls?

                         ROGER
          My last name is Royce.

                         MANDY
          That's the only reason?

Pulling the cardigan over his stomach:

                         ROGER
          If you already know, why ask?

Touching his arm and leaving it there:

                    MANDY
          I have a vicious streak.

With a quick glance at her eyes boring into his:

                    ROGER
          How long've you known Dickie?

                    MANDY
          You mean how long did it take him
          to get into my pants?

                    ROGER
          I didn't say that.

                    MANDY
          Uh huh.

                    ROGER
          Your family tragedy—what is it?

Definitely darker:

                    MANDY
          My mother.

                    ROGER
          My mother   and . . . your   boy-
          friend's father . . .

                    MANDY
          Dickie's father?

He backs off, holding his tongue.

                    MANDY (cont'd)
          What about him?
                         (beat)
          What about him!

                         ROGER
                    (blurting out)
          I caught him in the market groping
          my mother.

                         MANDY
          Oh yeah right. Hey, he's an old
          fox. I dig him.

                         ROGER
          Old fox. Attacking my mother in
          the Winn-Dixie.

                         MANDY
                    (ironically)
          He's a big deal in town . . . do
          you actually think he'd . . .

Not getting her irony:

                         ROGER
          I just saw them. Today.

                         MANDY
          Is that why you're so pissy?

                         ROGER
          How'd you like to . . .

                         MANDY
                    (ironically)
          Hey, you got the wrong guy. Or the
          wrong mother. Or the big imagina-
          tion. Because Dickie's dad . . .

                         ROGER
          Is an overblown ball of shit. I
          teach him to play golf. I know.

She gives him a look. Then gets silent.

                         ROGER (cont'd)
          What . . . ?

                    MANDY
          We're here . . .

Roger pulls in front of a small tidy house. A name plate on
the mailbox reads: SILVERA.

Roger gets out and walks around the car, holding open the
door for her.

She steps to the sidewalk. They're inches apart, clothes
touching.

They walk up the path toward the front door. Through the
window Roger sees a WOMAN, about 38, beautiful, dark like
Mandy, moving around inside.

                    ROGER
            (re: woman in house)
          Your family tragedy?

She nods.

                    ROGER (cont'd)
          Sorry for the tirade.

                    MANDY
          Thanks for the ride.

At the door: They stand very close. Neither of them is moving. She drips sex and has violet eyes, for crissakes. He
falls into them, under their spell. Can't help himself.

                    ROGER
          Any time.

Surprising them both, Roger kisses her full on the lips. And
holding there . . .

IN HIS MIND: quick flashes of her eyes, her hair, the shape
of her neck.

His hand trails down her back, his eyes roll, into slits,
losing himself in the kiss.

And now she responds, taking his face in one hand, kissing him back, lingering, tongue on tongue, pressing against him. Finally, she pushes him away, breathless.

                         MANDY
              Aren't you the impulsive one.

He's about to say something, but can't. He can't do anything but turn and march back down the path toward the car.

                                        CUT TO:

Here it is, around page thirty, Plot Point 1. The kiss itself. This is another bomb thrown into Roger's life, which has created another big shift.

He has kissed a girl, but what does he know? He's done it and he's about to become a changed man. Now he has something else to fight for—love. This will give him the *courage* to fight for other things. This kiss is transforming.

He's seen his mother and Victor Ferris, and a few pages later he kisses the girl. Two shocks hit him at once. Good? Let's hope.

In the structural paradigm I gave you earlier, this moment comes at the end of Act I. The question I ask myself: Is what I've written to this point strong enough to sustain the reader's interest?

Who cares how well written or poorly written it may be. If you don't know what the story is by page fifteen, is there a problem? You tell me.

Yes. There is a problem. So far, are you still interested in finding out what happens to Roger, and why? If not, why is that?

I could move the kiss up. I could pare down the scenes or get rid of the ones that might be superfluous. Tighten, tighten, tighten.

By this time I've dragged all the main characters on stage. Act I is the setup act. We have set up the characters and plot and the problem Roger faces. And now, in Act II, we're going to squeeze them all together to see what shakes out.

ACT II

(Don't put "Act II" in your own scripts; this is just to show you where it falls.)

IN PLYMOUTH
Roger, driving, in some other world. IN HIS MIND: reliving the kiss, over and over, on a loop.

                                        CUT TO:

EXT. HOME—DAY
Pulling into the driveway. Leaving the car door open, he
drifts cloudlike toward the door. SEEING: Mandy standing
seductively in the neighbor's yard waving to him.

IN HOUSE
On automatic, Roger heads for the kitchen.

AT FRIDGE
Throwing open the door, staring at a milk carton on which
Mandy appears shaking her head no.

He closes the door into darkness.

IN LIVING ROOM
On the couch, Roger, staring through the screened patio
toward the pool—where Mandy swims through the frame.

                              TIME CUT TO:

IN LIVING ROOM—DUSK
Mandy still swims out there. Roger, calmer now, watches her.
The sun is going down.

                              TIME CUT TO:

IN BED—NIGHT
Roger, wide awake, staring into space. Boy in love.

                              SLAM CUT TO:

IN WINN-DIXIE MARKET/FLASHBACK/LATER—NIGHT
Victor Ferris kisses Darlene on the neck—to the sound of:

                                   CUT TO:

IN BEDROOM—MORNING
The BASHING GOLF BALLS alarm clock. Roger, dead asleep, is
unmoved.

Standing over him:

                         BANG
             Roger, c'mon, get up!

Bang gives up and leaves. Roger's eyes fall open.

INT. LIVING ROOM
Roger, half-dressed, stumbles out to find his mother at the
table, in a housecoat, drinking coffee, smoking a cigarette.

                    DARLENE
                 (looking up)
            Good morning, honey.

                    ROGER
            What were you doing?!

                    DARLENE
            Doing?

                    ROGER
            In the market!

                    DARLENE
            What . . . ?

Through the window, in the driveway, he sees Bang climb into
the SUV beside Lloyd.

                    ROGER
             The market!

Roger turns and races out.

EXT. HOUSE
Lloyd Royce starts the SUV. Roger, crazed, exits the house
and heads toward the Plymouth, climbs in, and starts it up.

Bang jumps out of the SUV, rushes to the Plymouth, and hops
in.

                                        CUT TO:

NEIGHBORHOOD STREET/IN CAR—MOVING

                    BANG
            Wanna talk about it?

> ROGER
No.

> BANG
Whatever's making you weird . . .

> ROGER
No.

> BANG
Are you sick?

> ROGER
No.

> BANG
Light-headed?

> ROGER
(beat)
Somewhat.

> BANG
Strange in your stomach?

> ROGER
Yuh.

> BANG
Soapy feeling?

> ROGER
Soapy? Exactly.

As Bang stares at him.

You'll notice all the white space on the pages. In other words, there are *few* words to describe the action. The dialogue moves forward through conflict.

In screenplays characters rarely agree with one another. When information needs to get out, do it dramatically and not through simple exposition. White space, not clutter or clunky, thick paragraphs filled with ponderous details, is the key.

                                        CUT TO:

IN ZELLER'S PAPER SHACK
Folding papers:

                    BANG
          C'mon, who is she?

                    ROGER
          No one.

Mr. Zeller walks up, checking out Bang.

                    MR. ZELLER
          My nephew wants another 10 percent
          to fold your papers.

                    ROGER
          Tell him to go fuck himself!

Bang goes wide-eyed.

                    ZELLER
          What did you say?

                    ROGER
          You heard me.

                    ZELLER
          You're fired!

                    ROGER
          And so will you be when I tell
          your boss how you like to ogle
          young girls around here, Mr.
          Zeller.
                    (to Bang)
          Let's go.

Leaving Zeller, mouth open, worried.

                                        CUT TO:

ON PAPER ROUTE—DRIVING
Flinging papers:

                    BANG
          Short, eats with her hands. Honor
          Society. Cheats on tests. Drama
          Queen. Can't act.

                    ROGER
          Not Louise Winkler.

                    BANG
          Rich, wears thong underwear, has a
          massive inferiority complex . . .

                    ROGER
          Not Allegra Hamilton.

                    BANG
          Has a Malamute . . .

                    ROGER
          For*get* it!

IN CAR—DRIVING IN SILENCE
Bang sits in back, watching her brother.

By now we've all figured out that Roger's buddy is Bang. They love each other and they have issues. She is there for him, to care for him and to protect him (mainly from himself), and she doesn't at all like what's happening to him—at least how he's acting. Plus she knows him well enough to know that he's not telling her everything.

As the buddy, one of her jobs is to discover what it is that's eating away at him and to try to fix it. This brings complications and woes, but that's what screenplays are all about.

                                        CUT TO:

EXT. STREET OUTSIDE VICTOR FERRIS'S HOME
Roger drives by and keeps on going.

                    BANG
          What about your golf lesson?

Roger, dark, moody, silent, drives on.

                                                    CUT TO:

INT. SCHOOL CLASSROOM—DAY
In English class. Lloyd lectures. Next to Roger, Mandy's
seat is empty.

Roger abruptly gets up and leaves the class. Lloyd, perplexed, watches him go.

                                                    CUT TO:

INT. ROGER AT HOME—LATER IN THE DAY
Bang sits silently in a deck chair on the screened-in porch.
Roger paces.

                            BANG
                Why are you being such a jerk?

                            ROGER
                For you, aren't I always a jerk?

                            BANG
                This jerk is different. I can tell.

The phone rings. Roger answers it.

                            ROGER
                Hello . . . Mr. Ferris. Yeah. I
                couldn't make it. I won't be able
                to make it tomorrow, or the next
                day. Or. Actually. Ever.

INT. BIG-TIME LAW OFFICE—DAY
Victor Ferris, in suspenders and bow tie, sits behind his
big desk. Out the twentieth-floor window is a fabulous view.
A sign reads: FERRIS, WHEELER AND CATES, Attorneys at Law.

                            VICTOR
                Roger, we have an unwritten verbal
                contract. You have agreed to help
                me, for which I have agreed to pay
                you. If money is an issue . . .

                              ROGER
          It's not.

                              VICTOR
          You can't abandon me now. The
          tournament is next week.

                                              CUT TO:

THE HOUSE
Bang on the kitchen extension, covering the receiver:

                              BANG (O.S.)
                         (loud whisper)
          Do it!

Roger turns and sees Bang.

                              ROGER
          Just a minute, Mr. Ferris.

With their hands covering the receivers:

                              ROGER (cont'd)
                         (to Bang)
          What are you doing?!

                              BANG
          What are *you* doing?! That's five
          hundred dollars for five hours!
          That's camp next summer. A boogie
          board. My subwoofer. You heard
          him, that's, that's . . . *ethics!*

                              ROGER
          You don't get it.

                              BANG
          Five hundred dollars! Say yes!
          What're you, stupid?!

                              ROGER
          I can't!

                              BANG
               You'd better!

On Roger, backing down, filled with torment and indecision.
Into the receiver:

                              ROGER
                  . . . okay, Mr. Ferris, since you
                  put it like that . . .

                              VICTOR
               Wise   decision.   Tomorrow,   same
               time.

Hanging up. Now's the time to talk.

                              ROGER
               Bang, I have to tell you some-
               thing.

                              BANG
               It's done. Honor it. No excuses.

She heads out of the house. He follows.

EXT. HOUSE
Bang hops on her bike and takes off down the street.
Roger, dejected, confused, watches her go.

                                              CUT TO:

EXT. VICTOR FERRIS'S HOME—NEXT MORNING
The door swings open, revealing Victor Ferris, with the dis-
consolate Mrs. Ferris standing behind him.

                              VICTOR
               Come on in, son.

On the reluctant Roger, with Bang in tow.

                              ROGER
               How are you, Mrs. Ferris?

>   MRS. FERRIS
> As usual, suffering his insensi-
> tivity, but thank you, Roger, for
> asking.

>   VICTOR
> She's fine. Let's get going.

Victor leads Roger and Bang into the room—where they meet Dickie and Mandy.

Roger tenses. A look passes between him and Mandy, which Bang picks up on.

More pressure on Roger. What's with Mandy and Dickie? What is she *doing* with him? What's the attraction? Does this bring up Roger's insecurities? You bet it does.

>   MANDY
> Hello, Roger. Who's this?

>   ROGER
> My sister, Bang.

>   MANDY
> Bang, huh?

Eyeing her suspiciously:

>   BANG
> Yeah.

>   MANDY
> I'm Mandy.

>   BANG
> Wow, Mandy, huh? How 'bout that.

>   DICKIE
> Rolls, my man.

>   ROGER
>   (ignoring him; to Victor)
>   I have to be at school, Mr. Fer-
>   ris, so if we could start.

>   VICTOR
>   Sure, sure.

They head for the back patio. Roger turns and looks at
Mandy, who shows him nothing, driving a big pain through his
heart.

>   TIME CUT TO:

BACK PATIO
Roger hits one ball after the other, sweating, banging them
out like a pro.

>   VICTOR (cont'd)
>   Roger, if you don't mind. I'd like
>   to hit a couple.

>   ROGER
>   Check my setup. Watch my take-away.
>   See where my right elbow is.

In a frenzy, Roger keeps hitting and hitting.

>   VICTOR
>   I see it.

>   ROGER
>   Good. Pay attention. You'll learn
>   something.

>   TIME CUT TO:

HOUSE FOYER
Victor leads a perspiring Roger out, handing him five twenties.

>   VICTOR
>   We'll hit some tomorrow.

                              ROGER
          Yeah.

                              VICTOR
          Is everything all right?

At the front door, Roger glances over his shoulder into the
house. Bang's face pops into his line of vision.

                              BANG
          If you're looking for someone, she
          left for school.

                              VICTOR
                         (to Roger)
          I can't have you less than 100
          percent—when we're so close to
          game day.

As they walk out, the phone rings. Mrs. Ferris answers it.

                          MRS. FERRIS
                         (to Victor)
          It's the club, about your testimo-
          nial dinner.

                              VICTOR
          Take a message.

Putting his arm around Roger, who slips out of it.

                         VICTOR (cont'd)
          Testimonial dinner.

                              BANG
          For what?

                              VICTOR
          Honoring my service to the commu-
          nity. It's part of being an adult.

Roger gives him a look.

EXT. FRONT OF HOUSE
Roger and Bang move toward the car.

> VICTOR (cont'd)
> In repayment for an exemplary
> life. Take a lesson, kids.

Victor realizes that Roger and Bang are not taking a lesson.
In fact, they are already in the car, about to drive off.

More or less to his wife, who has turned away and is on her
way back into the house:

> VICTOR (cont'd)
> Attention deficit disorder. They've
> all got it.
>   CUT TO:

EXT. SCHOOL HALLWAY
Walking along.

> BANG
> Her parents just got divorced.

> ROGER
> Who?

> BANG
> Your new girlfriend. Mandy babe.

> ROGER
> She's not my new girlfriend.

> BANG
> Dickie's father is handling it.

Roger looks at her with sudden awareness.

> BANG (cont'd)
> That's how Mandy and Dickie met
> and fell in love.

> ROGER
> Knock it off, Bang.

                              BANG
               The truth hurts.

Exasperated, he splits off in another direction.

EXT. NEIGHBORHOOD STREET—DAY
Roger drives through Mandy's neighborhood, passing her mailbox, with "Silvera" on it.

He pulls over and gets out and is about to walk up the path
when the front door opens.

Roger dives back inside his car, looking up over the dash-
board, to SEE: Victor Ferris emerging with a beautiful
woman: MS. SILVERA.

Victor kisses Ms. Silvera's neck (just as he did with
Roger's mother in the market), with Ms. Silvera responding,
but in a more resigned way.

Victor now moves quickly down the walk, passing the ducked-
down Roger, toward his Lincoln. He climbs in and drives off.

Ms. Silvera stands in the door, resentment plastered on her
face.

Roger is about to drive off when he sees an SUV parked up
the street. *His own family SUV! With HIS MOTHER behind the
wheel*. She is glaring at Ms. Silvera at the front door, then
driving off.

ON ROGER, *sick* about this.

                                           CUT TO:

EXT. ROAD—DAY
Roger drives along. He's on his cell phone.

                              ROGER
               I have to see you . . . No, now.

**Okay, where have we been? After he kisses Mandy and we've entered
the great desert of Act II, we have to start working on the relationships.
Movies are not about characters but relationships.**

Roger tries to quit Victor's golf lessons, until Victor flashes cash and Bang tells him to do it. We also establish Bang and Roger as a strong but conflicted relationship, as all relationships in movies should be. In movies, nobody ever agrees with anybody. We have also seen Mandy Silvera slide into the picture: Her mother's been through the same emotional wringer that Roger's mother is about to enter.

We also have to get the plot rolling. A plan has to be set in force: What is Roger going to do about all this hell he's facing? This evil divorce lawyer is not only screwing around with his mother, but Mandy's, too!

                                                         CUT TO:

EXT. SCHOOL GROUNDS—DAY
Roger pulls into the parking lot and jumps out, moving with
determination.

This leads to the action toward the end of Act II. Roger and Mandy team up to get rid of the evil lawyer. They have to plot and plan the demise of the bastard—to save their families, or what's left of them. We're on the plot: tormented teens battle evil divorce lawyer. This is the three-act structure we're talking about here. It won't be easy. They have to contend with Victor and son Dickie, and one another, and all the insecurities of self.

Act I. The problem is established.

Act II. The main characters confront all the twists and turns the problem presents. They've established their objective—Victor Ferris. Now they have to plan and execute, plan and execute. And they will screw up royally.

Roger and Mandy are about to implement their plan to sabotage Victor. E-mails, videocam footage. Does Roger sabotage Victor's golf game? But where do all these lead? That's the big question. How do you get to the target—Victor—who seems impenetrable? Victor is powerful, rich, handsome, charismatic.

These teens don't have all the answers, but there is too much at stake for them not to make one hell of an effort to break into Victor Ferris's fortress.

One thing that must be made clear at this point: Whatever plan these two have has to be spelled out. One thing should lead to the other. They think they have it all figured out and then make adjustments along the way.

Their plan is going to collapse and meet reversals of fortune, and they will be forced into backup positions, which they might not have.

Reversals are plans that, for one reason or another, go awry. That's why it's essential to show the reader a plan, so that when the stuff happens and fails, the reader can laugh or cringe or at least follow their travails.

INT. CAFETERIA
Roger hustles through the tables, spotting Mandy—sitting with Dickie.

MANDY'S POV: of Roger approaching. She sees his wild, nutty expression. Roger continues across the cafeteria and out through a door.

> MANDY
> (to Dickie)
> Excuse me.

She rises and leaves, following Roger out.

EXT. CAFETERIA—OUT BY THE DUMPSTERS
Mandy bursts out. Looks around. No Roger.

> ROGER (O.S.)
> Over here.

She follows the sound and finds him behind a Dumpster.

> ROGER
> (fast, babbling)
> I heard your parents are getting divorced.

> MANDY
> Who told you?

> ROGER
> And Dickie's father is her lawyer.

> MANDY
> Yeah. He's helping her.

> ROGER
> Helping himself to her.

> MANDY
> What?

ROGER

A half-hour ago, at the front door
of your house, I saw your mother
with Mr. Ferris, in a clinch! Just
like my mother and that bastard.
What's going on here!?

MANDY

That's bullshit.

ROGER

Yeah? It looks like Mr. Ferris
preys on women with marriage problems. Your mother. My mother.
Other mothers?

MANDY

There are a lot of lawyers . . .

ROGER

Who one hour ago I saw groping
your mother at her front door?

MANDY
    (pacing, gathering thoughts)
You're trying to fuck me up here,
Roger. This has to do with me and
Dickie, not his father.

ROGER

Oh yeah? Your family tragedy has
to do with what again?

MANDY
    (beat)
I mean, I've heard my mom on the
phone with Mr. Ferris. I heard him
say: "I'm here in your time of
need. I will deliver you from the
evil of your husband."
    (beat, thinking)
Like this evangelist, and she's
part of the flock. Like she's under
his spell of something . . . jeez.

                    ROGER
Can she fire him?

                    MANDY
Well, sure, but . . . as she puts
it: his hooks are in—emotionally,
financially. On his advice, Mom
moved down here. Oh my God!

                    ROGER
What?

                    MANDY
I don't want to believe it.

                    ROGER
He's ruining our families.

                    MANDY
Yeah, well, the truth is, families
ruin   families. Divorce lawyers
profit from it.

                    ROGER
My mother never had a chance. Or
yours. Vulnerable women . . .

                    MANDY
                 (beat)
 . . . in shaky marriages. I gotta
think about this.

                    ROGER
Do you?

                    MANDY
No, not   really. I see them
together, but you don't think
they. . . .

                    ROGER
I'm going to kill him.

MANDY
(she's convinced)
I'll help you.

But will they? I have to come up with good stuff for these two to do to Victor—not just regular stuff, but attacks that Victor can turn back on them. Stuff with clout. At this point this is a problem with the script: What can these two do to really make the story cook from now on?

This has been the problem all along. How to put a plan into gear that is straightforward yet complex enough to drive them forward and make what they do interesting.

They will go forth, be turned back, have to regroup—back and forth, back and forth—until at the end they are able to throw the bastard into hell, while at the same time making it all dramatic and convincing.

ROGER
First, you have to get away from
Dickie.

MANDY
That's the last thing I'm going to
do.

ROGER
What!?

DICKIE (O.S.)
Lover's spat?

They turn to find Dickie. Mandy snaps out of it, back to normal:

MANDY
(to Dickie, re: Roger)
Your   friend   should   be   a
detective . . .

DICKIE
That's Rolls, one big tub of
inquiry.

ROGER
Fuck you, Dickie.

Mandy likes Roger's defiance.

> DICKIE
> Whoa, your mouth.

Dickie grabs Mandy by the arm and they move off together. Roger is about to make a dumb move—when Mandy shakes her head.

Roger backs off—as Dickie pulls Mandy against him and they start off. Turning back to Roger, smug, menacing:

> DICKIE (cont'd)
> Give my best to your little sis-
> ter.

> CUT TO:

EXT. MINI-MALL—DAY
In the car: Roger and Bang pull over and park in front of OLD SPORT: Experienced Athletic Equipment.

Roger gets out and stalks up to the front door, with Bang following.

> BANG
> What are you doing?

> ROGER
> Getting prepared.

> Bang
> For what?

IN OLD SPORT STORE—CHECKOUT LINE
ON Roger pushing a basket filled with used free weights and a workout bench, with Bang trailing behind—looking at him, wondering what the hell . . . ?

> TIME CUT TO:

THE CHECKOUT
With the loaded basket.

                         ROGER
                       (to Bang)
              I'm gonna have to dip into what I
              owe you. Is that okay?

                          BANG
              What am I supposed to say, no?

EXT. ROAD—DAY
The Plymouth, with the weight bench sticking out of the
trunk. Under heavy weight, the rear end is scraping the
pavement.

> Here we go. Roger has to save his mother from Victor. He's falling in love
> for the first time in his life, but Mandy's got something going with Dickie
> that Roger's not sure about. Talk about spinning incestuous wheels. His
> parents' marriage is falling apart. Roger hates his own fat and wants to get
> rid of it.
>   We've loaded Roger up with enough crap for one kid, right? Right?

INT. HOUSE—DAY
In the screened-in beautifully decorated (by Darlene) patio
overlooking the pool, Roger has set up a mini-gym.

ON: Roger, already working out.

                          BANG
                  Mom will kill you.

                         ROGER
                  How well does Mom know Mr. Ferris?

                          BANG
                  Mom? She doesn't . . .

Off his silence:

                       BANG (cont'd)
                  Does she?

                                        TIME CUT TO:

PATIO—LATER
Roger, sweaty and exhausted, continues working out.

                    LLOYD (O.S.)
          What's all this, Sport?

Lloyd, in a shirt and tie, puts his briefcase down and picks
up a 20-pound weight.

                              TIME CUT TO:

PATIO—LATER
Lloyd, sweaty and exhausted, working out. Roger is collapsed
in a chaise, tense, listening to his father.

                    LLOYD
           . . . it's been on my mind,
          so . . .

                    ROGER
          You're a good teacher, Dad. And
          what about the golf team? Without
          you, we wouldn't be a tenth the
          players we are.

                    LLOYD
          I need a better-paying job.

                    ROGER
          Because you see a change coming
          up? Around here? With the family?

                    LLOYD
          You have to keep your eye on the
          ball.

                    ROGER
          Maybe you're looking at the wrong
          ball, Dad.

                    LLOYD
          What do you mean?

                    DARLENE'S VOICE
          For God's sake!

They both look up.

                         DARLENE
              This is a home, not a gym.

In a huff, she stalks off. When she's out of earshot:

                         ROGER
              Are you and Mom breaking up?

                         LLOYD
              We've had problems. We're trying
              to work them out.

                         ROGER
              How?

                         LLOYD
              We've been going to a counselor.

                         ROGER
              Is it working?

                         LLOYD
              These things take time.

                         ROGER
              But there isn't much left, is
              there?

Lloyd looks at him quizzically. Roger is trying to make a
decision: Should he tell him what he knows?

                         ROGER (cont'd)
              I'll get this equipment out of
              here.

                         LLOYD
                    (with conviction)
              Leave it.

IN KITCHEN
Roger at the open fridge—on which signs are posted: "GO
AHEAD, TUBBO, EAT IT ALL," etc.—eyeing a piece of cake.

He sees an image of Mandy shaking her head. He closes the fridge door.

You have to start thinking about your main character changing his ways in order to accomplish what's necessary. You have to enroll your hero in a kind of training camp—while at the same time driving him nearly crazy with all the hell you throw at him. Once again: If this is not the most critical moment of your protagonist's life, the story is not worth telling. Never be too easy on your main character.

When in doubt, confront. One of the ways in which your character can get moving is to take chances.

                                              CUT TO:

EXT. LOCAL UPSCALE MALL—DAY
Roger pulls the Plymouth into a parking space. Through the windshield he's facing a sign: INHOUSE DESIGNS.

INT. INHOUSE DESIGNS
Roger marches through the fashionable office.

Ahead is Darlene, in a business suit, looking over some plans with a couple MEN.

As if sensing something, Darlene looks up.

                    DARLENE
          Roger . . . ?

                    ROGER
          Could I speak with you?

                    DARLENE
          Of course.
                    (to the men)
          Excuse us.
                    (to Roger)
          Come on, honey. Right back here.

                                       TIME CUT TO:

INT. OFFICE—LATER
In a chair, Darlene is shocked, unnerved:

DARLENE
(stiffening)
In the market? . . . Mr. Ferris?

ROGER
Accosting you.

DARLENE
What are you . . . ?

ROGER
. . . talking about?

DARLENE
Well, yes, this is a terrible
accusation. Why didn't you
just . . .

ROGER
Run up and kill him? I should
have. Then I saw you parked outside Mrs. Silvera's house. When
Mr. Ferris was coming out.

DARLENE
Roger, I don't know what you're
trying to do here . . .

ROGER
How much have you paid him?

Off her silence:

ROGER (cont'd)
For legal services? The financial
hooks he's got into you. Not to
mention the emotional ones.

DARLENE
In the market I was having a conversation with Mr. Ferris. I
slipped. He caught me. Your imagination, I must say, is stunning.

                    ROGER
          He's handling the Silvera divorce.
          He's doing the same for you, isn't
          he?

This really throws her. She has to make a decision.

                    DARLENE
          There've been discussions . . .

                    ROGER
          Whose fault is it, Mom, huh? Did I
          have anything . . .

                    DARLENE
          No no no. These things have more
          to do with . . . erosion than with
          fault.

                    ROGER
          So that's why you've gone to Mr.
          Ferris? To stop the erosion?

She looks at him, defeated.

I've tried to show Roger as a regular teen from a middle-class family. He has no driving ambition yet. He's a hard worker (paper route), a good golfer (which takes discipline), but he's also on hold, generally speaking. The tools are here; how are we going to make him use them?

He's confronted his mother, thinking that might work. He's already said no to Victor on the golf lessons, but after money pressure, he caves. He's made plans with Mandy. His mother is in utter denial. No help there.

His father is caught in the crosshairs of divorce. No help. Roger is forced to deal with the wrath himself—Victor Ferris. Even his name—VICTOR—is daunting.

                                        CUT TO:

EXT. PLANTATION GOLF CLUB—DAY
Roger in a deep SAND TRAP, pounding out balls—horrible shots, all of them. The rest of the golf team, with Coach Lloyd, watches this awful display.

LLOYD
What's the trouble, Champ?

As Roger continues to screw up:

LLOYD (cont'd)
Loosen your grip. Get rid of the
tension. Open your face.

Then, CRACK. A ball flies at the group itself. Everybody
dives for cover.

Lloyd rights himself and looks at his son, who has left the
trap and is heading across the field toward his car.

Lloyd hurries after him.

LLOYD (cont'd)
Roger!

Roger climbs in the Plymouth and speeds away.

CUT TO:

EXT. MANDY'S HOUSE
Roger's Plymouth is parked outside.

INT. HOUSE
Mandy's black-walled bedroom. Very Goth but meticulously
clean and organized.

Mandy sits at a computer; she's sending e-mail. Roger looks
over her shoulder.

MANDY
Can he trace this?

ROGER (O.S.)
(pointing)
Delete this. Okay. We're safe.
Speaking of which. You still hanging out with Dickie?

                         MANDY
          Why not? He handsome, rich, a
          hunk . . .

                         ROGER
          Yeah, sure.

                         MANDY
          Think *strategy*, Roger. We're going
          after Mr. Ferris, the big fox.
          Boom boom boom. He won't know what
          hit him.

                         ROGER
          Okay, right.

                         MANDY
          If I break up with Dickie, I lose
          access to his dad. Get it?
                    (typing)
          "In other news, Victor Ferris, se-
          nior law partner of Ferris,
          Wheeler and Cates . . ."

INT. SWANK OFFICE OF FERRIS, WHEELER AND CATES, ATTORNEYS AT
LAW—DAY

ON A COMPUTER SCREEN: An e-mail appears. A key is hit. The
e-mail reads: "In other news, Victor Ferris, senior law
partner of Ferris, Wheeler and Cates, has been having sex
with his divorce clients, who have filed complaints with law
enforcement authorities . . ."

On Victor, doing a double take. He sees that the e-mail has
been copied to his partners, Wheeler and Cates.

                         MALE VOICE (O.S.)
          Oh, Victor . . . ?

Victor turns to sees his two LAW PARTNERS, Wheeler and
Cates, standing solemnly in the doorway.

                         WHEELER
          A word?

Here's their first foray into knocking Victor off his pedestal. The question is: Does this work? Does the e-mail have additional consequences? Can Victor turn it back on the kids? Each part of the plan needs to have legs. We are not interested in one-shot deals or still water. Actions beget reactions, beget actions, etc.

INT. ANOTHER OFFICE AT FERRIS, WHEELER, AND CATES
Victor at the table, with Wheeler and Cates looming above him.

> CATES
> . . . a prank?

> VICTOR
> . . . what else would it be?

> WHEELER
> If this gets into the community,
> or to the press . . .

> VICTOR
> It won't.

> CATES
> There's no truth to this allega-
> tion?

> VICTOR
> Don't worry.

> WHEELER
> Because if there is . . .

> VICTOR
> I'll bring this prick to justice.
> Quietly.

> CUT TO:

EXT. VICTOR FERRIS'S REAR PATIO
Victor hooks a shot to the left, as Roger, aggravated, watches.

Roger tees up a ball for him.

> ROGER
>
> Right thumb. Move it down the
> shaft.

> VICTOR
>
> It doesn't feel right.

> ROGER
>
> Stop whining.

Victor, with a look at Roger, makes the adjustment, and now
slices one.

> VICTOR
>
> See.

> ROGER
>
> I want you to keep doing that.

> VICTOR
>
> You're sure?

> ROGER
>
> Yes.

> VICTOR
>
> Well, all right, but . . .

> ROGER
>
> Do you want my help or not?

> VICTOR
>
> Of course.

Roger takes the club.

> ROGER
>
> Tee one up.

Victor gets down on one knee and sticks the tee in the
ground. His head is right there, an easy poke with the

driver. An honest mistake. Just one perfectly timed swing
and *KAPOW!*

As Victor places the ball on the tee, Roger loads up. Big
backswing. Eyes riveted on the Victor's head, he swings.

A SOUND like a pumpkin exploding. Sinew and blood and bone
splatter and splash. Roger executes a perfect follow-
through, watching Victor's head blow out there in all directions.

                    HOLLOW MALE VOICE
          Roger . . . ? Roger?

Roger looks down into Victor's eyes.

                    VICTOR
          Are you going to hit it?

Roger comes out of his daze.

                    ROGER
          No, you are. That'll do it for me.

He turns and leaves.

AT FRONT DOOR
Victor catches up to him. He pulls out three twenties and
hands them to Roger. Roger looks at them.

                    VICTOR
          You were not all here today.

                    ROGER
          Who wants to be tournament cham-
          pion?

                    VICTOR
          I do.

                    ROGER
          Then honor your commitment, sir.

Victor does not appreciate this tone of voice.

                    VICTOR
          Quite right.

Victor hands him two other twenties.

                    VICTOR (cont'd)
          By the way, what's your e-mail
          address?

Roger looks up suddenly, trying to keep his cool. Is this a
test?

                    ROGER
          E-mail?

Wouldn't you know it, just as Roger and Mandy are making inroads into
the toppling of this guy, Dickie now will come on the scene. Like father, like
son. It's like a tag-team match, giving Roger and Mandy little chance
against the power-packed Ferris men.

This is called a reversal. Just when it looks as if the protagonist's plan
is working, something is thrown into the mix that reverses their fortunes.
They have to retreat, regroup, and find another way in.

The plot, in other words, is rolling along, action-wise. But the emotional
subplots—the Mom-Victor, Dickie-Mandy axis—throw Roger off.

                                        CUT TO:

OUTSIDE HOUSE
As Roger, unnerved, heads to his car . . .

                    DICKIE (O.S.)
          Good job, son.

Roger turns to find Dickie leaning against the hood of his
Lexus, smoking. He's in boxing gear, with boxing gloves
hanging out of his gym bag.

                    DICKIE
          Quite the popular one these days.

Roger keeps walking to his car. Following him:

                              DICKIE (cont'd)
          Mandy. My dad.

Roger reaches the Plymouth.

                              DICKIE (cont'd)
          Stay out of my shit, Rolls. I'm
          warning you.

As Dickie tosses his cigarette to the driveway, crushing it
with his shoe, and moves casually by Roger . . .

                              DICKIE (cont'd)
          You hear me?

As Roger turns to get in the car, Dickie feints and throws a
punch, catching Roger in the eye, sending him sprawling.

                              DICKIE (cont'd)
          Sorry, old man. You moved.

As Dickie strolls off, Roger holds his eye, in pain.

                                                  CUT TO:

INT. CLASSROOM—DAY
Roger, in sunglasses to hide his black eye, lost in thought,
stares out the window. The class is in progress, with Lloyd
lecturing to the class—including Mandy.

                              LLOYD
          . . . and so, Roger, could you
          repeat to the class, if you will,
          what I've just been saying?

Pulled abruptly from his thoughts, Roger says, by rote:

                              ROGER
          . . . as superb a writer, person-
          ality and wit as the great French
          novelist Colette was, she paid
          scant attention to her child,
          always trying to shake herself

         free of what she referred to as
         "the maternal yoke . . ."

                      LLOYD
      . . . okay . . . good . . .

Roger turning back to the window, as Lloyd continues . . .

                  LLOYD (cont'd)
      Alchemy. Who can give me a defini-
      tion?
               (beat)
      Anybody want to take a stab at it?

A hand goes up . . .

                  LLOYD (cont'd)
      Mandy.

                  MANDY
      From among the ruins, wherein
      nothing should rightly grow,
      springs love, out of an unexplain-
      able, call it magical, source. The
      alchemy of love.

This catches Roger's attention. They look at each other;
hard to read.

                  LLOYD
      That's lovely, and exactly
      right . . .
              (sadly but hopefully)
      Sometimes love can transcend ruin,
      to perhaps grow anew.

                  ROGER
              (blurting out)
      Not unless you work at it!

Lloyd and Mandy shoot him a look. The bell rings, and the
students pour out, with Roger moving among the chairs.

Stopping him, inspecting his face:

>   LLOYD
>   (re: Roger's blackening eye)
>   What's with the dark glasses,
>   Champ?

>   ROGER
>   I fell.

>   LLOYD
>   On your eye?

                                        CUT TO:

HALLWAY NEAR EXIT—LATER
Roger, harried, catches up to Mandy.

>   ROGER
>   Mandy . . .

>   MANDY
>   (re: black eye)
>   What happened?

>   ROGER
>   That was beautiful, your alchemy
>   of love definition . . .

>   MANDY
>   Beneath all love lies madness.
>   What happened to you?

Roger is mute.

>   MANDY (cont'd)
>   He hit you.
>   (beat)
>   Dickie hit you, didn't he?

>   ROGER
>   His father's suspicious about the
>   e-mails.

                              MANDY
          Fuck.

Touching her cheek:

                              ROGER
          You're wonderful.

He turns and wheels off toward his car.

                                        SLAM CUT TO:

EXT. NEIGHBORHOOD STREET—DAY
A bike, moving fast. TRACKING with: Mandy, peddling, racing
around corners, her thigh muscles straining, perspiration
beading on her olive skin.

She wears a studded sports bra, halter, tight studded jeans,
and low black boots—hauling ass toward and up to:

Roger's driveway, moving in and dismounting like a pro,
right in front of Lloyd Royce, watering the lawn:

                              LLOYD
          Hello, Mandy.

                              MANDY
          Mr. Royce. Is Roger in?

                              LLOYD
          In his room. Through the door,
          down the hall, first one . . .

She's already moving.

                              LLOYD (cont'd)
          . . . on the right . . .

                                        CUT TO:

INT. BEDROOM
Roger does strenuous floor exercises to blasting music. He's
definitely more fit than he was.

The door blows open and there's Mandy—the perspiring Madonna.

>   MANDY
>   Hey, looking good. Got a sec?

He pulls on a sweater.

Mandy enters, closing the door behind her—but not before we see Bang, in the hall, wide—eyed, watching this. Mandy sits on the bed, looking at a wall poster of a bleak desolate stretch of earth.

>   ROGER
>   Hell's fifth fairway.

>   MANDY
>   We have to cool it.

Off Roger's silence:

>   MANDY (cont'd)
>   Dickie will hurt you.

>   ROGER
>   What about our mothers—in the
>   clutches of that Machiavellian
>   fuck machine?

>   MANDY
>   Separate issue. As far as you and
>   I are concerned—we never began.

>   ROGER
>   For you maybe . . .

She looks sharply at him:

>   ROGER (cont'd)
>   I had to say that. Besides, you've
>   climbed into my heart . . .

>   MANDY
>   Evict me.

Back to business: Roger reaches under his bed and pulls out a VIDEOCAM.

>   ROGER
>   My dad's.

>   MANDY
>   Which we're gonna do what with?

>   ROGER
>   Gather evidence.

>   MANDY
>   Let's see.

She reaches for it. Roger takes her hand, kisses it.

>   MANDY (cont'd)
>   Roger, romantic fool.

Inspecting the videocam, handing it back.

>   ROGER
>   That's me.

>   MANDY
>   You're hopeless.

>   ROGER
>   Not entirely.

Mandy turns and goes to the door. Opening it, she finds Bang.

>   MANDY
>   Bang, eavesdropper.

She steps into the hall, closing the door behind her.

Here's where Mandy needs to straighten this guy out, but also to keep the plan going. She has to keep him on track. This is a problem, which has to be fixed. Any suggestions?

IN BEDROOM
Roger throws himself back against the headboard, stoned in
love.

IN HALLWAY
Mandy and Bang move toward the living room.

> MANDY (cont'd)
> I've been meaning to ask you.

> BANG
>
> What?

> MANDY
> How'd you get your name?

Rattling it off, as if she's done it a million times before:

> BANG
> As a kid. When my parents fought.
> They slammed doors. I would scream
> *Bang!* The name stuck. Bang! That's
> *your* door slamming, Saliva. Beat
> it.

> MANDY
> I'm not going anywhere.

> BANG
> Is that so? You're ruining my
> brother.

> MANDY
> You give me too much credit.

**Roger is losing it, getting off track. Mandy, for whom revenge has become
to both business and personal, warns him about his priorities. This is about
taking Victor down, not their nonexistent love affair.**

**So Roger, who is lathered in love, knows she's right but he can't help
himself. He starts to work out to take his mind off it.**

                                                  CUT TO:

INT. ROYCE SCREENED-IN PATIO—NIGHT
Roger pumps iron, one repetition after another. Sweat pours
out of him.

MONTAGE OF WORKOUT MOMENTS as Roger, overextending himself
but trying hard, he:

—jumps bad rope.

—reads confusing manual directions.

—stretches until it hurts.

> BANG (O.S.)
> Who gave it to you?

> ROGER
> What?

> BANG
> The shiner. Saliva?

Off his silence:

> BANG (cont'd)
> You should have heard her.
> (mimicking, throaty)
> "I'm not ruining your brother."

> ROGER
> She said that?

> BANG
> She's been watching too much Span-
> ish Channel.

> ROGER
> Knock it off.

> BANG
> Poor, deluded toad.

The phone rings. Through the open counter in the kitchen,
Roger sees his mother whispering into the receiver. She
hangs up, grabs the SUV keys, and exits.

Getting up from the bench:

ROGER
Gotta go.

BANG
To find Saliva-girl?

Roger, throwing on a jacket, grabs the videocam and takes off after her.

BANG (cont'd)
She will devour you!

ECU on Bang's wide open mouth:

MATCH AND MORPH TO:

From the TUNNEL of Bang's wide-open MOUTH, we enter: A TUNNEL through trees, with a set of emerging headlights.

EXT. LONELY ROAD—MOONLIT NIGHT/LATER
Roger drives, videocam on the seat beside him. We HEAR:

VICTOR (O.S.)
Darlene, that is not the life you
deserve. With a man for whom you
no longer care? Who no longer
cares for you?

DARLENE (O.S.)
I don't know what I want.

VICTOR (O.S.)
I'm here to guide you.

DARLENE (O.S.)
I can't see you anymore.

VICTOR (O.S.)
I'm afraid that's not possible.

DARLENE (O.S.)
What do you mean . . . ?

                         VICTOR (O.S.)
You owe me too much.

                         DARLENE (O.S.)
Owe you?

                         VICTOR (O.S.)
Devotion. Financial *and* emotional.

Off her stunned silence:

                         VICTOR (O.S.) (cont'd)
I'm in charge now.

In the distance, Roger sees two vehicles—Victor's big black
Lincoln and his mother's SUV—parked by the side of the road.

                         DARLENE (O.S.)
                         (struggling)
Please, Victor, I don't want to. I
met you to tell you that . . .

                         VICTOR (O.S.)
But I'm so tense. Do it!

                         DARLENE (O.S.)
Victor . . .

Her gagging sounds.

Roger drives slowly, snapping off his headlights.

                         VICTOR (O.S.)
You're so beautiful. The best. I
love to touch you. Touch me.

                         DARLENE (O.S.)
                         (muffled)
Mmmmmm . . .

                         VICTOR (O.S.)
Magnificent! You're the world!

MOVING CLOSER, Roger sees Victor's head thrown back against the seat, mouth agape in ecstasy. Roger holds up the video-cam, aiming it through the window.

Tears in his eyes, he holds it there, barely able to look.

With both hands, Victor is forcibly holding down a head—a woman's—in his lap. By the cut of the red-blonde hair, Roger knows who it is.

The back of her head pops up, protesting. He forces her down.

A stricken Roger, tears running down his cheeks, pulls the videocam in and continues down the road. He stops and does a U-turn, heading back.

> **How hard is it for a kid to videotape his mother having sex with a man, and somebody other than his own father? But he does it because he has to, no matter how awful it is. Courage grows.**

                                                        CUT TO:

SAME ROAD
Passing by them again, Roger sees them in the same posi-tions.

He takes more footage. Then, when he can't bear it anymore, HE BLASTS THE HORN. Darlene jerks her head, and Victor cries out in agony!

Roger steps on the gas and speeds off.

ON ROAD
Roger slows and pulls to the side, behind a tree.

                                                    TIME CUT TO:

SIDE OF ROAD/ROGER—MOMENTS LATER
In the rearview mirror he sees two pairs of approaching headlights.

After they pass—one set belongs to the SUV, the other to the Lincoln—Roger pulls onto the road and follows.

ON PLYMOUTH
Tailing Victor's Lincoln—to the SOUND of loud, crashing waves.

IN LINCOLN
Victor, listening to some cheesy '80s song, his face in agony from Darlene's penis chomp, feels a BUMP from behind. Wincing, he looks in the rearview mirror, seeing nothing but darkness.

He feels a bigger BUMP, and checks the side mirror—nothing.

IN PLYMOUTH
Roger, moving closer, gives Victor's car a crushing blow, sending the Lincoln swerving out of control—until Victor finally rights it.

IN LINCOLN
Victor, in a panic. He's banged his head on the steering wheel. A bruise forms.

IN PLYMOUTH
Roger, preparing for a final assault, revs the Plymouth's engine. Pulling back for the final thrust, he throws it into gear and lurches forward—straight at the Lincoln.

IN LINCOLN
Victor, sensing something awful about to happen, guns the car into the passing lane and starts to pull ahead of the SUV.

IN PLYMOUTH
Roger watches the Lincoln pull out—and now sees, dead ahead, his mother's SUV!!!

He swerves to the right—over the shoulder and into a ditch.

ON PLYMOUTH
As it plows through the ditch filled with rubbish and beer cans, and into a pile of driftwood . . . coming to a stop.

Roger's head is pressed against the wheel.

                                                  CUT TO:

EXT. GOLF CLUB MOUND/ABOVE 18TH FAIRWAY—DAY
Roger, glum, sits on the hood of the banged-up Plymouth.
Mandy sits beside him, her arm around him.

                    ROGER
          It was awful.

                    MANDY
          I'm sorry.

Roger brings out the videocam, handing it to her.

                    ROGER
          You sure you want to do this?

She takes it from him, determined.

                                        CUT TO:

EXT./INT. MANDY'S HOUSE—TWO NIGHTS LATER
SOUND of whirring and whispers by a male and female:

                    VICTOR (O.S.)
          You're so beautiful. The best. I
          love to touch you. Touch me.

A red light blinks from a VIDEOCAM tracking through the
darkness.

                    MS. SILVERA (O.S.)
                    (muffled)
          Mmmmmm . . .

                    VICTOR (O.S.)
          Oh, yes!

VIDEOCAM POV COMES UP ON Victor standing and Mandy's mother
on her knees, back to the camera, giving Victor a blow job.

Mandy in profile, aiming the videocam at:

                    VICTOR (cont'd)
          Be gentle. Ohhhh. Oh!

(in pain)
Oohhh!!!

                    MS. SILVERA
What?

                    VICTOR
I had . . . an accident.

                    MS. SILVERA
Sorry to hear it.

Wincing, closing his eyes:

                    VICTOR
My   darling.   Now   move   your
thumb . . . that's   it . . . down
the shaft . . .

                    MS. SILVERA
                     (muffled)
Mmmmm . . .

                    VICTOR
Magnificent!!! You're the world!!!

ON Mandy, in agony, eyes barely open, continues to shoot.

                              CUT TO:

EXT. SCHOOL PARKING LOT—DAY
Roger, in a daze, parks the car and gets out.

IN PARKING LOT
Roger turns the corner. Up ahead he sees Mandy hurrying down
stairs, moving toward him—though she doesn't see him yet.

Stepping up the pace, he closes the distance between them.

Mandy suddenly veers off, into Dickie's arms, with both of
them heading off together.

ON ROGER: watching this display, a boulder rolling over his
heart . . .

Now we have Roger on the run. In a series of potential disasters—video-taping his mother giving a blow job to Victor, Mandy recording the same with her mother, and now Roger seeing Mandy and Dickie together—Roger is about to fall off the end of the earth.

He's angry and agrees to fight Dickie, for what? Bragging rights to Mandy? The things Dickie says about Bang and his mother? Come on, Roger, wake up. Mandy can't convince him.

He's so pigheaded or wrongheaded that he can't see the obvious.

                                                  CUT TO:

EXT. SCHOOL—LATER THAT DAY
In bright sunlight, a distracted, frustrated Roger and a
yapping Dickie walk through the schoolyard.

                         DICKIE
            . . . are you listening to me?

                         ROGER
            No, I am not listening to you.
            I've never listened to you,
            Dickie, because you're an idiot.

                         DICKIE
            Lighten up, Rolls. I thought you
            might wanna make a couple hundred
            bucks.

                         ROGER
            Doing what?

                         DICKIE
            My sparring partner is sick. I
            need somebody to fill in. It's
            nothing, just some light dancing
            around.

He reaches into his pocket and pulls out a wad of cash.

                         DICKIE (cont'd)
            One now . . .
                    (peels off two fifties)
            One when it's over.

                    ROGER
Not interested.

                    DICKIE
Come on, Rog.

                    ROGER
No.

                    DICKIE
            (dead calm, eerie)
Okay. Then take some advice. Stay
away from Mandy. I don't like your
dewey-eyed fucking attitude toward
her. Just like you don't like my
father grabbing a blow job from
your mother whenever he feels like
it . . .

Roger pulls up, stunned, anger sprouting out of him.

                    DICKIE (cont'd)
Got your attention? Or gum-fucking
Mandy's mother. Or the fucking
relationship I have with your
heartthrob, the ever-fuckable
Mandy Silvera . . .

Roger throws a stupid punch. Dickie, easily avoiding it,
spins Roger around so that he's now behind him, in a body
lock.

Whispering in Roger's ear:

                    DICKIE (cont'd)
    . . . or the fucking relationship
that I will have one day soon with
your sweet little sister, the
extremely fuckable Bang.

Roger struggles to break free. Dickie stuffs the two fifties
into his mouth.

                              DICKIE (cont'd)
            Tomorrow. Four o'clock. Towne Gym.

Dickie corkscrews Roger's arm. Roger lets out a scream.
Dickie releases him, turns, and saunters off.

                                                  CUT TO:

EXT. NEIGHBORHOOD STREET—DAY
Roger, sweat pouring out of him, jogs alongside Bang, who is
riding her bike.

                              BANG
               I'll say you came down with some-
               thing you can't see. Let me think
               about it.

                              ROGER
               I'll kick his ass.

                              BANG
               Dickie will kick *your* ass. But
               that's not what we're talking
               about, is it? This is about
               Saliva-girl, who doesn't know you
               exist. Hel—*lo!*

Roger runs faster.

                              BANG (cont'd)
               If you're willing to have your
               internal organs, not to mention
               your face, mangled for life over
               some   misguided   notion   of
               honor . . .

He runs even faster.

                              BANG (cont'd)
               That's it. Pick up the pace. Maybe
               exhaustion will kill you first.

Now Bang tries to get Roger off this campaign. He has no allies left. He's confused as hell. Just where you want your main character. Moving forward, blindly but with purpose.

                                                    CUT TO:

INT. KITCHEN—AFTERNOON
A manic Roger, in sweats, at the refrigerator—plastered with
more "EAT ALL OF IT, YOU GARGANTUAN PIG"—type slogans. He
pulls out a giant container of META MUSCLE powder and carries it to the table, where he pours some into a glass of
juice.

The phone rings. Picking it up:

                    ROGER
          Hello?

                    MANDY'S VOICE
          I've got to see you.

                    ROGER
          I'll bet you do.

                    MANDY'S VOICE
          I thought we had a deal. We're
          supposed to be working together.
          You've become a one-man wrecking
          crew . . . on yourself!

                    ROGER
          I'm real busy, so . . .

                    LLOYD (O.S)
          Trouble, champ?

                    ROGER
                (into receiver)
          I've got an appointment . . .

                    MANDY'S VOICE
          I know you do, that's why I . . .

Roger hangs up.

>   LLOYD
>   (inspecting him)
>   Let's see. A black eye. Distracted
>   in class. Golf game in shambles.
>   Working out. Car smashed up. Have
>   I left anything out?

>   ROGER
>   I've been on edge.

>   LLOYD
>   What about? A girl?

>   ROGER
>   Yeah, right. Girls. Women. They
>   love you. They don't know you.
>   They think you're an idiot. They
>   wanna be your pal. Tease me, but
>   don't touch me . . .

>   LLOYD
>   It is a girl.

Into Lloyd's face:

>   ROGER
>   Love me, I loathe you. Stay. Get
>   out of my face. I love my family,
>   they're fucked! I'm great, you're
>   a failure! I make money, you make
>   shit . . . ! I hate you, don't
>   leave me. Got it?

>   LLOYD
>   Talk to me, son.

>   ROGER
>   How much more can you take, Dad,
>   huh? How much more can *we* take,
>   Bang and me? Do something, for
>   crissakes. Don't just stand there.

                    LLOYD
          Roger . . .

                    ROGER
          You're losing her.

They both know what the subject matter is.

                    LLOYD
          I know. I've been trying.

                    ROGER
          You've got to try harder. There
          are things going on.

                    LLOYD
          And have been for some time.

                    ROGER
          Well then why don't you . . .

                    LLOYD
          I love your mother. We've been
          having trouble. I *am* trying.

                    ROGER
          Not good enough!!!

Roger shoves him against the refrigerator, but Lloyd does
nothing.

                    ROGER (cont'd)
          Come on, Dad, be a man. Too pussy
          whipped!? Fight back. Hit me!

Roger goes to shove him again. Lloyd takes him by the shoulders, holding him, staring him down.

                    LLOYD
          Your mother wants out!

                    ROGER
          Fight for her!!!

              LLOYD
She doesn't love me.

              ROGER
Bullshit. What do *you* want?

              LLOYD
Her. I want her. But this has been
going on for too long.
       (long beat)
There's nothing left.

Roger pulls away from him and runs out. Lloyd stares after him, defeated and very worried.

> So here we have Roger, all pissed off. Has a fight with Mandy, attacks his father in the kitchen, goes to the gym to battle the far superior Dickie. What is this guy doing? But you gotta love him. He's moving forward, against all odds.

                        CUT TO:

EXT. TOWNE GYM PARKING LOT—DUSK
In an old rundown part of town. Roger, in sweats with a gym bag, marches toward the building.

Mandy, a vision in blue incandescent hair, suddenly appears beside him.

              ROGER
Here for the slaughter?

              MANDY
You are not going to do this. This
is not part of the plan.

              ROGER
That plan has failed.

              MANDY
Oh?

>   ROGER
> The e-mails got nothing. Trying to
> run Victor down didn't work. The
> video stuff was disgusting. I'm
> done with it.

Trying to block him:

>   MANDY
> You're not going in there.

Continuing around her:

>   MANDY (cont'd)
> He will mutilate you.

>   ROGER
> Why should you care? I know—
> because I mean so much to you.

>   MANDY
> You're doing this for the wrong
> reasons.

>   ROGER
> Why don't you tell me what the
> right reasons are, and while I'm
> on my way in, I could shift my
> focus.

>   MANDY
> You think you're so clever. But
> all you are . . .

>   ROGER
> I know. A stubborn overweight
> prick.
>   (a beat)
> Victor's got my mother. Dickie's
> got you and chasing after my sis-
> ter. You might wonder why I have a
> resentment against that family!

                            MANDY
Roger . . .

                            ROGER
What do you do to the enemy? You
said it. You wear them down. I'm
never going to give up. If nothing
else, *that'll* kill 'em. You see?

                            MANDY
Or you!

As he moves around her she tries to block him. He grabs her
and kisses her.

                            ROGER
                          (fiercely)
I love you.

He moves by her and into the gym, leaving her shaken.

                            SLAM CUT TO:

INT. TOWNE GYM—RING
A body shot to Roger's mid-section, doubling him over—followed by a shot to the head, with Roger reeling back against
the ropes.

Before a small crowd, in a ratty fight ring, Dickie, a lean-
muscled gazelle, stalks a bloody Roger.

The bell sounds, the fighters return to their corners.

Roger wipes blood off his face.

                         MANDY (V.O.)
Roger, please! Two rounds! Give it
up! Nobody thought you'd last two
seconds!

Spotting Mandy at ringside, mumbling through fat lips:

                            ROGER
I got him right where I want him.

Across the ring Dickie is dancing and primping before the crowd of locals. The bell goes off.

>   MANDY (O.S.)
>   Keep your head down! Dance!

Roger glances over, inspired by Mandy rooting for him.

He heads into the ring and catches Dickie with an overhand right, staggering him—to Roger's (and everyone else's) surprise.

>   MANDY (O.S.) (cont'd)
>   Hit him again! Hit him again!

Hearing Mandy, Dickie stops and looks over at her—realizing that she's rooting for Roger! Now hugely livid, he chases Roger down, pummeling him, driving him to the canvass.

>   MANDY (O.S.) (cont'd)
>   Ref! Do your job!!!

Finally the REF jumps in and protects Roger from Dickie's blows.

>   MANDY (O.S.) (cont'd)
>   We give up! We give up!!!

Dickie, now a maniac, shoves the ref to get at Roger—until Roger, with his remaining strength, takes a HUGE BITE out of Dickie's ankle.

Yowling, Dickie hops around on one leg—as Roger, bloody-faced and puffy-eyed, collapses.

ON CANVASS/ROGER'S POV: Through gradually closing eyelids, of Mandy, at ringside, staring bleakly at him—now seeing her through a diminishing rosy-pink filter.

> **Nobody's surprised that Roger got the shit beat out of him. What's that line: If it doesn't kill you it will make you stronger. Obviously, Roger is the proponent of that philosophy.**

FADE TO BLACK . . . AND UP ON:

EXT. GOLF CLUB—DAY
Roger, beat up, and Bang sit on a bench above the 18th green.
The course spreads before them like a fuzzy green blanket.

                    BANG
          What will you do now? That is, if
          you live through the week.

                    ROGER
          Direct confrontation. Full frontal
          attack. It's the only thing they
          understand.

                    BANG
          What about laying low?

                    ROGER
          I'm gonna bring them down.

                    BANG
          This crusade you're on. All for
          Mandy Saliva, Goth creep!

He wants to tell her everything, but can't.

                    ROGER
          Bang.

                    BANG
          What?
                    (beat)
          Wait a minute! *Them?* What do you
          mean *them?* You're going to bring
          them down?

                    ROGER
          Them. Him. What difference does it
          make?

Off her wariness:

                    ROGER (cont'd)
          Bang, you've made mistakes, felt
          things . . .

With a disturbing look:

> BANG
>
> You're in love with her . . .
> aren't you?

Off his silence:

> BANG (cont'd)
>
> Oh, jeez.

Taking his hand:

> BANG (cont'd)
>
> Be careful will you? Please?

CUT TO:

INT. SCREENED-IN PATIO-DUSK
Roger, bruised and swelling, sits on his weight bench with workout gloves, sweating, listening to pounding techno.

The music stops. The lights snap on. Roger looks up to see his mother, standing in the doorway.

> DARLENE
>
> My God, what happened . . .

> ROGER
>
> I fell down.
> (beat)
> I saw you.

Off her cautious look:

> ROGER (cont'd)
>
> Again. With Mr. Ferris.

Off her silence:

> ROGER (cont'd)
>
> On Fowler Street. In the front
> seat of his car.

                    DARLENE
                    (aghast)
          Why, that's just. . . .

                    ROGER
          I passed you. Remember? The guy
          who honked?

                    DARLENE
                (starting to lose it)
          I   cannot   even . . . I   mean,
          that's . . . Oh, Roger . . .

                    ROGER
          Don't leave, Mom. We can all make
          it work. I mean it. Just say okay.
          Okay?

                    DARLENE
          Roger, this is not the time.

                    ROGER
          Yes it is.

                    DARLENE
          Your father shut me out, long ago.

                    ROGER
          That's what he said.

                    DARLENE
          What?

                    ROGER
          That there's no intimacy.

                    DARLENE
          He's right.

                    ROGER
          Mom.

                    DARLENE
          What?

                    ROGER
        We're all pitching in here . . .
        to make this work . . . okay?

A moment of silence, as they stare at one another . . .

                                  CUT TO:

EXT. VICTOR'S BACK PATIO—DAY
Victor Ferris whacks balls but not nearly as well as he has
been. Roger enters.

                    ROGER
        You're not concentrating.

                    VICTOR
          (noticing Roger's bruises)
        What happened to you?

                    ROGER
        Had an accident.

Indicating his bruised head:

                    VICTOR
        Me, too.

                    ROGER
        Motor vehicle?

                    VICTOR
        How did you know?

                    ROGER
        Your car. I saw the fender.

                    VICTOR
        I saw yours, too.

Victor inspects him as he would an antagonistic witness.

                    ROGER
        This divorce law business of
        yours, Mr. Ferris . . . ?

> VICTOR
>
> I'm paying you a hundred bucks for
> your expertise in golf. You have
> legal questions? It'll cost you a
> hell of a lot more than that.

Victor tees it up and hits a big slice.

> VICTOR (cont'd)
> Look at that! What am I doing
> wrong?

Roger tees one up for Victor, who addresses the ball.

> ROGER
> This way you have of freeing women
> from marital hell.

> VICTOR
> What about it?

Victor hits a banana slice into the neighbor's yard.

> VOICE FROM NEXT DOOR
> Hey!

> ROGER
> Try another one.

Roger tees another one up for Victor, who banana slices
another one.

> VOICE FROM NEXT DOOR
> Hey!!!

With a cold hard stare:

> VICTOR
> I don't appreciate what you're
> doing, on *any* level. That'll be
> enough for today.

> ROGER
> But don't you . . . ?

> VICTOR
>
> No I don't.

With a cold hard stare:

> VICTOR (cont'd)
>
> Don't fuck with me, Roger. You
> can't afford it. Be here tomorrow,
> same time. With a better attitude.
> Now get out of here.

                                        CUT TO:

EXT. STREET/THE PLYMOUTH

INT. ROGER'S BEDROOM—EARLY MORNING
Wide awake, Roger stares at the ceiling. The GOLF BALL ALARM
goes off. His eyes open. The clock reads 5:00 A.M.

                                        CUT TO:

EXT. DARK NEIGHBORHOOD STREET—VERY EARLY MORNING
In the newspaper-laden Plymouth, top down, Roger drives—to
the crashing waves tape.

> BANG
> (shouting)
>
> Talk to me! There's something
> going on. What is it?! What I
> don't need is a dead brother.

                                    TIME CUT TO:

EXT. NEIGHBORHOOD STREET—DAWN

IN THE CAR: from the back and front seats respectively—Bang
and Roger sling newspapers onto lawns.

> BANG
>
> You'd better get smart . . .

> ROGER
>
> I am. About certain relationships.

                    BANG
Like yours with Saliva?

                    ROGER
That's one.

                    BANG
You have got to tell me what's
going on!

                    ROGER
You don't want to know.

                    BANG
Tell me!!!

                    ROGER
     (a pause; blurting it out)
I saw Mr. Ferris groping Mom in
the Winn-Dixie.

                    BANG
What . . . ?

                    ROGER
I also saw them parked out on
Fowler Avenue. Having oral sex.

                    BANG
What???!!!

                    ROGER
I told you you didn't want to
know.

On Bang, stunned.

                    ROGER (cont'd)
You missed the Fergusons . . .

                                   CUT TO:

EXT. ROYCE HOUSE/FRONT PORCH
Roger and Bang, sitting on the flagstones, stern expressions,
facing each other, listening to the conversation inside:

> DARLENE (O.S.)
> Do you know how lonely I've been?

> LLOYD (O.S.)
> The only thing I've ever wanted
> was you, until this river of ice
> formed between us.

> DARLENE (O.S.)
> You've blamed me all this time for
> your inability to . . .

> LLOYD (O.S.)
> Get it up? Go ahead, say it. I had
> some trouble there for a while and
> all I got from you was ridicule.

> DARLENE (O.S.)
> I'm not totally responsible for
> your loss of desire. When you made
> me feel so misshapen, repug-
> nant . . . as if I caused it.

> LLOYD (O.S.)
> I never said that.

> DARLENE (O.S.)
> I see it in your eyes . . .

> LLOYD (O.S.)
> That's loneliness, Dar, and pain.
> Sick to death and forsaken. All
> these months on that couch, long-
> ing to . . .

> DARLENE (O.S.)
> Then why didn't you?

                              LLOYD (O.S.)
          One night about a month ago, when
          you came in late, I got up and
          went over to the bed and stood
          over you, and was about to lie
          beside you, and try . . . when I
          smelled it. The cologne. You
          reeked of it. A man had been all
          over you.

                            DARLENE (O.S.)
          Lloyd . . .

                              LLOYD (O.S.)
          I'm sorry.

SOUND of Lloyd walking out of the kitchen.

Roger and Bang climb to their feet and quietly enter the
house.

IN HOUSE
Roger and Bang slip across the living room.

                            DARLENE (O.S.)
          Hey you two. Where are you going?

At a dead stop:

                            BANG/ROGER
          . . . to the bathroom . . . for-
          got something in my room . . .
          nowhere . . .

                                     TIME CUT TO:

KITCHEN TABLE
Where Roger and Bang are seated. Darlene stands at the
counter, mascara running, red-eyed.

                            BANG
          Statistically, ninety-seven per-
          cent of couples who separate never
          get back together again.

>   DARLENE
>   Ninety-seven?

What does Roger need? Utter focus. He brings Bang in on the deal. He challenges Victor. He brutalizes Dickie. But what about his mother? And her marriage to Lloyd? Can he save them? Should he even bother?

                                                  CUT TO:

EXT. DRIVING RANGE—DAY
Roger bangs out four irons like a machine, sending the balls in beautiful arcs way out there. Onlookers have put down their clubs, watching in awe.

Mandy walks up, unnoticed by Roger, and sits on the ground next to his bag, watching.

With sweat pouring off him, and utterly focused, Roger is in the zone . . . bang, bang, bang . . .

                                                  CUT TO:

EXT. STREET—DAY
With Mandy beside him, Roger, lathered in sweat, drives through the village center. He spots his mother's SUV parked on the palm-lined street.

Pulling into INHOUSE DESIGNS, Roger and Mandy climb out and head for the front door . . .

INT. INHOUSE DESIGNS
Roger and Mandy enter. They hear the SOUND of a woman's voice.

>   DARLENE (O.S.)
>   . . . I don't know what I've done.
>   I mean, I know what I've done, but
>   I don't know how I've done it.
>   Rather, I know how I've done it,
>   but I don't know how it happened.
>   *How* it happened, but I don't *know*
>   how it happened . . . how I *let* it
>   happen . . .

Roger and Mandy angle toward the rear of the office, approaching Darlene's voice.

Peeking around the corner, they SEE: Darlene, looking crazed, seated behind a desk, wedged into a cubicle, the listener out of sight.

> DARLENE
> I mean, I know how I let it hap-
> pen, but I don't know how I
> allowed *myself* to let it happen.

Roger and Mandy angle in for a better look, still unable to see to whom she's speaking.

> DARLENE (cont'd)
> (holding back tears)
> I know how I allowed it to happen,
> but I don't know how I put myself
> in a position to *allow* it to hap-
> pen . . .

She puts her head in her hands and tears flow out between her fingers.

Roger and Mandy peek around a corner. From their POV: of Darlene speaking—to an empty chair . . .

As they look at each other, we . . .

> DISSOLVE TO:

INT. CAR—LATER
Roger and Mandy, in the Plymouth, driving.

> MANDY
> My mother was just as bad. Worse.

> ROGER
> Remember that thing my father said
> in class—"To bring a man down,
> discover what matters to him most,
> and take it from him."

MANDY
(bitterly)
His dick.

DISSOLVE TO:

EXT. NEIGHBORHOOD—EARLY NEXT MORNING/PAPER ROUTE
In the Plymouth, Roger, intense, drives. Bang, in the back
seat, tosses papers.

BANG
(shouting)
What else can happen?

ROGER
Don't ask.

BANG
Mom and Dad splitting. You off the
deep end . . .

ROGER
It's under control.

BANG
Of course it is.

ROGER
I'll *get* it under control.
(turning to face her)
With some help.

The same BULLDOG we saw in an earlier scene runs into the
street, yapping. Roger aims the car at it, chasing the dog
back to its yard.

FROM THE CARPORT
The dog's owner races out, yelling.

ROGER (cont'd)
(to Bang)
Can you handle the Murphys?

Grabbing a paper, she holds it up with a thumb and two fingers and slings it.

FOLLOWING the paper's flight through the air and across the lawn, it CATCHES the bulldog smack on the forehead, sending it sprawling into Old Man Murphy.

But this time the bulldog quickly recovers and starts down the street after the car.

It somehow claws its way up the back of the Plymouth and into the rear seat—snarling and barking and attacking Bang.

With the car swerving all over the road and Bang screaming, Roger slams on the brakes, thrusting the dog into the front seat—where Roger opens the passenger-side door and kicks the dog into the street, where it goes tumbling and plows into Mr. Murphy.

Roger starts moving forward again, leaning back over the seat—where Bang, out of breath, looks demented.

                    ROGER (cont'd)
          Bang?!

                    BANG
          Don't mind me. *It was just a bull-
          dog trying to kill me!*

He drives a bit farther, pulls over, stops.

                    ROGER
          Mandy and I need you.

Off her patented withering look:

                    BANG
          If I'm in, Saliva's out.

                    ROGER
          Let me tell you what we're think-
          ing.

                              BANG
          I mean it, not with her.

                              ROGER
          She's in.

                              BANG
          Fine. Let me out.

                              ROGER
          Bang . . .

                              BANG
          Stop the car!

Roger pulls over, Bang climbs out and walks on—and stops,
dropping her head into her hands, starting to shake, tears
flowing out of her.

Roger hops out and goes to her.

                              BANG (cont'd)
          What's going to happen to us,
          Roger, huh?

Roger uses his shirtsleeve to wipe her eyes. Putting his
arms around her:

                              ROGER
          We're going to beat this.

                                             CUT TO:

EXT. VICTOR'S HOUSE—NEXT MORNING
Roger pulls up, marches to the front door, and knocks. The
door opens on Mrs. Ferris, looking more resentful than
usual.

Pointing to the rear of the house, she turns and vanishes.

ON PATIO
Victor hits balls furiously. Stopping in mid-swing, he looks
up and sees Roger. All is icy as they size each other up.

                         VICTOR
Roger.

                         ROGER
Mr. Ferris.

                         VICTOR
I want to talk about my weight
shift.

                         ROGER
If you overcompensate you lose
your balance, and your evidence.

                         VICTOR
My what?

                         ROGER
As a lawyer you rely more on evidence than instinct, right?

                         VICTOR
Are you going to start this again?

                         ROGER
What's the worst thing you could
ever imagine losing?

                         VICTOR
The tournament. Which is tomorrow!

                         ROGER
Seriously, the worst thing. What
would you hate to lose more than
anything?

                         VICTOR
What's that?

                         ROGER
 . . . what?

                         VICTOR
That noise.

Victor takes Roger by the shoulders and literally lifts him up. Victor listens. He hears a whirring SOUND, like a tape winding.

                    VICTOR (cont'd)
        That! What's that!

                    ROGER
            (panicking, wild)
        You took advantage of my mother!!!

                    VICTOR
        What?

                    ROGER
        Had sex with her! Didn't you!
        Admit it!

The whirring sound doesn't stop; in fact, it starts skipping and getting louder. Victor looks at Roger's pocket, from which the sound seems to be coming, and reaches inside.

Roger tries to squirm away, but Victor has him in a grip. Victor comes out with a mini-tape recorder that's stuck on fast-forward.

Victor puts Roger down and holds up the tape recorder, turning it off.

                    VICTOR
        What in hell do you think you're
        doing?!

Off Roger's silence:

                    VICTOR (cont'd)
        This is a felony, you little prick.

                    ROGER
        What about screwing your clients?
        Ruining lives? Destroying fami-
        lies?

                              VICTOR
                    (leaning close; very calm)
                Here's the deal. I could ruin *you*,
                and your family, with trials, and
                legal fees. Your parents go broke
                defending you. You go to jail.
                Your life is over. There's no end
                to it. And for what?

                              ROGER
                I'll call the newspapers.

                              VICTOR
                Do you really want to go up
                against me, Roger?

Victor opens the recorder, pops out the tape.

                         VICTOR (cont'd)
                I'll keep this.

They turn to find Dickie, limping in from the shadows, a bandage around his ankle from where Roger bit him during the
fight.

                         VICTOR (cont'd)
                Hello, Dickie! Roger and I were
                talking about the takeaway.
                         (at Roger)
                Take away this. Take away that.

Looking ill:

                              ROGER
                I have to go.

He turns and walks off, passing Dickie. A look of utter
loathing passes between them.

Big sequence here. Roger confronts Victor and, below, he tackles Dickie, head on. But he's not going to let them know what's ahead. He might be headstrong to let Victor in on his feelings, but he's got to let him know that he loathes him for how he's contributed to the ruination of his family.

Victor throws his weight around. He is a big-time lawyer who will crush Roger, and his family, if he feels like it. Something really big has to be done. Are Roger and his little team of commandos up to it?

AT FRONT DOOR
Roger's about to leave when Mrs. Ferris suddenly appears.

> MRS. FERRIS
> I was thinking, Roger, about your
> quite interesting question: about
> the worst thing one could imagine
> losing.

Roger looks carefully at her.

> MRS. FERRIS (cont'd)
> I would say, in this particular
> case, the respect of one's peers.
> Without that, one is nothing, a
> man adrift. Disgraced. A shell. No
> man at all.

Mrs. Ferris smiles faintly (the first he's ever seen) and vanishes back into the shadows.

> CUT TO:

EXT. HOUSE
Roger moves down the driveway toward his car. Dickie peg-legs out from the side of the house.

> DICKIE
> How many times do I have to say
> it, you fat piece of shit—stay
> away from my family!

> ROGER
> Don't worry, I'm done with all of
> you.

> DICKIE
> And as soon as I fuck your sister,
> I'll be done with you.

Something snaps in Roger, who smashes Dickie in the face.
Roger then kicks him in his bad leg. Dickie goes down yowling.

Roger climbs in the Plymouth and drives off.

With bloodied lip, Dickie struggles up, shouting:

                    DICKIE (cont'd)
            You're fucked, Royce! Fucked!!!

                                            CUT TO:

EXT. STREET—DAY (LATER)
Roger drives the Plymouth, with Bang beside him.

                    BANG
            Where we going?

                    ROGER
            Into battle.

Rolling her eyes:

                    BANG
            Roger of Troy.

                                            CUT TO:

EXT. SCHOOL PARKING LOT—DAY
Roger pulls in, they both get out.

IN PARKING LOT
Roger and Bang head toward school, splitting off.

IN HALLWAY
Roger passes a herd of warlike, impressionistic student
Goths and Visigoths.

IN CLASSROOM
Already in progress. Roger enters. He notices Mandy's empty
chair and frowns.

CUT TO:

EXT. SCHOOL YARD—DAY
Bang walks through school.

> FEMALE VOICE (O.S.)
> Bang . . .

Turning and seeing Mandy, in dark glasses, punked-out.

> BANG
> Mandy Saliva, big as life. I
> understand we'll be working
> together.

> MANDY
> (following her)
> Which doesn't suit you?

> BANG
> No.

> MANDY
> Bang, listen . . .

> BANG
> My name coming out of your mouth
> makes me want to vomit.

> MANDY
> What is your problem?

> BANG
> My brother thinks he's in love
> with you.

Mandy waits.

> BANG (cont'd)
> Which presents a problem.

> MANDY
> Got a solution?

>   BANG
>   I do.

IN ROGER'S CLASSROOM
Distracted, Roger gazes out the window, paying scant attention to Lloyd's lecture:

>   LLOYD
>   On the subject of martyrs, we'll
>   discuss a play written by one of
>   our   own   students,   with   the
>   intriguing   title: *The   Further
>   Adventures of Joan of Arc,* consid-
>   ering what might have happened to
>   Joan . . .
>   (looking at Roger)
>   . . . had she lived . . .

On the lawn below the window, Roger sees Bang motioning to
him.

>   TIME CUT TO:

ON LAWN
LONG SHOT of Bang talking (MOS) insistently to Roger, who is
very upset by what he hears.

Roger turns and races off. Bang tries to follow, but Roger
shouts "No!"

>   CUT TO:

EXT. NEIGHBORHOOD STREET/MOVING—DAY
In the Plymouth, Roger speeds along. Up ahead, in his family's driveway, he sees Victor's big Lincoln.

Pulling to the curb, Roger climbs out. As he starts across
the lawn he hears Victor's laughter and his mother's
anguished cries.

>   DARLENE (O.S.)
>   I don't want this, Victor. Please
>   leave.

                         VICTOR (O.S.)
          The Silvera business means noth-
          ing. I have to get clients to open
          up . . .

                         DARLENE (O.S.)
          Their legs. I know all about it.

                         VICTOR (O.S.)
          Who said that, Roger? Who threat-
          ened me?

                         DARLENE (O.S.)
          What?!

                         VICTOR (O.S.)
          You're all I ever wanted.

The front door opens and Roger enters quietly. TRACKING with
him, he follows the voices.

                         DARLENE (O.S.)
          You can't just barge in here . . .

                         VICTOR (O.S.)
          And you can't just throw me out.

                         DARLENE (O.S.)
          Stop it!!!

                         VICTOR (O.S.)
          There's my girl.

Roger enters the porch, knocking over a chair. He sees: On
the couch, Victor pinning Darlene.

Looking up sharply:

                         VICTOR (cont'd)
          What the hell?!!!

Victor attempts to get up—*just as Roger's fist plows into his
jaw.*

Victor topples to the floor, his nose bloodied. He starts crawling around on the tiles.

Moving beside him:

>   ROGER
>   Lost your edge, Mr. Ferris?

With the most evil glare Roger has ever seen:

>   VICTOR
>   I'm not finished with you.

Victor, shaking, crawls toward the door. With his foot, Roger applies pressure to his back.

>   ROGER
>   Yes sir, you are. Finished with
>   me, my family, my mother. Pay
>   attention. Keep your head down.

With Victor struggling forward.

>   VICTOR
>   (muttering)
>   I warned you, Roger.

>   ROGER
>   Watch that weight shift.

Roger moves besides Victor as he crawls toward the door.

>   VICTOR
>   You'll be sorry.

Roger sees an opportunity and STEPS on the THUMB of Victor's left hand. Victor howls in pain.

>   ROGER
>   Thumb down the shaft.

>   DARLENE
>   Roger, please stop . . .

She tries to pull him off.

                    ROGER
          Snap out of it, Mom!

Victor takes advantage of the moment by spurting out through the door.

Roger lets him go. He hears the SOUND of Victor's heavy feet clumping on the pavement, the Lincoln's door slamming, and the car taking off.

                    DARLENE
          What am I going to do?

                    ROGER
          First off, no more lies.

                    DARLENE
          You can't understand.

                    ROGER
          Yes I can.
                    (taking her hand)
          Be strong. There is so much love
          here, Mom, in this family. *Feel*
          it.

Darlene looks at her son, tears rolling out of her eyes.

Here we are with Roger taking charge. He humiliates Victor and faces down his mother. But this is not the end of it, not by a long shot.

                                        CUT TO:

EXT. STREET OUTSIDE SCHOOL—DAY
Mandy is walking along. In his car, Roger pulls up.

                    ROGER
          Hop in.

As she does:

                         ROGER (cont'd)
          "There is nothing more important
          than the respect of one's peers."

                         MANDY
          Yeah?

                         ROGER
          A direct quote from the wife of
          Victor Ferris, Esq., who, by the
          way, is on to us.

                         MANDY
          Oh no.

                         ROGER
          He caught me with my tape recorder.
          He threatened me and my parents
          with lawsuits, poverty, and jail.

                         MANDY
          You're saying we should back off?

                         ROGER
                    (very close to her)
          We go in harder and faster than
          ever.

                         MANDY
                    (kissing him)
          My Roger.

Pointing though the windshield:

                         MANDY (cont'd)
          There's Bang. Stop.

Roger pulls up beside Bang, who's walking along. Seeing who
it is:

                         BANG
          Why don't you just drive off a
          cliff.

                    ROGER
    Get in.

As she continues walking:

                    BANG
    To the Death Car? No thanks.

                    ROGER
    Come on, Bang-o.

Detecting something in his voice, she turns and, with Mandy
opening the door, climbs in the back.

                              CUT TO:

EXT. GOLF COURSE—DUSK
The Plymouth sits on a small rise behind the 18th tee, looking up the fairway toward the majestic clubhouse.

In the car with Roger, Bang, and Mandy, in intense conversation.

                    ROGER
    You can get your hands on one?

                    MANDY
    This is precisely why I stayed
    close to that disgusting family.

                    ROGER
                (to bang)
    And you can make those invitations
    appealing?

                    BANG
    Irresistible.

                    ROGER
    Then here we go.

The three of them, eyes riveted on one another, join hands
across the Plymouth's front seat, in a pact.

ACT III

This is where the main character makes a decision to get the bad guy. Will he succeed? Who knows? That's the joy, the mystery.

Act III itself is the working out of the decision made by the protagonist(s) at the end of Act II. Hamlet made a decision to kill Claudius after seeing him give himself away in the Player King's scene. Hamlet did not plan to die in the end. Neither does Roger.

BEGIN MONTAGE:

INT. GOLF COURSE CLUBHOUSE OFFICE—NIGHT
In dim light, Roger scrolls through the computer until he finds: DICK FERRIS CHARITY INVITATIONAL AND TESTIMONIAL DINNER—INVITATIONS AND SEATING PLAN.

He begins rearranging things.

INT. CLUBHOUSE AUDIO/VISUAL EQUIPMENT ROOM—NIGHT
Roger fiddles with a REAR PROJECTION MACHINE.

                                        CUT TO:

INT. DEPARTMENT STORE/JEWELRY SECTION—DAY
Three sets of unique, very expensive identical EARRINGS sit on the counter.

                         CLERK
              That will come to four thousand
              eight hundred and sixty-four dol-
              lars, please.

Across the glass counter, Mandy slides a credit card, with V.R. FERRIS Jr.'s name on it and an ID with her photo under V.R. Jr.'s (Dickie's) name.

                                        CUT TO:

EXT. THE SILVERA MAILBOX
Into the mailbox Bang slips a gift-wrapped package and a card, addressed to Marla Silvera, reading: "My Darling, please wear these to the testimonial dinner on Saturday. Your Victor."

CUT TO:

EXT. THE FERRIS MAILBOX
Into the box Bang slips a gift-wrapped package and a card, addressed to Mrs. Victor Ferris, with the same message.

CUT TO:

EXT. THE ROYCE MAILBOX
Into the box Bang slips a gift-wrapped package and a note, addressed to Ms. Darlene Royce. The end of the message reading: "This is as much about honoring Roger."

END MONTAGE

CUT TO:

EXT. GOLF CLUB—TOURNAMENT DAY
A gala event. The town's who's who is here. Giant banners, announcing: FERRIS, WHEELER AND CATES 10th ANNIVERSARY CHARITY GOLF TOURNAMENT. Ladies and gentlemen parade across the immaculate grounds. This is the event of the year.

EXT. FIRST TEE
A huge crowd gathers around Victor and his foursome, ready to tee off.

> ANNOUNCER
> On the tee, our esteemed host and
> tournament chairman, from Ferris,
> Wheeler and Cates—Victor Ferris.

To big applause, Victor steps forward and tees it up.

Victor's three PLAYING PARTNERS watch. He's confident, even with a BANDAGED THUMB, as he addresses the ball.

IN VICTOR'S IMAGINATION: We see Roger giving him instructions. Victor repeats after Roger:

> ROGER/VICTOR (V.O.)
> . . . weight   on   the   rear
> foot . . . strong right hand . . .

> right eye on the ball . . . club
> back with right hand . . . shift
> weight to the right side . . .
> thumb down shaft . . . hip turned
> in . . . head   still . . . slow
> takeaway . . .

Victor takes a mighty swing and shanks the shot into the trees.

He's humiliated beyond words. The other guys don't know what to say. The gallery murmurs, looks away.

                    VICTOR
              (trying to shrug it off)
          Hey, it's just a game.

                                        CUT TO:

EXT. FT. LAUDERDALE STRIP—LATER THAT EVENING
Roger and Bang drive the beat-up Plymouth down a busy Saturday night street, top down.

                    BANG
          This is so not going to work.

                    ROGER
          Don't be a pessimist.

                    BANG
          It's filled with holes. As big as
          the one in your head.

                    ROGER
          We're committed.

                    BANG
          How can we do this to Mom?

                    ROGER
          It's a little late for that. It'll
          be good for her. For everybody.

> BANG
> No, no, no, no, no.

Pulling to the curb:

> ROGER
> Okay.

> BANG
> What're you doing?

> ROGER
> I understand your reluctance.
> You're free to go.

> BANG
> Like that's a possibility.

Putting the car in gear, and pulling away from the curb:

> ROGER
> Okay, then.

> CUT TO:

EXT. JERRY'S DRIVE-IN—NIGHT
Pulling into a retro '70s drive-in joint with carhops and spots for cars. Roger and Bang see kids from school—who watch them cruise around the horseshoe drive.

Through the cars, Roger spots Dickie in his Lexus, with Mandy beside him.

> ROGER
> There they are.

> BANG
> Oh jeez.

Roger pulls into a slot. To the approaching CARHOP:

> BANG (cont'd)
> Two hemlocks, please.

                         CARHOP
We're out of hemlock, miss.

                         BANG
What else have you got for a quick
demise?

                         CARHOP
I'm busy, guys. What's your pleasure?

                      ROGER/BANG
Coffee/tea.

Roger signals Mandy to meet him by the Dumpster.

Mandy says something to Dickie and slides out of the Lexus,
moving toward the restroom beside the Dumpster.

ON ROGER leaving the Plymouth:

                         ROGER
                     (to Bang)
Be right back.

                         BANG
        (with a look toward Dickie)
You hope.

Roger angles toward the Dumpster where, in the shadows,
Mandy joins him—coming up to each other, face to face.

                       MANDY
Hi.

                       ROGER
Hi.

                       MANDY
Ready.

He nods and moves closer to her:

                    ROGER
          Together we can do anything.

Taking his hand:

                    MANDY
          Then let's.

    . . . and bringing it to her lips. She leans against him.
He takes her in his arms, holding her. She closes her eyes.

                    DICKIE (O.S.)
                 (shouting)
          What the fuck!!!

Looking up, Roger and Mandy spot Dickie by his Lexus, staring at them, inflamed!

                    ROGER
          Okay. Round one. Let's go.

They dart across the parking lot toward the Plymouth.

DICKIE
Throwing open the Lexus trunk, he grabs a GOLF CLUB (a four
iron) and marches across Jerry's Drive-In at them.

IN PLYMOUTH
Bang stands up in her seat, motioning for them to hurry!

DICKIE
Angles through cars at them, the four iron raised high.

ROGER AND MANDY
Reach the Plymouth, jump in. Face to face, lips almost
touching:

                    MANDY
          Clyde . . .

                    ROGER
          Bonnie . . .

                          BANG
              Pu-lese!

Roger starts the car.

And WHAM! They turn back, to SEE: Dickie plowing the four
iron into the trunk, again and again, and now moving around
to the driver's side—toward Roger.

Roger slams the Plymouth into reverse, throwing Bang and
Mandy against their seats. The carhop, carrying their
drinks, dives out of the way.

The Plymouth peels out—with Dickie's four iron narrowly
missing Roger's head and shattering the windshield.

HORSESHOE DRIVE
Dickie chases after them across the divide. Roger throws the
Plymouth into low, laying rubber. People scramble out of the
way.

Dickie cuts across the median—over a car or two—to intercept
and demolish Roger.

THE PLYMOUTH
A dented disaster, racing around the horseshoe—toward Las
Olas Boulevard, the main drag and freedom, dead ahead, WHEN:
Dickie jumps in front of the car, the four iron raised.

Roger jams on the breaks. It's a standoff.

Approaching menacingly:

                          DICKIE
              Rolls, you made a big mistake.
              When I'm done with you, I'm going
              after that fucking sister of
              yours, with the big mouth.

                          BANG
              Oh, Dickie! You're such a man!

                          DICKIE
              Mandy, get out of the car!

Nobody's moving.

                      DICKIE (cont'd)
        You shouldna fucked with me,
        Rolls.

Moving forward and banging the four iron into the palm of his hand:

                      DICKIE (cont'd)
        Mandy! Out!

Leaning in from the backseat, into Roger's ear:

                      BANG
        Run him over.

                      DICKIE
          (to Roger)
        Got any last words before I take a
        divot out of your face?

Mandy and Bang look at each other. On a silent signal, Bang grabs the wheel and Mandy steps on the gas—and the Plymouth leaps forward.

Letting out a horrific cry, Dickie raises the four iron and lunges at them.

Trying to regain control of the Plymouth, Roger hits the brake but instead finds Mandy's foot on the accelerator.

The Plymouth swerves toward Dickie, who reaches out with his free hand and GRABS the windshield frame—with the BROKEN GLASS CUTTING into his fingers.

THE PLYMOUTH
Racing out of Jerry's, now dragging Dickie—who is hanging on with one hand and trying to slam the four iron into Roger with the other.

The Plymouth careens into busy Las Olas Boulevard traffic.

IN TRAFFIC
With Dickie's head right beside Roger, who is driving and
taking his blows. Mandy and Bang reach across the driver's
seat, trying to extract the four iron from Dickie's
clutches.

ON: Mandy's lips, in Roger's ear.

                         MANDY
              You're beautiful.

Roger tries to smile.

THE PLYMOUTH
Swerving down Las Olas, taking a wild right, then another—
finding themselves back at the rear of Jerry's Drive-In.

The Plymouth plows through a fence and back into Jerry's
horseshoe drive.

With Bang and Mandy screaming and trying to wrest the four
iron from Dickie, the Plymouth swerves around a corner of
the horseshoe.

Staring into Dickie's manic eyes:

                         MANDY (cont'd)
              Your stop, Dickie.

As she digs her nails into his hand, he releases his grip on
the car and goes tumbling into the pavement.

But the resilient Dickie rolls up to a standing position and
is after them again.

Bang reaches down to the floorboard and comes up with an old
folded newspaper, which she expertly flips at the attacking
Dickie—hitting him, and throwing him off, so he misses Roger
with the four iron, by inches, and flies into the curb.

The Plymouth storms into Las Olas traffic.

LOOKING BACK
Roger, Bang, and Mandy see a battered Dickie climbing into his Lexus, gunning it across the medium, and the chase is on.

With their half-crazed look that says: So far, so good.

                                                    CUT TO:

EXT. PLANTATION GOLF CLUB—A PERFECT EVENING
TRACKING up the moonlit 18th fairway toward the clubhouse banquet room lights, to the escalating SOUND of music and a testimonial dinner in progress.

BANQUET ROOM
In this crowded, jovial country club with the community's most respected citizens, the MASTER OF CEREMONIES steps to the podium.

TRACKING THROUGH THE DINERS—where we find: Darlene and Lloyd at a front table marked with a card, reading: "1" and "VIC-TOR FERRIS TESTIMONIAL DINNER."

ON GIANT SCREEN
Behind the podium, a film honoring Victor Ferris runs. It's like a political campaign self-congratulatory documentary, with Victor accepting awards, playing with children, and kissing babies—along with a chronology of Victor growing up with the community.

THE PODIUM
Where Victor, flush with a sense of self-importance and fueled by alcohol, stands beside the MASTER OF CEREMONIES, wearing a bandage on his thumb.

                          MC
          . . . we are here this evening to
            honor my favorite fellow and . . .

He takes a look at the Club Championship Leader Board, where Victor Ferris's name is way down near the bottom.

                    MC (cont'd)
        . . . all-around superior guy,
        who might need some work on his
        golf game but is otherwise on top
        of the world. It's my great plea-
        sure to present a compatriot, a
        true community leader—and, the
        rumor is, soon to be club presi-
        dent, and might even be running
        for public office in our fair city.
        The sky's the limit for our man of
        the hour! My good friend, and
        yours! Victor Ferris!

To applause, as Victor steps to the podium. He's particu-
larly handsome and larger than life tonight.

                    VICTOR
        It's an honor to be here among
        you—Senator Buchanan, Congressman
        Whitman, Mayor Black, along with
        dear friends Darlene and Lloyd
        Royce, our wonderful golf coach,
        whose son Roger, our city junior
        champion, has been instrumental in
        my appreciation of this demanding
        game—although I must exonerate
        Roger from all responsibility for
        my poor play. I found more lost
        balls today than at any time in my
        career.

Laughter. Looking out over the sea of faces, he places his
hand over his heart. With a humble smile:

                    VICTOR (cont'd)
        Please forgive me. I'm overwhelmed
        tonight. Wondering what I've ever
        done to deserve such an outpouring
        of love.

Let's pause for a moment. Here's where I am running into difficulty and
need help. First of all, the tone is changing here. This last act is turning into
a rollicking fast car chase. Is that what I want? Isn't this betraying the more

subtle, internalized struggle of the previous pages? Is this what it's all for, an action-adventure Act III?

It's not clever enough. It's not a slam-bang. It doesn't have the sophistication and feeling it promises. It's a cop-out. I'm torn here, but I have to listen to my doubts.

This is a work in progress all right.

My question to you: How can this be clever and still keep the tone of the earlier pages? I'm stumped for now.

                                        SLAM CUT TO:

EXT. BROWARD BOULEVARD TRAFFIC—OVERHEAD SHOT OF: TWO SPEED-ING CARS

TIGHT ON: the lead car, Roger's Plymouth, as it whips through traffic, closely followed by Dickie's Lexus.

TIGHTER ON: Roger, Mandy, and Bang, all very intense, check-ing behind to see Dickie.

With Mandy in one of Roger's ears, and Bang, leaning over the seat, in the other—both whispering encouragement.

                                        CUT TO:

INT. GOLF CLUB BANQUET ROOM
Victor drones on:

                    VICTOR
          . . . to my mind there is nothing
          more important than a strong fam-
          ily, and the togetherness it fos-
          ters . . . especially   in   my
          profession, where the family unit
          is tantamount to God's grace . . .

Victor looks up, startled, to see: his wife, Mrs. Victor Ferris, elegantly dressed in black but as gaunt and bitter as ever, being led in by a white-coated waiter to table "1" and seated beside Darlene and Lloyd.

They nod to one another, with Darlene looking suspiciously at the earrings on Mrs. Ferris—which are identical to her own!

ON: Victor, who also notices the identical earrings:

                        VICTOR (cont'd)
                . . . and of course, in life as
                in my law practice, I try to bring
                the very highest standards to bear
                upon the . . .

Victor looks up, startled to SEE: Marla Silvera, Mandy's
mother, all dressed up, subtly oozing sex, being led in by
the same white-coated waiter to the Ferris table, where she
is seated between Mrs. Ferris and Darlene.

Marla gives a little wave to Victor, who blanches. There,
just a few feet from the podium, are the three women in his
life.

Mrs. Ferris, confused by the presence of this strange woman,
glares at her earrings—which are identical to her own!

Darlene, smoldering at Marla Silvera, sees that not one but
two women, at her own table, wear identical earrings to her
own!

ON GIANT SCREEN
A *startling scene appears:* In the front seat of Victor's
car. Victor is apparently getting a blow job from a woman
whose face we can't see—this is Roger's videocam footage.

The audience gradually becomes aware of what it's seeing and
gasps. The screen reverts back to Victor's testimonial
footage.

                                        SLAM CUT TO:

EXT. PLANTATION GOLF CLUB ENTRANCE
Roger's Plymouth roars through the country club gates, followed closely by Dickie's Lexus.

NEAR THE BAG DROP/IN LEXUS
Dickie cuts off Roger, sending the Plymouth through a hedge,
and down along a cart path—and onto the 18th fairway.

Headlights blaring, the cars, side by side, careen up the fairway, toward the clubhouse lights.

                                              CUT TO:

IN CLUBHOUSE BANQUET ROOM/AT PODIUM
Victor in the midst of a rapidly disintegrating speech. The giant screen behind him is dark. The audience mumbles, puzzled.

                    VICTOR (cont'd)
          . . . in the matter of my own
          life, I can honestly say . . .

The three women are interested in hearing this one.

                    VICTOR (cont'd)
          . . . that I have been faith-
          ful . . .

The women, narrow-eyed, glare at this lying sack of shit.

                    VICTOR (cont'd)
          . . . to the notion that the game
          of golf and a strong sense of pro-
          priety go hand in hand . . .

ON THE SCREEN
Another scene appears: Shot by Mandy. An ecstatic, sweating, half-naked Victor stands in some strange living room, with a woman (an unrecognizable Marla Silvera) on her knees, performing fellatio on him.

                    VICTOR ON SCREEN
          Magnificent! You're the world!

The audience gasps.

ON: Darlene, Marla, and Mrs. Ferris, all of whom have heard his expression before.

Victor can't figure out what all the hubbub is. He turns back toward the screen.

He's interrupted by BLARING CAR HORNS and the sweep of headlights crossing his paralyzed expression.

OUT THE PICTURE WINDOW
Two sets of headlights zigzag up the 18th fairway—heading
straight for the clubhouse.

IN BANQUET ROOM
The dinner guests flock to the window, where they see
approaching cars heading straight for them, at high speed.

                         MC
                     (to Victor)
          Why, Victor! Isn't that your son's
          car?! And young Roger Royce he's
          chasing?

Victor races to the window to see the two cars.

Victor's face contorts in anger when he sees Roger, who he
now knows is behind everything: his wife, Darlene, and Marla
at the same table; the identical earrings.

                       VICTOR
          You little bastard.

He turns back to the video screen, where he sees himself
getting the blow job. The audience is torn between the
screen and the scene outside.

                         MC
          What on earth are you doing up
          there, Victor! Oh, my word!!!

**Okay, so this is what Act III should do: work out the decision made by the
character at the end of Act II. It's lumpy, though, and insincere. This is the
stuff we all face. How to make it work? How to remain consistent? How not
to cop out? We need to build rising dramatic action toward the climax.
The scenes get shorter; the action and tension escalate. We are heading
for the climax.**

But he's speaking to air, because Victor is fighting his way
out the door.

ON 18TH FAIRWAY
The two cars, neck and neck, sideswipe one another. They blast through a shallow sand trap and over the green, toward the clubhouse.

ON Mandy, in Roger's ear:

                    MANDY
          My Spartacus . . .

Off Roger's manic grin.

                                        CUT TO:

COURTYARD OUTSIDE CLUBHOUSE
Led by an anguished and ripping mad Victor, guests pour into the courtyard—as the speeding cars nearly run them down!

Victor hurries toward the golf carts. "Victor" is emblazoned on one of them. He hops in, giving chase.

OVERHEAD SHOT/TRACKING
The Plymouth (with Roger, Mandy, and Bang) and the Lexus, top down (with Dickie, wielding his four iron), race through the grounds.

A frantic Victor, in his golf cart, races across the grounds.

DARLENE, MRS. FERRIS, AND MARLA SILVERA
In a tight knot, watch in horror—suddenly realizing where they are, and with whom—and the terrible humiliations they have had to endure from Victor.

Through a series of quickly exchanged glances, the women are transformed from enemies to allies and turn toward the cause of their woe—Victor himself.

Victor, in his golf cart, arrives on the scene, recoiling from the women's ferocious stares.

Roger, Mandy, and Bang, in the Plymouth, approach the scene too fast. Roger loses control of the car.

                              BANG
          Yikes!

                             MANDY
          Slow down, baby.

The Plymouth trades paint with the clubhouse wall and spins
out, coming to a dead stop.

SMALL ALCOVE
Dazed, the trio stumble out of the Plymouth to find themselves
wedged into the alcove, trapped against a bare wall, like
firing squad targets—holding on to one another for dear life.

DICKIE
Sees an opportunity for revenge, guns the Lexus toward the
defenseless trio—swinging the four iron like a bolero.

FROM THE OPPOSITE SIDE OF THE COURTYARD—VICTOR
In his golf cart, his dignity in shambles, spots Roger and
the two girls trapped in the alcove.

He aims his cart at this unholy trio that ruined his life
and presses down on the accelerator.

OVERHEAD SHOT
Dickie's Lexus roars in from one side, with Victor's golf
cart from another—both aimed at the defenseless Roger, Bang,
and Mandy.

Dickie lets the four iron fly. It sails through the air, narrowly missing the trio, and crashes into the wall behind
them.

They huddle together, waiting for the end.

To the SHOUTS and SCREAMS of the onlookers—seeing both Victor and Dickie heading for the three defenseless kids.

ON: Victor and Dickie's dark, determined faces, moving in
for the kill.

ROGER
Snatches the four iron off the tarmac and grips it as he
would a newspaper on his route. He hurls it through the air,
in the general direction of the approaching vehicles.

THE FOUR IRON
In SLO-MO, sails high above them—with everyone watching. The
glint from the club's shaft somehow fuses with the silver of
the moon, freezing time for a moment.

All of this to the SOUND of Roger's sea-crashing-against-
rocks tape playing from the wrecked Plymouth.

DICKIE
In the Lexus, sidetracked by the four iron glint, veers off-
course.

VICTOR
In his cart, just a few feet from kids, swerves abruptly to
avoid his son's car. But too late!

The two vehicles CRASH INTO EACH OTHER, missing Roger,
Mandy, and Bang, by inches.

TO SHOUTS and CRIES and the reverberations from the terrible collision.

                              LONG DISSOLVE TO BLACK:

                         ROGER (V.O.)
                Nothing good came out of all
                this . . . at first.

                                   FADE UP ON:

INT. HOSPITAL ROOM—DAY
IN BED: an immobilized Victor.

                         ROGER (V.O.)
                . . . we sow what we reap. A
                shattered pelvis. Making it impos-
                sible for Mr. Ferris to tee off
                the next morning, among other

                    things. Not that it mattered. By
                    his actions he lost the club pres-
                    idency. And the respect of his
                    peers.

Mrs. Ferris sits beside the bed, rocking, wearing an oddly
satisfied smirk.

                              ROGER (V.O.) (cont'd)
                    Mrs. Ferris divorced Victor, got
                    the house, most of the money.
                    Whatever Victor couldn't hide.

                                              CUT TO:

INT. PRISON—DAY
Dickie, in prison gray, irons a shirt . . .

                              ROGER (V.O.)
                    Dickie was charged with assault
                    with deadly weapons—his four iron
                    and his automobile—and attempted
                    murder.

 . . . belonging to a VERY BIG AND MEAN LOOKING INMATE,
dwarfing Dickie, his new bitch.

                              ROGER (V.O.) (cont'd)
                    Though I hear he's worked a pretty
                    good deal for himself at the cor-
                    rectional facility.

                                              CUT TO:

EXT. ROYCE DRIVEWAY—DAY
Roger, Bang, Lloyd, and Darlene stand in a family cluster,
tears flowing. Together again. Mandy Silvera takes their
photo. FLASH!

                              ROGER (V.O.)
                         (halting, choked up)
                    We beat the odds. We're four
                    again, a family. Troubled, beaten,

suspicious, still iffy, but
together.
                    (long beat)
There was one last thing.

                                                    CUT TO:

INT. ROGER'S BEDROOM—DUSK
Roger lies on his rumbled bed, in his underwear, dozing. His
eyes pop open. In the doorway he sees: MANDY, in jeans and a
top. She approaches and sits on the bed beside him.

                          MANDY
          Hello, tiger.

A little tentative:

                          ROGER
          Hi.

                          MANDY
          I'm leaving today.

Sitting up, very upset:

                          ROGER
          You are . . . ?

                          MANDY
          With my mother, who is not doing
          well, as you can imagine. We're
          going back to live with my dad.

                                                    CUT TO:

IN ROGER'S ROOM

                          ROGER
          I'm going to miss you.

                          MANDY
          You're quite courageous.

                        ROGER
        Oh, sure.

                        MANDY
        You save things, Roger. By making
        a valiant effort.

Off his bewilderment:

                        MANDY (cont'd)
        Like me, for instance.

                        ROGER
        All I wanted to do was to save my
        parents' marriage.

                        MANDY
        You can only save yourself.

Leaning forward to give him a kiss, and lingering.

She swings one foot out and catches the door, closing it.
But not before seeing Bang in the hallway. The girls' eyes
lock on each other's, sealing a pact between them.

                        MANDY (cont'd)
                      (to Roger)
        You are very special . . .

She lets down her hair and starts removing her blouse, no
bra.

                        ROGER
        I am?

                        MANDY
        You might not know it yet, but you
        are. You'll see.

Roger stares, mesmerized, at her extraordinary body. She
reaches under the covers, grabbing him, and smiling.

                    MANDY (cont'd)
        Nice.

Removing her jeans. No underwear. And holding up a condom.

                    MANDY (cont'd)
        This will be our secret.

Roger nods.

Now naked, Mandy throws back the covers and pulls down
Roger's underwear.

Now moving beside him, holding him gently, as a kind of sadness shows on her face. Roger turns to her. They begin to
kiss, tenderly.

We begin PULLING AWAY, toward the window.

                    ROGER (O.S.)
        Oh, man . . .

                    MANDY (O.S.)
        I'm not going to have to do all
        the work myself, am I?

We slowly leave them, moving out through the window, and up
the side of the house, toward the sky.

                    MANDY (O.S.) (cont'd)
        That's my Roger. Mmmmm. You like
        that?

                    ROGER (O.S.)
        Not really.

                    MANDY (O.S.)
                (beat)
        Not really?

                    ROGER (O.S.)
        Just kidding . . . ha ha . . .

                         MANDY (O.S.)
          I dig you, Roger.

                         ROGER (O.S.)
          I dig you, Mandy.

                         MANDY (O.S.)
          Don't say it if you don't mean it.

                         ROGER (O.S.)
           . . . oh. Okay.
                              (beat)
          I love you.

                         MANDY (O.S.)
          I'll be back.

                         ROGER (O.S.)
          You will?

                         MANDY (O.S.)
          I hope so.

We're now high above the house, moving east, away from the
setting sun. Roger's waves-crashing-against-waves tape
plays in the b.g.

While down below we hear: the SOUND of a golf ball being
struck.

                         MANDY (O.S.) (cont'd)
          Frisky boy . . .

And now we're moving more quickly, over the neighborhood and
the big highway and across the flat plains of the city,
toward the beach.

                         ROGER (V.O.)
          My heart cracked open. I long for
          her. You can't imagine how much.
          But I have to face it—she's gone.
          As Bang says, one day I'll wake up
          and Mandy won't be the first
          thought in my mind, or even the

second or third; in fact, she
might not cross my mind until
sometime in the late afternoon.
And then I'll know that the heal-
ing process has begun . . .

> BANG (V.O.)
> I never said "healing pro-
> cess . . ."

> ROGER (V.O.)
> Oh, okay. Well, what then? How did
> you put it?

> BANG (V.O.)
> I don't know, but I distinctly
> remember not saying "healing pro-
> cess," which is so not an expres-
> sion I would use.

Crossing above the top of the hotel, we're now over ocean,
heading into accelerating darkness.

As their voices fade and the music rises, we finally lose the
light . . .

> FADE OUT:

I'm just going to have to keep working on it. I have some ideas, most of
which are not that great. But this is the nature of the beast. You work and
work and get to a point where you think you might have something, and
then you work some more.

It beats going to an office and working for someone else every day—
at least it does for me. But the wolf is at the door and I can't afford to sit
around and wait for the muse to ride down in her Lexus or on her alu-
minum broom with the answer.

I have to ask the one person who knows what to do, which I have not
done enough. Maybe because I don't know him well enough yet to get a
satisfactory answer—or even to ask a satisfactory question.

My main character. My best collaborator. There's my muse. The
answers lie in him, in good old Roger.

I have to get to work.